Sir Syed, Aligarh Muslim University and National Politics

By the same author

Indian Muslims Against British Rule

About the Author

Aijaz Ahmad was born on 16th August, 1969, at Motipur village in Sant Kabir Nagar district of Uttar Pradesh. He studied in Khair Inter College, Basti, AMU Aligarh and Jamia Millia Islamia and completed B.A. (Hons.), M.A., M. Phil. and Ph. D. in History. He also qualified NET and JRF test conducted by UGC from the AMU. In 1994, he was appointed as a lecturer in History in YMD College, Nuh in Mewat District of Haryana. Now, he is promoted as Associate Professor in History at the same college. During his service career in the YMD College, Nuh, he got published nine research papers in national and international journals and proceedings of the Indian History Congress. In the same period, he also got published six books: 1. *Aligarh Muslim University: An Educational and Political History, 1920-47*, Ghaziabad, 2005. 2. *Mewat: A Retrospective*, Ghaziabad, 2013. 3. *Indian Muslims Against British Rule*, New Delhi, 2014. 4. *Uprising of 1857: Some Facts about Failure of Indian War of Independence*, New Delhi, 2014. 5. *Heritage of Mewat*, Nuh, 2015. 6. *Mewati Rebellion of 1857*, New Delhi, 2016.

Sir Syed, Aligarh Muslim University *and* National Politics

Revised and Enlarged Edition

Aijaz Ahmad

CONCEPT PUBLISHING COMPANY PVT. LTD.
NEW DELHI-110059

ISBN-13: 978-93-5125-293-1

Edition: 2017

Published and Printed by

Concept Publishing Company Pvt. Ltd.
Regd. Office:
A/15-16, Commercial Block, Mohan Garden,
New Delhi-110059 (INDIA)
Phones : 25351460, 25351794, *Fax* : 091-11-25357109
E-mail : publishing@conceptpub.com
Website: www.conceptpub.com

Cataloging in Publication Data—DK Courtesy: D.K. Agencies (P) Ltd. <docinfo@dkagencies.com>

Ahmad, Aijaz, 1969- **author.**
Sir Syed, Aligarh Muslim University and national politics / Aijaz Ahmad. — Revised and enlarged edition.
pages cm
Includes bibliographical references and index.
ISBN 9789351252931

1. Aligarh Muslim University—History. 2. Aligarh Muslim University—Political activity. 3. Muslims—Education (Higher)—India—Aligarh—History. 4. Aligarh movement. 5. Aligarh (India)—History—Autonomy and independence movements. 6. India—Politics and government—1919-1947. 7. Aḥmad K͟hān, Sayyid, Sir, 1817-1898. I. Title.

LG169.A45A36 2017 DDC 378.542 23

In Memory of My Father
Late Chaudhary Shafaat Mohammad
Who Will Always Survive in My Heart

Preface

The present book titled, "Sir Syed, Aligarh Muslim University and National Politics" is intended for the general reader to explain the historical facts about Sir Syed Ahmad Khan, Aligarh and Aligarh Muslim University, and their role in the freedom movement of India. In this preface, I have given a detailed introduction of all the topics included in this book and also explained the aim, purpose and need of writing this book. While briefly describing the role of Sir Syed Ahmad Khan and Aligarh Movement, this work deals with a very crucial phase of the Indian Freedom Movement until the Independence of India.

Sir Syed Ahmad Khan played the most important role to save the innocents during the rebellion of 1857. As he was in the service of the British Government, he tried his level best to solve the issues between the rebellious leaders and the British. In this process of mediation, he met a heavy loss by losing many of his relatives and even his mother. After the suppression of the rebellion, he tried to save the Muslim masses which were being massacred by the British on the charge of the revolt. Sir Syed Ahmad Khan followed the loyalist policy to save the Muslim masses from the heavy hand of the British. He became successful in persuading the British Government that the people of India, including all caste and creed, revolted due to the unfavourable policies of the Government.

After Sir Syed Ahmad Khan, his true followers also adopted the loyalist policy towards the British Government. These Aligarh loyalists devoted all their time and energy to ameliorate the position of the Muslim community with the help and cooperation of the

British Government. They tried to get the charter of Aligarh Muslim University, to get government grants, to open different departments of study in the AMU and also provide government jobs to their students. However, there was another section of AMU, which advocated national and political ideas along with the Indian National Congress and Muslim League. They devoted their full energy and strength in the Indian National Movement. They invited the reputed National leaders in AMU and mobilised and encouraged the students for freedom struggle. Most of the old boys and staff members of old MAO College and AMU also contributed to the national movement.

Although, a lot of work has been done on Sir Syed Ahmad Khan, but as far as political and educational history of AMU and its role in the national movement, no more work is noticed until now. It is this gap, which I have intended to fill-up by writing this book. The sources on the subject are wide spread, which have facilitated to complete this book. Among them the contemporary sources, the life sketch of the prominent personalities, related to this topic, needs to be reviewed here shortly.

Habibullah Khan has written the biography of Sahibzada Aftab Ahmad Khan with the name of *Hayat-i-Aftab*. In his book, he has covered particularly the contribution of Sahibzada Aftab Ahmad Khan to the AMU both as Vice-Chancellor and as well-wisher of the university. In his book, he has emphasised the Jubilee Celebrations of the AMU and personal differences between Pro-Vice-Chancellor Dr. Ziauddin Ahmad and Vice-Chancellor Sahibzada Aftab Ahmad Khan. The Rahmatullah Enquiry Report has also been very widely discussed in his book.

Another scholar Mohammad Amin Zuberi has written the life sketch of Dr. Ziauddin Ahmad *Zia-i-Hayat*. This is a very important work as it covers the whole period from Dr. Ziauddin Ahmad's Principalship of the MAO College to his last term as Vice-Chancellor of AMU up to 1947. It describes how Dr. Ziauddin Ahmad devoted his entire life to the institution and proved himself a real successor of Sir Syed Ahmad Khan. He made many changes in the curriculum of AMU and opened different departments in Aligarh Muslim University. The differences between Sahibzada Aftab Ahmad Khan and Dr. Ziauddin Ahmad have also been discussed in detail. Dr. Ziauddin Ahmad himself has written a book named *Bayan* in which he has discussed his experiences.

Another associate of Sir Syed Ahmad Khan was Shaikh Abdullah (Papa Miyan) who had devoted his whole life for the women's education and established Women's College in Aligarh. He has written a book *Mushahidat-o-Taassurat* in which he has discussed all his efforts regarding women's education in Aligarh. He also served AMU in various capacities. Another scholar Shamsur Rahman Muhsini has written a book about Shaikh Abdullah named *Hayat-i-Abdullah*. In this book, Muhsini has covered the contribution of Shaikh Abdullah to both the AMU and Women's College. The differences among Shaikh Abdullah, Dr. Ziauddin Ahmad and Sir Ross Masood have also been discussed in detail.

A careful scrutiny of these works has enabled me to throw new light on educational and political issues faced by AMU during the proposed period so far ignored. The contemporary English and Urdu newspapers, confidential files from Aligarh Library, various registers, different reports, many proceedings, related magazines and journals from Aligarh, Lucknow and Delhi Archives have been duly utilised.

Among the main chapters of this book, first chapter deals with Sir Syed Ahmad Khan and his Aligarh Movement. The second chapter deals with the establishment of Aligarh Muslim University. Next two chapters describe the educational developments in AMU. The other two chapters attempt to throw light on the political role of AMU in the national movement.

The first chapter "Sir Syed Ahmad Khan and Aligarh Movement" deals with the brief life sketches of Sir Syed Ahmad Khan, different views of various historians regarding thoughts and policies of Sir Syed Ahmad Khan and introduction of Aligarh Movement. Most of the scholars have admired the educational works of Sir Syed Ahmad Khan and appreciated his dream of developing MAO College into a university based on Oxford and Cambridge.

The second chapter "Establishment of Aligarh Muslim University" deals with the movement for establishing the Aligarh Muslim University, its Act and constitution, establishment of Jamia Millia Islamia, etc. After the death of Sir Syed Ahmad Khan in 1898, his friends and followers, in order to prove true to the dream of their godfather, started a movement to set-up a university at Aligarh. They collected the required money and sent the proposal to the government to grant the charter for the proposed AMU. Due to the First World War and controversy about the affiliation powers of the university, the movement had to be stopped in the midway. Nevertheless, at the time when Khilafat and Non-Cooperation movements were launched, the government found an opportunity to woo the Muslims from the national platform by granting them the charter of the AMU at the end of 1920. Surely, it was the long-cherished dream of Sir Syed Ahmad Khan and his Aligarh Movement. AMU's Act was different from that of the Banaras Hindu University. The AMU Court was given enormous powers.

This chapter also includes the establishment of Jamia Millia Islamia. This university was an offshoot of the Khilafat and Non-Cooperation movements. Mohammad Ali and Shaukat Ali, popularly known as Ali brothers, along with Mahatma Gandhi arrived in Aligarh in 1920 to convince the MAO College authorities about their national programme. On refusal of the college authorities, they founded an independent national university at Aligarh, which was known as Jamia Millia Islamia. Jamia Millia Islamia later on shifted to New Delhi.

The third chapter "Educational Activities in AMU, 1920-1928" deals with educational pattern, medium of instructions, spiritual teachings, nationalism, communal harmony, and culture and traditions of AMU. It also includes developmental works done by the Vice-Chancellors like, Raja Mohammad Ali Mohammad Khan, Nawab Muzammilullah Khan Sherwani, and Sahibzada Aftab Ahmad Khan. Special reference is given to the activities of the Pro-Vice- Chancellor Dr. Ziauddin Ahmad. The Golden Jubilee Celebrations of Aligarh Muslim University has also been given much attention. Special focus also has been made on the differences between the Vice-Chancellor Sahibzada Aftab Ahmad Khan and Pro-Vice- Chancellor Dr. Ziauddin Ahmad. Abdullah Inquiry Committee and Rahmatullah Enquiry Committee also have been very widely discussed.

This chapter also includes the expansion of the university and establishment of many departments of studies. In this chapter, the culture and traditions of AMU have been very widely discussed. It also includes the social life of the students residing in the hostels, particularly the cordial equation between Hindu students and Muslim students. The Hindu students took pride in having absorbed in the tradition and culture of the AMU.

When the AMU started functioning, many new departments of study were created. With the efforts of Dr. Ziauddin Ahmad and Sahibzada Aftab Ahmad Khan, many appointments were made to run the full-fledged departments. Substantial grants were collected for that purpose.

In 1925 in order to popularise the university among the Indians, particularly among the Indian Muslims, the Silver Jubilee Celebration of AMU was observed. Many political and educational organisations were also invited to hold their sessions as part of the university's Silver Jubilee Celebration due to which the celebration proved a grand success. In addition to these activities, enormous fund was also collected to start new departments of studies in the AMU.

Aligarh Muslim University faced a great crisis during the late twenties as a result of the differences among its authorities, who were true followers of Sir Syed Ahmad Khan. They were all dedicated and did their best for the welfare of the university in their own way, but lacked harmony of ideas. This led to mutual jealousy leading to a cold war between them. AMU Pro-Vice-Chancellor Dr. Ziauddin Ahmad was the main target of a group, who was very critical of his way of workings. A committee was appointed to enquire into the working of Dr. Ziauddin Ahmad. This committee came to be known as Rahmatullah Enquiry Committee. A few months later, the committee submitted its report and filially Dr. Ziauddin Ahmad was asked to resign from his post.

The fourth chapter is devoted to "Educational Progress in AMU, 1929-1947." At the beginning of this chapter, the educational developments in Aligarh Muslim University from 1929 to 1947, have been discussed. The developmental works under Sir Shah Mohammad Sulaiman, Syed Ross Masood and Dr. Ziauddin Ahmad have been discussed in detail. Many appointments were made to run the full-fledged departments. Substantial grants were collected for that purpose. A separate fund was collected for the establishment of the Engineering and Medical Colleges in AMU.

Towards the end of this chapter women's education in AMU has been very widely discussed. A great effort was made to educate the Muslim girls in Aligarh. It was a revolutionary step because the Muslims in general were rigid and orthodox on providing English education to their daughters. They were not prepared to send their daughters to English school and boarding. However, Shaikh Abdullah by his herculean efforts transformed the dream of educating the Muslim girls into reality. As a result, the boarding school was started with enough strength of the girl students. Later on, this school developed into a college.

The fifth chapter deals with "Contribution of AMU to the National Politics till 1937." This chapter consists of formation of the Muslim League, responses over Tripoli and Balkan wars, Khilafat and Non-Cooperation Movement in Aligarh. It also includes the influence of the Congress and Muslim League over Aligarh Muslim University. AMU's efforts of Hindu-Muslim unity and its national programmes are also the major portions in this chapter. The alumni's role in the national politics has also been widely discussed.

In this section formation of Muslim League and anti-British feelings in Aligarh are discussed in short. This chapter also throws light on the Khilafat and Non-Cooperation movements in Aligarh. The Khilafat committees were set-up on the provincial and central level in order to boycott British goods. The movement also embarked upon complete non-cooperation with the British Government. Mahatma Gandhi and other national leaders took it as a golden opportunity to mobilize the Indian Muslims into the nationalist fold. Mahatma Gandhi, who presided over the Khilafat Committee, appealed to the Hindus to cooperate with their Muslim brethren in their movements. This movement was greatly helped in bringing about unity between the Hindus and Muslims in India.

Since long it was the general belief that Aligarh played a negative role in the National Movement, but this chapter of the present work proves that almost all Aligarh old boys spread all over India and abroad and carried their national programmes to oust the Englishmen from India. They extended their cooperation to the political parties like, Indian National Congress, Muslims League, Khilafat Party, *Swaraj* Party, Communist Party, etc.

The sixth chapter "Political Activities in Aligarh from 1937 to 1947" deals with the very critical study of the reactions of AMU authorities and Student's Union to the Muslim League; responses to the Indian National Congress and British policies; activities of political parties and groups in AMU, responses of the AMU community over the demand for Pakistan; partition of India and its reaction in Aligarh Muslim University.

1940 was the very crucial year in the history of the freedom movement as the Pakistan resolution was passed by Muslim League. This resolution further forced the League leaders to motivate Muslim masses in favour of the movement for Pakistan. They toured throughout India and delivered speeches, especially in educational institutions to mobilize the Muslim support. They also tried to motivate the AMU students and received a positive response. The Congress also tried to bring the AMU students in their favour but except a handful of students no one paid any attention to whatever they said.

The Muslim League was successful in opening its branches in Aligarh city and in AMU. Even the children of Aligarh formed a 'Bachcha Muslim League'. These organisations passed many resolutions supporting Pakistan Movement and expressed their faith in the leadership of Mr. Mohammad Ali Jinnah. Mr. Mohammad Ali Jinnah succeeded in keeping his hold on the Aligarh Muslim University. Their resolutions confirm their strong faith and support in Jinnah and to his demand for Pakistan.

In 1946, under a proposal of the Cabinet Mission, the Interim Government was formed by the Indian National Congress and only after much persuasion Mr. Mohammad Ali Jinnah agreed to nominate a few members to the Interim Government. The purpose seems to serve as a deterrent to Congress programmes because the League by now had the only demand that of Pakistan for which only a few months back he had given the call for 'Direct Action' to achieve the objective.

The Direct Action day was followed by communal riots, first in Bengal and in the rest of India afterwards. Even after joining the Interim Government by the Muslim League, the communal riots did not stop. The Muslim League was bent upon to achieve its goal but Mahatma Gandhi was not in favour of partition of India. However, in order to stop the communal disturbances and keeping in view of the future prospects the Indian National Congress accepted the partition plan after much opposition of Mahatma Gandhi. Due to this acceptance of the partition plan by the Congress, the impossible dream of Mr. Mohammad Ali Jinnah became a reality. Aligarh Muslim University, though a stronghold of Mr. Jinnah, found itself in a state of shock, when the country was partitioned; perhaps, even Jinnah did not think to get it in his lifetime.

The seventh and last chapter of this book is the conclusion, and author's own opinion regarding all the above chapters of this book. The above resume would help the reader in forming the general idea of the main contents of the book as also of the line of thought and approach adopted by the author in attempting a descriptive, analytical and critical account of the educational and political history of the Aligarh Muslim University.

In the last, I feel it my pleasant duty to acknowledge the kindness, advice and help, which I received from my teachers, Professor Irfan Habib, Professor Iqbal Hussain and Professor Mujeeb Ashraf. I am also indebted to my colleagues, friends and relatives Dr. Mohammad Isa Gauhar, Dr. Tufail Ahmad, Dr. Siraj Ahmad, Master Nisar Ahmad, Mr. Mazharul Haque, Mr. Wahid Ali, etc. who are also worth praising, without whose encouragement, moral support and active co-operation, this work would not have been possible. I am grateful to my wife Imrana Anjum, my children Lubna, Iram, Anam and Sadaf for their kind support and constant encouragement.

I am also indebted to the authorities and staff of the National Archives, New Delhi; Nehru Memorial Museum and Library, New Delhi; Zakir Husain Library, JMI, New Delhi; UP State Archives, Lucknow; AMU Union Hall; AMU Archive; AMU Research Library Department of History; Maulana Azad Library, AMU, Aligarh; and YMD College Library, Nuh, for allowing me to use the source material preserved in their collection.

Aijaz Ahmad
Associate Professor in History
YMD College, Nuh, Mewat, Haryana

Contents

1
Sir Syed Ahmad Khan and Aligarh Movement

After the fall of the Mughal Empire and other Muslim Kingdoms and principalities, the positions of the Muslims in general and *Ulema* class, in particular, badly worsened. At the outbreak of the Rebellion of 1857, in order to gain their lost power and prestige, the Muslims along with other castes and communities actively took part against the British rule. However, after the suppression of the rebellion, the heavy hand of the British Government fell upon them. It left a deep impact on the entire Muslim community of India. At that crucial time Sir Syed Ahmad Khan, although being a government official, took the cause of the Muslims and worked for their betterment.

Sir Syed Ahmad Khan: A Brief Introduction

Sir Syed Ahmad Khan (October 17, 1817—March 27, 1898) was born to Mir Mohammad Taqi and Aziz-un-Nisa in Delhi. It is said that his forefathers had migrated to India at the time of Mughal Emperor Akbar from Herat in Afghanistan. His ancestors from paternal and maternal side were closely attached to the Mughal administration from many generations. His grandfather Syed Mohammad Hadi came from Herat and settled in Hindustan. His grandfather Syed Mohammad Hadi was given the titles of Jowahid Khan and Javed-ud-Daulah, a *mansab* of 1000/500, in the court of Mughal Emperor Alamgir-II. Syed Ahmed Khan's father, Syed Mohammad Taqi, was a man of deep religious feeling, and on his father's death, declined all titles from the Mughal Emperor Akbar Shah-II, though offered those of his father. His maternal grandfather Khwaja Fariduddin served as *wazir* in the court of Mughal Emperor Akbar Shah-II.[1]

On his father's death in 1836, the Emperor Bahadur Shah Zafar bestowed upon Syed Ahmad Khan, the title of his grandfather, 'Javed-ud-Daulah' with an additional title 'Aarif Jang'. He received education on the subjects like Persian, Arabic, Urdu, and Islamic jurisprudence at his home. He never received any formal instruction in English but through his own personal efforts, he gained some smattering of the language and could understand, speak, and write. In January 1837, he stopped his education, and, greatly against the inclination of his relatives, entered the British service as *Sar-Rishtadar* (an official) of the Criminal Department in the Sadar Amin's office at Delhi. In February 1839, he was transferred to Agra as Naib Munshi or deputy reader in the office of the Commissioner of that Division. In December 1841, he became Munsif or Sub-Judge of Fatehpur Sikri and was transferred to Delhi in January 1846. Here as Munsif in Delhi, he wrote his famous book, *Asar-us-Sanadid* (Archeological analysis on the historical buildings of Delhi).[2]

In 1850, Sir Syed Ahmad Khan was posted to Rohtak as subordinate judge; and in 1855, he was transferred in the same capacity to Bijnor, where he remained until the Uprising broke out in May 1857. When the news of the Meerut mutiny reached Bijnor on the 13th May, there were many European residents, whose lives were at stake. These were Mr. and Mrs. Shakespeare and their child; Mr. Palmer; Dr. and Mrs. Knight; Mr. R. Currie; Mr. and Mrs. Lemaistre, and three children; Mr. Johnson; Mr. and Mrs. Murphy, and four children; and Mr. Cawood. Mr. Shakespeare and Syed Ahmad Khan, in order to prepare them from any danger and to save the life of the Europeans, raised a body of 100 Pathan horse and foot for their protection and also arranged intelligence for the daily news regarding the progress of the Uprising.[3]

About the end of May, the Uprising erupted at Bijnor but Sir Syed Ahmad Khan convinced the Roorki mutineers to bye-pass the Bijnor and advised Mr. Shakespeare to hide the treasury in the well. However, after a few days, Sir Syed Ahmad Khan heard that the Europeans, who were all in one house, were being surrounded by

Mahmud Khan (nephew of Ghulam Qadir Khan who had put out the eyes of Emperor Shah Alam), and his 800 strong men. Sir Syed rushed to that place accompanied by Mir Turrab Ali, Tahsildar, Rahmat Khan, Deputy Collector, and Pratap Singh (later Raja) of Tajpur. Sir Syed urged to Nawab Mahmud Khan to save the life of Europeans and allow them to leave the city and congratulated the Nawab on receiving the country of his ancestors. The Nawab, after fully convincing with the suggestion of Sir Syed Ahmad Khan, provided the Europeans, the required carriage for the departure. The Nawab thereupon gave them two elephants, a bullock cart and Rs. 3000 for necessary expenditure. All the Europeans departed from Bijnor and safely reached to Meerut.[4]

Meanwhile, three Hindu landholders, the Chaudharies of Haldour and Tajpur, gathered their retainers together, and attacked and defeated the Nawab's forces. This created a political as well as administrative disturbance at Bijnor. Sir Syed Ahmad Khan was ordered by Meerut Commissioner to rule the district under the name of English with the assistance of Deputy Collector Mahmud Rahmat Khan and Tahsildar Turrab Ali. However, a month later the Chaudhary of Haldour attacked and plundered at a Muslim village Nagina and slaughtered a number of inhabitants. The Muslim people urged the Nawab Mahmud Khan to take over the administration at the district as the English administration failed to provide them protection. The Nawab accordingly attacked and captured Bijnor. Unfortunately, Sir Syed Ahmad Khan fled to Haldour which created suspicion among the Muslims that the Nagina attack was in connivance of Sir Syed Ahmad Khan. The Nawab attacked and took Haldour, and Syed Ahmad fled to another village, Chandpur, where he was surrounded by a crowd of Muslims who shouted out, "There is the man who brought about the massacre of Mohammadans at Nagina!" From Chandpur, Sir Syed Ahmad Khan, aided by some friends, escaped to Meerut at the end of September, after four months of anxiety and peril.[5]

Towards the end of September 1857, he visited his home at Delhi and heard that his mother had taken refuge in one of her horse attendant's houses. His biographer Graham wrote that on his calling out to her, she opened the door, crying out, "Why have you come here? All are being killed. You will be killed also!" Sir Syed

Ahmad Khan came to know that her mother had been living on the horses' grain for five days, and was very weak. For three days, she had no water. He took his mother back with him to Meerut, but the shock and anxiety of mind that she had suffered during the siege and at the assault were too much for her, and she died a month afterwards. Sir Syed Ahmad Khan's uncle and cousin, whose house adjoined his at Delhi, were slain unarmed by the infuriated Sikhs three days after the assault.[6]

In July 1858, he was transferred to Moradabad as Principal Sadar Amin[7] or Native Judge and for his services during the revolt, he received a special pension of Rs. 200 per month and a *khil'at* of one cap of four cones, one *gashwara* or outer turban, one *neem astin* or jacket, one pair of shawls, one belt, one *jugha* or coat, one *surpech* or turban of honour, one pearl necklace and one sword. His loss in goods and chattels at Delhi and at Bijnor, he estimates at Rs. 30,384.00.[8]

During the Uprising, the British Government experienced that it was happened due to the Muslims religious war or *Jihad,* and after the revolt they massacred mostly the Muslim theologians and innocent Muslim masses. The animosity between the British and Muslims before and after the rebellion of 1857 threatened to the marginalized Muslim communities across India. In this grave situation, Sir Syed Ahmad Khan firmly stood to defend the Indian masses in general and Muslims in particular. This knighted servant of the British Imperialism was, in the real sense, a first rebel in his own way, after the revolt of 1857.

He was the first person who declared that the British policies were the sole cause of the Uprising while defending the people of India. Sir Syed Ahmad Khan said that for a long period, many grievances had been rankling in the hearts of the people. In a course of time, a vast store of explosive material was collected. It wanted but the application of a match to light it, and that match was applied by the mutinous army. The English were living over a volcano ready to burst into deadly violence at any moment, but they could not, or would not, apprehend their danger.[9]

In 1858, Sir Syed Ahmad Khan wrote a booklet *Asbab-e-Baghawat-e-Hind* (The Causes of the Indian Revolt) in which he rejected the common notion that the conspiracy was planned by

Muslims. In this booklet, he blamed the British East India Company for its aggressive expansion as well as the ignorance of British politicians regarding Indian culture. Sir Syed advised the British to appoint the Indian people in their Legislative Councils. According to Sir Syed Ahmad Khan, there were five causes of Uprising, which compelled the Indian people to rise against the British rule. The causes were as follows:[10]

1. Ignorance on the part of the people: by which I mean misapprehension of the intentions of government.
2. The passing of such laws and regulations and forms of procedure as jarred with the established custom and practice of Hindustan and the introduction of such as were in themselves objectionable.
3. Ignorance on the part of the government of the conditions of the people; of their modes of thought and of life; and of the grievances through which their hearts were becoming estranged.
4. The neglect on the part of our rulers of such points as were essential to the good Government of Hindustan.
5. The bad management and disaffection of the army.

Sir Syed Ahmad Khan not only charged the British Government for their bad policies in India but also boldly defended the Indians and particularly Muslims who were more convicted in this regard. He tried a lot to save the Muslim community from the heavy hands of the British Government. As the Muslims and the *Ulema* class were the worst sufferers after failure of the Uprising, Sir Syed Ahmad Khan, while negotiating the British authorities, deliberately hided the real facts as well as participation of the Muslims in the Uprising. While hiding the facts of the participation of Muslim clerics and masses, he wrote a letter to Sir John Key of India Office, London, in December 1869. In this letter, he boldly asserted that the people who participated in the Uprising were of three groups as follows:[11]

1. Robbers and dacoits who were kept down by the power and strength of the government, now assembling in numbers, not only attacked way-farers but also plundered villages and even towns.

2. Some of the minor chiefs, whose families had fallen into decay, endeavoured the resuscitation of their ancestral power. This sort of mutiny occurred in four places only: Kanpur, Bareilly, Bijnor, and Farrukhabad. Some of these parties tried to have themselves restored, while others were compelled by the mutineers to make an effort.
3. Some of the lower classes, variously employed, entered the service of these rebellious chiefs.

In the same letter Sir Syed Ahmad Khan accused the British Army officers of Meerut for not handling properly to the Sepoys which became a spark for the Uprising. He wrote, "It cannot be denied that the use of the greased cartridges did violence to the superstition of the Sepoys, who consequently determined not to bite the same. Almost all the Sepoys had unanimously resolved never to bite the cartridge, which determination was the only charge that could be brought against them, till a very severe punishment was inflicted upon them at Meerut, a punishment which produced a strong impression on the minds of those men, that they must either bite the greased cartridges or suffer the punishment of their disobedience. And it was then and not before that the discontent of the Sepoys grew into a military mutiny. I am strongly of opinion that if before the infliction of punishment the alternative either of biting the cartridges or resigning the service had been offered to them, the Sepoys would undoubtedly have peaceably withdrawn themselves from the Company's service."[12]

Sir Syed Ahmad Khan advocated that the British Government was not acquainted with the unhappy state of Indian people. He requested the government that in order to know the public mentality; Indians must be included in the Councils. Sir Syed Ahmad Khan says, "I only wish to say that they were misconstructed by people, and that this misconstruction hurried on the rebellion. Had there been a native of Hindustan in the Legislative Council, the people would never have fallen into such errors."[13]

The criticism of Sir Syed Ahmad Khan received the due attention of the British Government, and next year nominated Raja Narendra Singh (Rais Patiala), Raja Devi Narain (Rais of Banaras), and Raja Dinkar Rao (Dewan of Gwalior) to the Legislative Council.[14]

His book *Asbab-e-Baghawat-e-Hind* was the first book of its kind about the Uprising of 1857, which boldly criticized the policies of the British Government and advised for reformation in the system according to the need of the time. His book first published from Agra, and he sent its copies to England and the British Parliament.

His friend Rai Shankar Das advised him to burn the copies rather than put his life in danger. Sir Syed Ahmad Khan said that he was bringing these matters to the attention of the British for the good of his own people, of his country, and of the government itself. He also said that if he came to any harm while doing something that would greatly benefit the rulers and the subjects of India alike, he would gladly suffer whatever befell him. When the Government of India had the book translated and presented before the Council, Lord Canning, the Governor-General, and Sir Barthold Frere favourably accepted it as a sincere and friendly report. When the House of Commons discussed the pamphlet, Mr. Sale Beadon, the Foreign Secretary, vehemently opposed it and asked the government to imprison such a revolutionary writer. However, Parliament did not support him. On the contrary, most of the British papers supported the views of Syed Ahmad and advised the government to act upon the valuable recommendations made by him. The foreign secretary Sale Beadon, however, severely attacked it, calling it 'an extremely seditious pamphlet'. He wanted a proper inquiry on the matter and said that the author, unless he could give a satisfactory explanation, should be harshly dealt with. Since no other member of the Council agreed to his opinion, his attack did no harm.[15]

In addition to the *Asbab-e-Baghawat-e-Hind,* Sir Syed Ahmad Khan wrote another book *The Loyal Mohammadans of India*, in 1860, to save the Muslims from the cruelties of the British Government. He emphasized that during and for long after the Uprising, the Muslims were under a cloud. To them were attributed all the horrors and calamities of that terrible time; and that this prejudice was to a very great extent unjust, and that it was regretted and resented by the Muslims, is undoubted. In this book, he reminded the government for the services rendered by the Indian Muslims during the memorable years of 1857-58.[16]

Defending his Muslim brethren, Sir Syed Ahmad Khan says in his book, *The Loyal Mohammadans of India,* "...Undoubtedly, if a man be guilty of a really culpable act, there can be no extenuation for it; but when he is enveloped by the sombre mantle of misfortune, even his good deeds are open to suspicion and misconstruction, and are either condemned *in toto*, or said to proceed from a latent sinister motive. Certainly, good and bad are to be found in every class and creed; but the proverb that 'a fish pollutes all water' has reference especially to a season of distress; for it is a peculiarity of the time, that if even one man has done ill, the entire class to which he belongs is held up to execration; and although a large number of that class may have done right well, nobody thinks of their good deeds, and they get no credit for them. Now the season of dire extremity to which I allude is that which befell the Mohammedans in 1857-58. There was no atrocity committed then of which the blame was not imputed to the Mohammadans, although the parties really guilty may have been Ramdin and Matadin....There was no prickly thorn in those awful times respecting which it was not said that it was planted by a Mohammedan! There was no fiery whirlwind that was not raised by a Mohammadan."[17]

In 1876, when Hunter wrote a book *The Indian Musalmans,* which defamed the Indian Muslims in all around, Sir Syed Ahmad Khan once again came forward in their defence. In 1872, he wrote a review of Hunter's book in which he answered the every aspect which had been discussed in that book. After their participation of the Uprising of 1857, the Indian Muslims were once again on the focus of British criticism. It was owing to three causes, viz., the Wahabi trials at Patna and Ambala, Dr. Hunter's book on '*The Indian Mussulmans*', and the murder of the late lamented Chief-Justice Norman. Sir Syed Ahmad Khan writes, as quoted by Graham, "Articles sneering at them, or misrepresenting their thoughts and feelings, sink deep into their soul, and work much harm. .... I had expected great things from Dr. Hunter's book. Alas that I should add one more to the long list of disappointed men! Friend to the Mohammadans as Dr. Hunter no doubt is, his friendship, as represented by this his last work, has worked us great harm. 'God save me from my friends!' was the exclamation which rose to my lips as I perused the author's pages.... he has used his 'power of the pen' in a way calculated still more to embitter the minds of Englishmen against the already little-loved Muslims."[18]

At the time of crisis, Sir Syed Ahmad Khan, tried his level best to prove the Muslim community loyal to the British Government based on the loyalty of a few people whose name he has mentioned in his book. However, the fact also could not be denied that the number of those people was like salt in the cooked food, and it is evident that these were the Muslim *Jihadis* or *Mujahideen,* who fought the war until their last breath.[19]

After the war of 1857, when the British Government started the persecution of the Muslims, and it appeared that the Muslims would not stand upon their feet again. The Mughal Empire was finally liquidated in the terrible blood bath of 1857. Sir Syed bitterly lamented on the plight of Muslims, and he thought that only modern education could improve their situation and change their mentality. That's why he established many schools wherever he was transferred.[20]

In 1859, he founded a primary school in Moradabad, in 1863 Victoria school in Ghazipur. In April 1864, Sir Syed Ahmad Khan got transferred at Aligarh where he continued his educational work of Scientific Society, which he had already established at Ghazipur in the same year. The idea of establishing an English medium school was born in his mind at Aligarh. In 1867, he was transferred to Banaras and on 1st April, 1869, Sir Syed Ahmad Khan, along with his two sons and servant Chajju, left for England to see the British system of education in England. Sir Sayed Ahmad Khan accompanied his sons Syed Mahmud and Syed Hamid, who were going to higher study in England, and after their return, they were appointed High Court Judge and Superintendent of Police in the North-West Provinces. Travelling across England, Sir Syed Ahmad Khan visited its colleges and was inspired by the culture of learning established after the Renaissance.[21]

Sir Syed returned to India towards the end of 1870 with determination to build a 'Muslim Cambridge' and resumed his duties of Native Judge at Banaras. Soon after his return from England, Sir Syed started a journal called the '*Mohammedan Social Reformer*', and wrote a series of articles combating the religious prejudices of his fellow-countrymen against the acquisition of modern science and art. Graham quotes, "He saw the weakness that had crept over Mohammadans through their estrangement from the thoughts and aspirations of the nineteenth century, and he proposed to himself the great task of makings Mohammadans changed, not their dogmas, but their policy, so that independence of mind and political liberation should no longer be accounted as symptoms of heterodoxy."[22]

In Aligarh, his work gained a further momentum. There he conceived the idea of establishing a college for imparting modern education to the Muslims. For this purpose, he formed the "Mohammadan Anglo Oriental College Fund Committee" in 1870 for collecting required money. He started his work with the establishment of a school "Madarsatul Uloom Musalmanan" in Aligarh, which was inaugurated on 24th May, 1875, on the occasion of the birthday of Queen Victoria, but the actual work commenced from first June of the same year. The school was affiliated to the Calcutta University for the matriculation examination. Its first batch of four students, Mahboob Alam, Harnath Singh, Ishrat Husain and Abdul Majid appeared in the matriculation examination and were declared passed. Mr. H.G.L. Siddon, an Englishman, was appointed as the first Headmaster and Mr. Baijnath Prasad was appointed as Second Master. On 12th November, the Governor of United Provinces, Sir William Muir visited the College and after a long address congratulated Sir Syed Ahmad Khan.[23]

In 1876, after thirty-seven years' service, Syed Ahmad retired on his pension, and took up his abode at Aligarh and continued the work of educational uplift of the nation. On 8th January, 1877, Honourable Edward Robert Lytton, Viceroy and Governor General of India laid the foundation stone of the College which was already running from 1875. At this occasion, Sir Syed Ahmad Khan gave expression to his earnest hopes that this College may expand into a University, whose sons shall go forth through the length and breadth of the land to preach the gospel of free enquiry, of large-hearted toleration and of a pure morality. Only to uplift the community Sir Syed Ahmad Khan accepted the membership of the Viceroy's Council for two terms from 1878-1882, but it crowned his long and honourable career.[24]

Through his articles in his journal '*Mohammadan Social Reformer*' and modern scientific ideology, Sir Syed Ahmad Khan was dubbed as an atheist. When the MAO College was started, a Mohammedan wrote to Mecca asking the priests as to their opinion on Syed Ahmad's proposed college. He said, "What is your opinion (may your Excellence continue) regarding the legality of an institution established by a man who does not believe in the existence of an Evil One; who denies the bodily night-journey of the Prophet to heaven; who does not believe the story of Adam; ... his institution was a school to teach atheism and spread irreligion, ... let me know whether it is religiously lawful for Mohammadans to aid this college or not." The Mecca priest accordingly wrote, "In this case no assistance is allowable to the institution. May God destroy it and its founder. No Mohammadan is allowed to give assistance to or countenance the establishment of such an institution. It is, moreover, the duty of the faithful to destroy it if it be established, and to chastise to the utmost those who are friendly to it." After this religious decree Sir Syed Ahmad Khan received numerous anonymous letters. One of the letters was quoted as, "Sher Ali, who assassinated Lord Mayo, was an idiot for doing so, as he could have ensured Paradise for himself by killing Syed Ahmad!"[25]

Sir Syed Ahmad Khan faced boldly all the hindrances came on his way and showed the right path of uplift and development to his Muslim community. Perhaps educationally upgrading the Muslim community was the only tribute to the Muslim martyrs of the Uprising of 1857. His efforts strengthened the Muslim community to cope with every future engagement and take active part in nation building by educating themselves in modern science and technology.

Political Ideas of Sir Syed Ahmad Khan

Sir Syed Ahmad Khan was the first modern Muslim philosopher, who not only saved the entire Muslim community in India from the British brutality, but showed them the right path following which the Muslims still flourishing and developing. No doubt his ideas and thinking were bitterly criticized by both Hindus and Muslims but his farsightedness forced them to realize the fact and need of the time.

Sir Syed Ahmad Khan realized that the Indian Muslims were educationally, socially, politically and economically backward and the panacea of all the evils was to persuade them to receive western education. For achieving these objectives, he founded an institution for imparting English education to the Muslims in 1875, which, later on in 1877, came to be known as Mohammadan Anglo Oriental College.

The MAO College, which he had founded, was gradually and systematically working towards his coveted goal. After Sir Syed Ahmad Khan, his efforts were carried on by his friends and disciples, the great luminaries of the age, Hali, Shibli, Zakaullah, Mohsinul Mulk, Viqarul Mulk, Nazir Ahmad etc., who clustered around his magnetic personality, extended their worthy help to the great reformer. Subsequently, this college was raised to the status of Aligarh Muslim University in 1920.

Sir Syed was one of those dynamic, progressive and radical revolutionary personalities of history, who have moulded the destinies of nations and changed the course of history. He began the work of regeneration of Muslims in the dreadful aftermath of 1857. The failure of the first war of India's independence not only resulted in putting an end to the political sway of the Muslims in India, but they, being the bitter enemy were persecuted by the British in all walk of life. They found themselves at the lowest ebb in the history of India. It was at this crucial turn of history that Sir Syed rose with courage, conviction, restlessness and burning passion to mould the destiny of the Indian Muslims.

Being an educational reformer in the interest of the Muslim community, the political attitude of Sir Syed Ahmad Khan was quite reactionary. He advised the Muslims to be completely devout themselves in western education to compete the need of the time. He also advised the Muslims not to take part in politics in view of the lessons of 1857 and nascent educational reform movement.

After great efforts, he had succeeded in changing the opinion and attitude of the British Government towards the Muslims. He totally opposed the active participation of the Muslims. In 1885, when the Indian National Congress was founded, the national leaders made an appeal the people of all-over India to join the Indian National Congress, irrespective of their caste and communities.

Following the appeal of the Congress, Sir Syed Ahmad Khan advised the Muslim community not to join the politics. He thought that at this stage, when the Muslims need to be equipped with western education with the cooperation of the British Government, their participation in politics may prove ruinous to their future. The Muslims, who had recently received a shocking treatment after 1857, were unable to afford any other shock. Sir Syed Ahmad Khan visualised Muslim's ameliorations in close ties with the British Government. A few years earlier, he also had declined to support the National Mohammadan Association founded in 1877 by Justice Ameer Ali of Calcutta. He said, "In my opinion, it is not proper for the Muslims to make any political agitation."[26]

Sir Syed thought that the Muslim's entry in the active politics would create a hindrance in British help, cooperation and in his mission of Muslim's upliftment. Keeping in view of this fact, Sir Syed's attitude towards Congress should not be given any communal colour. Pandit Jawahar Lal Nehru, while discussing Sir Syed's attitude towards Congress in his book, *The Discovery of India*, said, "He was not opposed to the Indian National Congress because he considered it predominantly a Hindu organization. He opposed it because he thought it was politically too aggressive and he wanted British help and cooperation.... He was in no way anti-Hindu or communally separatist."[27]

In opposing the Indian National Congress, Sir Syed Ahmad Khan had in his mind the Muslim welfare uppermost. His views had the following consideration:[28]

1. The Congress had tried to show that the Hindus and the Muslims were both united in this agitation. He was afraid that if something untoward happened as a result of this agitation, the Muslims would again be accused of all consequences.
2. He has realized as far back as 1857 that the Muslims would gain by allying themselves with the British.
3. Muslim's backwardness.
4. The Aligarh leaders were obsessed with an overweening idea of their political power and importance and consequently, held themselves aloof from the national movement.

Sir Syed once said that Indian Muslims must depend on the British for safeguarding of their interests and for their effective representation. He asked the Muslims to unite with British Government.[29]

His opposition to the Indian National Congress was based upon his personal experiences keeping in view of the ultimate good of the Muslims as understood by him. He had seen the unprecedented loss of life and property of the Indian Muslims as a consequence of their active participation in the revolt of 1857. The ruling class hated the Muslims and called them "conspirators, rebels and untrustworthy." Hence, the rulers did not trust the Muslim community.

Sir Syed wished to bridge the gap. He, therefore, began to work ceaselessly in bringing the British ruling class and the Muslim closer to each another through his writings, speeches and actions. It, however, does not mean that he was totally against the nationalist movement and spirit of nationalism. He was of the view that the participation of the Muslims at this stage in political activities would be premature. They should first acquire education, attain perfection in various worldly affairs and then decide their own political course.

After the death of Sir Syed Ahmad Khan in 1898, the circumstances turned the Muslims towards active politics. In 1906, a few Muslim leaders contributed to the formation of a political organization called as All India Muslim League. The purpose of formation of the All India Muslim League was not to oppose the British rule, but work for the betterment and safeguards of the Muslim interests. At the time of the establishment of the Aligarh Muslim University in 1920, the Indian political scenario was changed and it led to the involvement of Aligarh Muslim University in politics, though divided on the ideological basis.

Aligarh Movement

The Aligarh Movement was an effort of Muslim upliftment and awakening by Sir Syed Ahmad Khan. He felt that the Muslim community, in order to take its rightful place in the country, must undertake all-embracing reforms, including religious belief and practices, social life and education, manners and customs, etc. Sir

Syed Ahmad Khan wanted to make all Muslims realise the significance of the age and take up challenge of the time. This movement was necessary because the Muslims suffered from the depressing feelings that they had not only lost political power forever and were in danger for losing their culture and civilization. The entire Muslim community was frustrated and lacked the sense of direction and aspiration. They wanted real torch bearer, who could show them the right path according to the need of the time.

Sir Syed Ahmad Khan never wanted the Muslim community to become misled once again as he had the example of Wahabi Movement and Rebellion of 1857 and the brutal results. He was sure that the anti-British trend of the Muslim community did not last long. So he stressed more to improve the relations between Muslims and the British Government and by this effort, government adopted the policy of paternalism towards the Muslims.

The most important aspect of this movement was to educate the Muslim community. He started his work from Moradabad, then Ghazipur and finally Aligarh. In Aligarh, his work gained a further momentum and a school "Madarsatul Uloom Musalmanan" was started on 24th May, 1875. Maulvi Samiullah's son Mr. Hamidullah Khan was admitted as the first student. On 1st June, 1875, a boarding house was started with seven students on the roll. On 8th January, 1877, Lord Lytton laid the foundation stone of the MAO College and described it as an epoch in the social progress of India. In 1878, the college was affiliated to the Calcutta University and Mr. Ishwari Prasad got the credit of passing the BA examination in 1881 as first student.

Initially, the orthodox Muslims were not ready for modem education and they thought that it would convert them into Christianity. However, Sir Syed Ahmad Khan continued his work of persuading the Muslim community for English education.

The Government of India also drew its attention to the unsatisfactory condition of the Muslim education. Governor-General in Council directed the local governments to inquire why Musalmans refrained from availing themselves of the education offered by the State.[30] In these circumstances, Sir Syed Ahmad Khan worked very hard to mobilize the Indian Muslims in favour of the modern education.

The MAO College continued to be affiliated to the Calcutta University until 1877, when it got to be affiliated to the newly founded Allahabad University.[31] It was partly financed by the British Government. The MAO College was based on Oxford and Cambridge Universities in pattern of education and religious practices. Its medium of instruction was English. About the religious practices in the college, Sir Syed Ahmad Khan once said, "just as the students of Oxford and Cambridge have to visit the Church and attend the prayer regularly,... the students will have to offer the congregational prayer five times a day."[32] He also said that they would all eat, play and study at fixed times.[33] He considered an education without religious instruction to be a body without soul.[34]

Although MAO College was founded primarily for Muslims, it openly welcomed Hindu students both as day scholars and as boarders. Commenting on the secular atmosphere at the MAO College, S.K. Bhatnagar writes: "Co-existence of Hindus and Muslims in the college on terms of equality continued to operate effectively throughout the life of Sir Syed Ahmad Khan and his faith in secularism was never dimmed."[35]

Aligarh Institute Gazette has clarified the object of opening the MAO College that in addition of providing modern education to the Muslims, the most important object of the college was the improving of understanding between the English and Muslims.[36] M.S. Jain in his book *Aligarh Movement* has emphasized the aim of opening the MAO College that the college was such an institution as would suit not only the present but also the future needs of the Muslim community.[37]

While emphasising the future needs of Muslim community Sir Syed Ahmad Khan said, "If you wish to attain honour, prosperity and high position, strive your interest to acquire high English education, which is the only means for your real improvement. Your case is hopeless until you educate yourselves highly and learn to value of self-reliance, self-control and self-help."[38]

The main obstruction in the ameliorating work of Sir Syed Ahmad Khan was the interference of the Muslim theologians and the orthodox Muslim society. They continuously attacked Sir Syed Ahmad Khan by spreading different types of rumour. This resulted the circulation of many *fatwas*, declaring him a *Kafir* (infidel). Sir

Syed Ahmad Khan was called *Naturi* (believing in nature blindly), and an agnostic, an atheist and a *Dajjal*, and all sorts of bad names were associated with him.[39]

However, Sir Syed Ahmad Khan faced the Muslim theologians and the orthodox Muslim society very boldly and they never become successful in turning him from his goal of amelioration of Muslim community. Actually, Sir Syed Ahmad Khan was a man of farsightedness and he thought that only English and scientific education could make the Muslims equal to the other communities of the world. It was the talisman of Sir Syed Ahmad Khan to cope the present as well as problems of the Muslim society. However, at that time in the Muslim society, English education was considered to be hateful and regarded as dangerous to the Islamic faith and any move against this conception was challenged openly. Even the famous poet Akbar Allahabadi, while taunting the work of Sir Syed Ahmad Khan, his followers and Aligarh culture, expressed his views in the following couplet:

> *"Aiman Bechne Pe Hain Sab Tule Huye,*
> *Lekin Kharid Ho Jo Aligarh Ke Bhao Se."*

(All are now bending upon selling their faith only if it is bought at the rate fixed by Aligarh.)

In 1885, Indian National Congress was founded and it invited all the dynamic youths of all-over India. In its response, a lot of Indian youths began to join the newly established political organization. It was definitely a big jolt to the educational work of Sir Syed Ahmad Khan. Sir Syed Ahmad Khan was sure that only educated youths could bring the real political change in India, but until that time Muslims were uneducated and their participation in politics could prove dangerous to their community as well as the nation. In response to the Indian National Congress and to popularise the education, particularly western education among the Indian Muslims, Sir Syed Ahmad Khan founded All India Mohammadan Educational Congress in 1886.[40] In 1890, the word "Congress" was replaced by "Conference."[41]

Sir Syed Ahmad Khan was of the view that the healthy politics require the mature and well-educated people, who could understand the need of the time and following the farsighted policies could make better future of their people. Sir Syed Ahmad Khan thought that the Indian Muslims were not fit without acquiring proper western education. Because of these factors, Sir Syed Ahmad Khan was totally against the Muslim entry into politics, his only first and last aim was to educate the Muslims. To Sir Syed Ahmad Khan, the question of English education was essential to strengthen the mental faculties, to get government jobs and to improve the social, political and economic conditions of the people.

The famous politician Pandit Jawahar Lal Nehru had rightly understood the ideology of Sir Syed Ahmad Khan and said, "Syed's decision to concentrate on western education for Muslims was undoubtedly a right one, without that they could not have played any effective part in the building up of Indian nationalism."[42]

Sir Syed Ahmad Khan was a patron of Hindu-Muslim unity, a true patriot and a pure nationalist and also a man of secular outlook. In this regard, it is very essential to quote his speech of 27th January, 1873 to prove his nationalist ideology and secular thinking. He declared, "To be Hindu or a Muslim is a matter of inner faith and belief. It was nothing to do with the worldly matters and mutual social intercourse, India belongs to both of us (Hindus and Muslims). Both of us breathe the air of India and in equal measure drink the waters of Ganga and Yamuna. We share the happiness and sorrows of birth and death in an equal degree. Socially and culturally we have given to, and taken from each other. We have evolved a common language Urdu. We, by virtue of living in the same country are one nation."[43]

Sir Syed Ahmad Khan was the best icon of Hindu-Muslim unity, and he always tried to spread the communal harmony, brotherhood and nationalism. His famous quote regarding nationalism and Hindu-Muslim unity needs to be cited here. Sir Syed Ahmad Khan wrote in an article entitled "Hindu-Muslim Relations", "I have frequently said that India is a beautiful bride and Hindus and Muslims are the two eyes. Her beauty lies in the proper safety of these two eyes. If one of them is lost, this beautiful bride will become ugly and one eyed... In my opinion, the differences of religion as it exists between Hindus and Muslims cannot be an obstacle in their intercourse and sympathy for each other. Likewise, the political differences also cannot be an obstacle in maintaining close relations between the two. Without any doubt, as I want friendship, unity and love between the two communities in spite of religious distinction, similarly I want mutual cooperation, love sympathy and brotherhood especially without minding the political differences."[44]

Sir Syed Ahmad Khan appealed to the Indian people to unite together irrespective of their caste and creed. He logically described that the Hindu-Muslim unity or the unity among Indian people was the need of the time. In his speech at Lahore in 1873, he said, "I wish that all men irrespective of their religion and community may unite together for common weal. Our religions are undoubtedly different but there is no reason for enmity among us on this account."[45]

Sir Syed Ahmad Khan thought that nothing was more important than national unity or Hindu-Muslim unity. He stressed that if cow-slaughter was the reason of enmity between the two communities, the Muslims should abandon the beef eating. In this regard Sir Syed Ahmad Khan says, "I have repeatedly given my community to understand that it is a folly to annoy our Hindu brothers by resorting to cow-slaughter. If friendship can be established between us, then this is far better than cow-slaughter."[46]

Sir Syed Ahmad Khan was undoubtedly a symbol of Hindu-Muslim unity and nationalism. Somehow, he did not directly advocate for nationalism as that period was not ripe for that philosophy. However, Sir Syed Ahmad Khan always propagated those philosophies of unity of Indian people and Hindu-Muslim unity, which directly promoted nationalism and freedom of India. The social, political and educational work and philosophy of Sir Syed Ahmad Khan was known as "Aligarh Movement." Due to his long-life work of Hindu-Muslim unity and especially betterment of the Muslim community, the other communities of India and the nation also got a lot of inspirations from him.

Sir Syed Ahmad Khan died in 1898, but his work of the movement was carried on by his friends and pupils like Nawab Mohsinul Mulk, Nawab Viqarul Mulk, Dr. Ziauddin Ahmad, Sahibzada Aftab Ahmad Khan, Sir Agha Khan, etc. They continued the prime work of Aligarh Movement, including a new move of founding a Muslim University at Aligarh.

Sir Syed Ahmad Khan was succeeded by his son Syed Mahmud but in 1899, he gave way to Nawab Mohsinul Mulk the right-hand man of Sir Syed Ahmad Khan.[47] Nawab Mohsinul Mulk also followed the secular and unbiased policy of Sir Syed Ahmad Khan. During his Secretaryship, he started Sir Syed Memorial Fund to solve the monetary problems of MAO College. He also encouraged 'Duty Society,' which was set-up in 1890 for collection of funds for granting scholarship to the poor students. From 1907-12, the MAO College developed under the Secretaryship of Nawab Viqarul Mulk.[48]

Different Views about Sir Syed Ahmad Khan

About life and works of Sir Syed Ahmad Khan, most of his associates and historians have written a number of books and articles. The first among these works is the *Hayat-i-Javed* of Maulana Altaf Husain Hali. He was a close associate of Sir Syed Ahmad Khan. In his book, he has written every aspect of Sir Syed's life in detail such as educational, political, social, religious, etc.

Prof. H.K. Sherwani in his book *The Aligarh Movement* has defended Sir Syed's ideology and stated his secular attitude. He says that in 1877, at the time of the foundation of the Mohammadan Anglo Oriental College by Lord Lytton, a Christian H.G.I. Siddon was Headmaster and a Hindu Bhavani Chandra Chakravarti was the Second Master. He also says that along with the Muslim donors to the institution Sikh and Hindu donors such as Maharaja of Patiala, Maharaja of Vijayanagar and Maharaja of Banaras were in the fore. Sherwani also admits that the change in the political and ideological outlook of Sir Syed Ahmad Khan was due to influence of Theodore Beck, who was the Principal of MAO College from February 1884 to his death in September 1899.

Professor Shan Mohammad in his book *Sir Syed Ahmad Khan: A Political Biography* also testifies to the secular attitude of Sir Syed Ahmad Khan. He defended Sir Syed by referring to the first batch of MAO School, who appeared in matriculation examination, consisting of three Muslims viz., Mahboob Alam, Ishrat Husain and Abdul Majid and one Hindu student Harnath Singh. He also points out why Sir Syed adopted a different attitude after the formation of the Indian National Congress in 1885. Surayya Husain in her book *Sir Syed Ahmad Khan Aur Unka Ahad* also admits the same ideology.

S.K. Bhatnagar in his book *History of the MAO College, Aligarh* proves Sir Syed's love for Hindu-Muslim unity and secularism. He observes, "Co-existence of Hindus and Muslims in the college on terms of equality continued to operate effectively throughout the life of Sir Syed Ahmad Khan and his faith of secularism never dimmed." K.A. Nizami in his book *Sir Syed on Education, Society and Economy* also expresses the same opinion about Sir Syed and MAO College.

M.S. Jain in his book *The Aligarh Movement* gives entirely a different picture about Sir Syed and Mohammadan Anglo Oriental College. He says that Sir Syed's efforts and the college were basically for the Muslims. He further says, "The College was such an institution as would suit not only to the present, but also to the future needs of the Muslim community." Jain by quoting *Aligarh Institute Gazette* says that the most important object of the college was to bring about the better understanding between Muslims and the Englishmen.

The institution Mohammadan Anglo Oriental College was established no doubt basically for educating the Muslim community as it was the basic need of the time. However, the doors of his institution were always open for the other communities also. His attitude towards other communities was based on tolerance. This fact has been very wisely testified by Pt. Jawaharlal Nehru.

Jawahar Lal Nehru in his *Autobiography* admires the works of Sir Syed Ahmad Khan in the following words, "Syed's decision to concentrate on western education for Muslims was undoubtedly a right one, without that they could not have played any effective part in the building up of Indian nationalism." In his another book *The Discovery of India* Pt. Nehru says about Sir Syed Ahmad Khan, "He was not opposed to Indian National Congress because he considered it predominantly a Hindu organisation, he opposed it because he thought it was politically too aggressive and he wanted British help and cooperation ... he was in no way anti-Hindu or communally separatist."

Prof. Mujeeb Ashraf in his book *Hayat-ul-Bashir* has written the life and works of Maulvi Bashiruddin, a close associate of Sir Syed Ahmad Khan. In this book, Prof. Ashraf has thrown some light on the educational and political trends as developed in MAO College during the lifetime of Sir Syed Ahmad Khan as well as after his death. He has touched upon the contribution of various prominent Muslims to the establishment of AMU and the role of Educational Conference in the making of that great institution.

Another historian Sita Ram Singh in his presidential address of the Indian History Congress (54th Session 1992, Mysore) comments about Sir Syed that before 1885, he was the ardent supporter of the Hindu-Muslim unity. He quotes Sir Syed's words, "Now both of us live on the air of India, drink the holy water of Ganga and Yamuna, we both feed upon the products of the Indian soil, we both belong to the same country, we are a nation." Sita Ram says that after the formation of the Indian National Congress his attitude was changed. He believed and declared that the political interests of the Hindus and Muslims were not only different but also opposite. He then spoke of the Hindus and Muslims that they are not only the two nations but two warring nations who could not lead a common political life, if once the British retired from India.

From all the statements, it becomes clear that most of the historians have admired his movement of social and educational upliftment of the Muslim community. However, a few of them tried to prove him a man with secular outlook. In his social and educational mission, he was no doubt a secular, but when come to deal with political issues he tends to show his communal leanings. Surely, he was fearful of majority rule and exploitation of the Muslim community in the present democratic set-up. His utmost concern was the well-being of the Muslim community in India. It is because of this political thought of Sir Syed Ahmad Khan, the works of M.S. Jain, etc. reach to the conclusion that Sir Syed Ahmad Khan possessed a separatist and communal outlook.

NOTES

1. Graham, G.F.I., *The Life and Work of Sayed Ahmed Khan*, Edinburgh, 1885, pp. 1-2 (Hereafter cited as *The Life and Work of Sayed Ahmed Khan*).
2. *Ibid.*, pp. 6-8.
3. *Ibid.*, pp. 18-20.
4. *Ibid.*, pp. 20-25.

5. *Ibid.*, pp. 25-27.
6. *Ibid.*, pp. 27-28.
7. The Native Commissioners were of three kinds — Sadar Amins, Amins and Munsifs, who were subordinate to the District Judge. Sadar Amins sat at the headquarters of the Judge and Magistrate and were empowered to dispose of suits of which the subject matter did not exceed Rs. 100 in value, referred to them by the Judge. The Amins were nominated by the Judge and confirmed by the Sadar Diwani Adalat. They sat in the interior of the district. Each had a jurisdiction of about 10 square miles and could hear suits of which the subject matter did not exceed Rs. 50 in value referred to him by the Judge. A Munsif was appointed for each Thana and had an original jurisdiction in the case of suits of which the subject matter did not exceed Rs. 50. The Munsifs could receive plaints whereas Sadar Amins and Amins could only take up cases referred to them by the Judge. (Dewar, Douglas, *Hand-book to the English Pre-mutiny Records in the Government Record rooms of the United Provinces of Agra and Oudh*, Allahabad (ND), p. 1).
8. *The Life and Work of Sayed Ahmed Khan*, pp. 28 and 31.
9. Ahmad, Aijaz, *Uprising of 1857: Some Facts About Failure of Indian War of Independence*, New Delhi, 2014, p. 20.
10. *The Life and Work of Sayed Ahmed Khan*, pp. 202-204.
11. Khan, Syed Ahmad, *Asbab-e-Baghawat-e-Hind*, (Eng. Trans.), Patna, 1999, pp.15-16, see also *The Life and Work of Sayed Ahmed Khan*, p. 39.
12. *Ibid.*, p. 114.
13. *Ibid.*, p. 113.
14. *Ibid.*, p. 16.
15. Mohammad, Shan, *Writings and Speeches of Sir Syed Ahmad Khan*, Bombay, 1972, p. 20.
16. *Ibid.*, p. 15.
17. *The Life and Work of Sayed Ahmed Khan*, p. 58.
18. *Ibid.*, pp. 205-207.
19. Ahmad, Aijaz, *Indian Muslims Against British Rule*, New Delhi, 2014, p. 185.
20. *Ibid.*
21. *The Life and Work of Sayed Ahmed Khan*, pp. 59-60.
22. *Ibid.*, pp. 95-98 and 116.
23. Mohammad, Shan, *Sir Syed Ahmad Khan; A Political Biography*, Meerut, 1969, p. 9; see also Husain, Suraiya, *Sir Syed Ahmad Khan Aur Unka Ahad*, Aligarh, 1993, pp. 324-328, (Hereafter quoted as 'Suraiya Hussain'); Sherwani, H.K., *The Aligarh Movement*, New Delhi, 1969, pp. 25-27 (Hereafter quoted as Sherwani).
24. *The Life and Work of Sayed Ahmed Khan*, pp. 194 and 201.
25. *Ibid.*, pp. 252, 259, 267, 275 and 289-290. Finally, the dream of Sir Syed Ahmad Khan became true and in 1920 this MAO College was elevated to the Muslim University, after his death.

26. Muhammad, Shan, *Sir Syed Ahmad Khan*, Delhi, 1981, p. 229 (Hereafter cited as *Sir Syed Ahmad Khan*).
27. Nehru, Pandit Jawahar Lal, *The Discovery of India*, Calcutta, 1996, pp. 410-411.
28. Jain, M.S., *The Aligarh Movement*, Agra, 1965, pp. 119-121; see also *Aligarh Magazine*, July-October, 1921, p. 1.
29. *The Pioneer*, 11th January, 1888; see also Zakaria, Rafiq, *Rise of Muslims in Indian Politics,* Bombay, 1970, pp. 54-55.
30. *The Pioneer*, 8th January, 1877.
31. *Sir Syed Ahmad Khan*, p. 81.
32. *Tahzibul Akhlaq*, 1st Rajab, 1289 H.; see also Lelyveld, David, *Aligarh First Generation*, New Delhi, 1878, p. 129.
33. Lelyveld, David, *Aligarh First Generation*, New Delhi, 1878, p. 129.
34. *Aligarh Institute Gazette*, 21st August, 1874.
35. Bhatnagar, S.K., *History of the MAO College Aligarh*, New Delhi, 1869, p. 28, (Hereafter quoted as Bhatnagar); see also Nizami, Khaliq Ahmad, *Sir Syed on Education, Society and Economy*, Delhi, 1995, p. 90.
36. *Aligarh Institute Gazette*, 1st May, 1886.
37. Jain, M.S., *The Aligarh Movement*, Agra, 1865, p. 33.
38. *Aligarh Institute Gazette*, 1st March, 1890; see also Muhammad, Shan, *The Aligarh Movement*, Vol. III, Meerut, 1978, p. 995.
39. *Sir Syed Ahmad Khan*, p. 69.
40. Bhatnagar, S.K., *op.cit.*, p. 17.
41. *Sir Syed Ahmad Khan*, p. 85.
42. Nehru, Pandit Jawahar Lal, *An Autobiography*, New Delhi, 1962, pp. 458-459 (Hereafter quoted as *An Autobiography*).
43. Bhatnagar, S.K., *op.cit.*, p. 17.
44. *Aligarh Institute Gazette*, 12th June, 1897.
45. *Sir Syed Ahmad Khan*, p. 245 (taken from *Mukammal Majmua Lectures va Speeches of Sir Syed from 1863-1896*, Lahore, 1990, p.120).
46. Ahmad, Syed Tufail, *Musalmanon Ka Roshan Mustaqbil,* Delhi, 1945, pp. 316-317.
47. Sherwani, H.K., *op.cit.*, p. 317.
48. *Ibid.,* p. 37; see also Ashraf, Mujib, *Hayat-ul-Bashir*, New Delhi, 1997, p. 100.

2
Establishment of Aligarh Muslim University

The dream of Sir Syed Ahmad Khan was materialized in 1920, when Aligarh Muslim University established by his pupils and friends with their day-night continuous efforts. When the Indian Muslims were targeted after the Rebellion of 1857, Sir Syed Ahmad Khan continuously made efforts to free the Indian Muslims from the heavy hands of the British Government. Sir Syed Ahmad Khan came to the conclusion that only education can save them and mould their destiny in India. Consequently, Sir Syed Ahmad Khan conceived the idea of establishing a vernacular university in 1869, but he abandoned this idea after his visit to England.[1] He decided to lay the foundation of an educational institution which could fulfil the demand of the time and scenario. Scientific and modern education was the need of those days.

Movement for Establishing Aligarh Muslim University

Unfortunately, the dream of establishing a university could not be transformed into reality during the lifetime of Sir Syed Ahmad Khan. After his death, the alumni of the MAO College, the College Management and the well-wishers of the Muslim community launched a movement for establishing a Muslim University.[2]

The movement for establishing a Muslim University continued for a long time, and the British Government fully exploited the sentiments of the Muslim community. A group of the Indian Muslims, including the launchers of the Muslim University blindly followed the British Government. Perhaps on the government's instigation, the loyalist Muslims also formed a political party in 1906, parallel to the Indian National Congress. However, the British Government was not true to the Muslim loyalists. Undoubtedly, their ultimate aim was 'divide and rule'.

The British Government was deliberately delaying the demand, playing a double game and using the sentiments of the Indian Muslims, who were keen for the establishment of a university. In January 1911, a committee was constituted to establish a Muslim University at Aligarh with Sir Mohammad Agha Khan as the President and Nawab Viqarul Mulk as the Honourary Secretary.

The British Government also instigated the Hindu leaders to launch a similar movement for establishing a Hindu University. In order to materialize the divide and rule policy, the British Government wanted an equal and opposite Hindu University parallel to the Muslim University. On the eve of the visit of King George V to India in 1911, the British Government of India asked Hindus and Muslims to raise a sum of Rs. 30 lakhs for obtaining the charter for their respected universities.[3] But a little later, the British Government changed its stand on the questions of affiliating the colleges and the word "Muslim" of the name of Aligarh Muslim University.[4]

The changed attitude of the British Government caused a great setback to the university movement. The Indian Muslim youths realized the dubious attitude of the British Government and became sure that the British Government was no more their well-wisher as claimed since long. Subsequently, the attitude of the Indian Muslims about their loyalty to the British Government, to some extent, changed over the years and new section of nationalists stood against the government.[5]

The international incidents also adversely affected the Muslim University movement and consequently, delayed the foundation of the Muslim University. Definitely, the First World War and the Turkey's stand against the British and its allies adversely affected the campaign for a Muslim University. In between the Hindus under Madan Mohan Malviya became successful in obtaining the charter for the Banaras Hindu University, which was established at Banaras in 1916.

It is also true that during the First World War, Muslims were not much active in getting their university. They were fearful about the Turkey's fate, which was claimed as the religious and political centre of entire Muslim World. After the termination of the First World War, a session of the Muslim University Association was held at Aligarh on 15th October, 1919 in order to accelerate the Muslim University campaign.[6]

In 1919, an India Act was passed by the British Parliament. This Act further delayed the establishment of the Muslim University. Act of 1919, placed the university education under the control of the Provincial Government. This provision completely shattered the perception of the protagonists of the university. By and large, they were of the view that the Muslim University after its establishment would enjoy an all-India status and would be out of reach of Provincial Government.[7]

Efforts were made to establish the Muslim University under Central Government. It was decided to send the University Bill in the Central Legislature. Fortunately, Sir Mohammad Shafi, the Old Boy of the MAO College was serving as the education member in the Viceroy's Council. He came to Aligarh and had a discussion with Mr. Sharp (Secretary, Department of Education) and Dr. Wali Ahmad (Asstt. Secretary, Department of Education), on 23rd and 24th March, 1920. As a result of these discussions a few amendments were made in the proposed Constitution of the University. These amendments were approved by the Muslim University Association. After the amendments, the Honourary Secretary published a statement, "This constitution is more liberal than the Constitution of the Hindu University and the Decca University and there is no hope to get a better constitution than this."[8]

After the passage of the Act of 1919, the supporters of the foundation of the Muslim University felt that the proposed university bill should be delayed until the situation became favourable for its placement before the Central Legislative Council.[9] The proposed Muslim University constitution was, thereafter, sent to the Indian Government in July 1920. The Secretary of State for India approved the Muslim University constitution.[10] In the meantime Syed Mohammad Ali, the Secretary of the MAO College and Muslim University Association was given the additional membership of the Central Legislative Council so that he could represent the bill whenever introduced.[11]

The post-war situation cemented the understanding among the Muslims League, Congress and the Khilafat Committee leaders. In order to show the political unity and prepare a consensus on Khilafat and Non-Cooperation issues, the special session of Indian National Congress held in September 1920. It was remarkable that in this session of the Indian National Congress, a large number of Muslim League and the Khilafat leaders were present at that session.

In this period of communal harmony and national unity, the supporters of the foundation of the Muslim University found an opportunity to materialize the long cherished dream of founding the Aligarh Muslim University. There was no doubt of being opposed to the AMU Bill by any Legislature. Sir Mohammad Shafi, an Old Boy of the MAO College and education member in the Viceroy's Council along with the other Aligarh loyalists considered it an opportunity to put the AMU Bill in the Central Legislative Council. It was also hoped that the British Government also would amen.[12]

The AMU Bill was thus introduced in the council and came up for discussion, the newly appointed Legislature and the Secretary of the MAO College and Muslim University Association Syed Mohammad Ali while defending the Bill delivered a memorable speech. An excerpt of his speech is being given below:[13]

> "It is nearly 10 years ago that Mohammadans were first promised their university. My Lord, Aligarh was the first institution in this country which followed the best residential system of the public schools of England. It is the matter of history that the Banaras constitution was modeled on the lines of proposed constitution of Aligarh and that of Decca does not introduce any new ideas except slight changes in the nomenclature."
>
> "Even since the first definite proposals for the university were made, the whole controversy has mainly centred round two points firstly, the extent of jurisdiction of the university and secondly, the government control. About the first, the Muslim community was compelled to accept that there

> would be no room in future for affiliating type of university, but about the latter community favoured autonomous university."
>
> "My Lord without real power there can be no sense of responsibility and without responsibility there can be no efficiency."

The report of the Select Committee, regarding the AMU Bill, was placed in the Indian Legislative Council on 2nd September, 1920.[14] On 9th September, 1920, Sir Mohammad Shafi spoke, "Sir, after having a careful study of the Indian political conditions, I have arrived at conclusion that the backwardness of this community was due to their neglect of modern education...."[15]

During these days, the British Government in India was facing a serious threat from the Indian nationalist youths. The joint Khilafat-Non-cooperation Movement also caused great concern to the British authorities in India. The government thought it wise to keep the loyalist elements happy by granting the fulfilment of their demands. So, the Bill when introduced in the Council, was passed and the Government of India assured the yearly aid of one lakh of rupees.[16]

His Excellency the Viceroy congratulated the Muslim community on the passage of the AMU Bill.[17] Honourable Sir D.R. Sarbadhikari said, "Sir, I congratulate my Muslim fellow subjects upon 'the appointed time' having arrived, upon the approaching materialization of an educational organization of their own for which they have long been waiting.... [18] Honourable Mr. Surendra Nath Banerjee also congratulated on the passage of the AMU Bill.[19]

Aligarh Muslim University Act of 1920

After passage of the Aligarh Muslim University Bill, the MAO College attained the status of a university under Aligarh Muslim University Act of 1920. The AMU Act came into force from 1st December, 1920. The Act gave enormous powers to the Aligarh Muslim University. The university now could provide instructions in such branches of learning as it might think fit and make provisions for research and for advancement, and dissemination of knowledge.[20]

Under the Act of 1920, the Aligarh Muslim University was empowered to promote oriental and Islamic studies and give instruction in Muslim theology and religion and to impart moral and physical training.[21] Under this Act the university was given the right to hold examination and to grant and confer degrees and other academic distinctions. The Act also empowered the university to confer honourary degrees or other distinctions on approved persons and grant diplomas. The university was authorised to appoint Professors, Readers, Lecturers and other posts as required by it. It was empowered to institute and award fellowships, scholarships, exhibitions and prizes in accordance with statutes and ordinances.[22]

The Aligarh Muslim University Act of 1920 also empowered the university to institute and maintain halls for the residence of the students of the university, demand and receive fees and other charges as might be prescribed by the ordinances, and to supervise and control the residence and discipline of students and make arrangements for promoting their health. The Act of 1920 also gave freedom to the university to provide and promote arts, science and other branches of learing including professional studies, technology, Islamic learning and Muslim theology, and to promote interests of its students.[23]

The Act clearly provided that the university would function under the Act, and it would be open to all persons of either sex and of whatever race, creed or class. All recognised teachings would include lecturing, laboratory work and other teaching conducted in the university by the teachers in accordance with the syllabus prescribed. The recognised teachers would also include tutorial instructions.[24]

According to the Act, the university also had power to establish and maintain Intermediate Colleges and schools within the limits of Aligarh district. It was also directed that the instruction in the Muslim religion and theology would also be provided in such colleges and schools.[25] As far as the admission to the university was concerned, it was said that all admissions were to be made by a committee, consisting of the Pro-Vice-Chancellor, the Principal of an Intermediate College who would be selected by the Vice-Chancellor and other officials appointed by the Academic Council.[26]

For the smooth conduct of the examinations, it was maintained that the Academic Council would appoint Examination Committee consisting of members of its own body or of the other persons or of both. The committee was to moderate examination questions, prepare the results of the examinations and to report such results to the Executive Council for publication.[27]

Another important rule according to the Act was that every salaried officer or teacher of the university, and any of its officers or teachers would be referred to a tribunal of arbitration consisting of one member appointed by the Executive Council, one member nominated by the officer or teacher concerned, and an umpire appointed by the Visiting Board. The decision of the tribunal would be final, and no suit would lie in any civil court. The university was also empowered to constitute, for the benefit of its officers, teachers and servants, such as provident and pension funds as it might think fit.[28]

The Court

The Act of 1920 had the provision of a Court, to act as the supreme governing body of the university and to exercise all powers of the university. The Court was empowered to review the acts of the Executive, and Academic Councils and direct them for necessary action in accordance with the recommendations of the Lord Rector. The Court was, however, to function within the framework of the provisions of the Act in:[29]

(a) Making statutes and amending or repealing it.
(b) Considering the ordinances.
(c) Considering and passing resolutions on the annual report, the annual accounts and the financial estimates.
(d) Electing the persons to serve on authorities of the university and of appointing the officers.

The composition of the Court was clearly defined by the AMU Act of 1920. It consisted of the Chancellor, the Pro-Chancellor and the Vice-Chancellor and other persons for the time being. However, no person other than a Muslim would get the membership of the Court.[30]

It was provided that the Court would meet once in a year on the date fixed by the Vice-Chancellor, but by requisition in writing signed by at least 30 members of the Court, the Vice-Chancellor was empowered to commence a special meeting. However, 25 attendances of the members in the Court were required for the quorum.[31]

The Executive Council

As the Court was a too-large body to meet frequently, its executive powers were delegated to an Executive Council, consisting of not more than 30 members. Four of them were exofficio members, i.e. Vice-Chancellor, Pro-Vice-Chancellor, the Principal of an Intermediate College and Treasurer. Six persons were elected by the Academic Council and the rest by the Court. The elected members were to hold office for three years. It was necessary that at least eleven members of the Executive Council were to be present in the meeting or form a quorum. The Executive Council was to administer their revenue and property of the university, regulate the finances, accounts and investments and perform all such duties and acts as could be necessary for the business of the university.[32]

The Executive Council had the power to make and vary investment, purchase, accept and sell movable and immovable property. The Executive Council was having also the responsibility to maintain the buildings, premises, furniture and apparatus needed for the work of the university.[33]

The Executive Council also had the power to grant leaves to officers, teachers and servants and deal with their grievances. It was also to see that a register of donors to the university was maintained. Since the founder of the MAO College had understood the importance of press for publication of books, college magazines, this tradition was retained and the Executive Council was made responsible to maintain the university press. The Executive Council also had power to consider the recommendation of the Academic Council in regard to the fixation of fees and charges payable by the students; payments of the fees and allowances of examiners, moderators and other persons engaged in the university examination work. The Executive Council was also to manage the Intermediate College and schools maintained by the university.[34]

The Academic Council

Apart from the powers to the Executive Council, the Act also defined as to how the Academic Council was to function. Under the provisions of the Act, the Academic Council was to consist of the Vice-Chancellor, the Pro-Vice Chancellor, the Chairpersons of the department of studies, the Librarian, the Proctor, two persons elected by the Court, two persons nominated by the Visiting Board, and five persons co-opted by the Academic Council, two of whom at least could be head of the halls, two Professors or Readers and one person not engaged in the teaching in the university. Eleven members of the Academic Council were to form a quorum and members other than ex-officio members were to hold office for three years.[35]

The powers of the Academic Council were defined as under:[36]

(1) To arrange and supervise the work of education in the university.
(2) To recommend to the Executive Council the creation and abolition of posts in the educational and tutorial staff.
(3) To fix the time, mode and terms of competition for fellowships, scholarships, studentships, medals, prizes and awards.
(4) To conduct the examinations and publish the results in the University Gazette.
(5) To have entire charge of the discipline of the students in the university.
(6) To publish and revise lists of prescribed and recommended books and prescribe syllabi in consultation with the departments of studies.
(7) To appoint library committee and publish the University Gazette.

These provisions were with the exception of the Department of Theology whose proceedings were subject to the approval of the Executive Council.

Departments of Studies

The Act of 1920 also defined the functioning of the departments of studies. The provisions made to run the departments were, by and large, uniform. It is interesting to note that the Act of 1920 provided the selection of the Chairman of the departments from among the Readers and Professors, who were to hold office for three years. This provision was totally different from the existing system in which the Chairman of the department was elevated to that position by right of seniority and not by the selection. The Departments of Studies recommended to the Academic Council about the courses and syllabi of studies, text-books, fellowships, scholarships, studentships, medals and prizes, in the subject with which it was concerned.[37]

The Lord Rector

The Act of 1920 made the university an autonomous body, but the government had retained some powers in authorities like Lord Rector and Rectors. According to the University Act, the Governor-General of India was to act as Lord Rector of the university. He had the right to order an inspection of the university or get it done by some persons appointed by him. Nevertheless, in every case, he was supposed to give notice to the university which had the right to be represented by a responsible person. The Lord Rector could address the Vice-Chancellor with reference to the result of such inspection and enquiry. The Vice-Chancellor was to communicate the views of Lord Rector to the Court with the advice as the Lord Rector might have given. The Court was to communicate through the Vice-Chancellor to the Lord Rector about the actions it proposed to take, as a result of such inspection and enquiry. If the Court did not take action within the reasonable time, the Lord Rector might issue such directions as he thought fit and the Court was bound to comply with that directions.[38]

The Rector

According to the provisions of the Act, next to the Lord Rector, there was the authority of Rector in the university. The Rector was a person from among the head of local governments, Princes and the rulers of the states in India. The Rector was appointed by the Lord Rector on his own motion or on the recommendations of the Court. The Chancellor might also, on the recommendation of the Academic Council, appoint the persons of eminence as Rector.[39]

The Visiting Board

According to the Act, another body of the university was the Visiting Board. It consisted of the Governor of United Provinces, members of his Executive Council, the Ministers, one member nominated by the Governor and one member nominated by Minister in charge of Education.[40] The Visiting Board had been conferred extensive powers under the Act, such as to inspect the university and to satisfy itself that the proceedings of the university were in conformity with the Act, Statutes and Ordinance, but not before giving a prior show cause notice to the university.[41]

Other Important Officers of the University

The AMU Act of 1920 made provisions for the smooth functioning of the university by providing a set of university functionaries or university officers. According to the AMU Act, five categories of the university officers were described. Of these officers, some were to be absolutely honourary and some were to be appointed on salary. The five categories of officers specified in the AMU Act of 1920 were as follows:

(a) The Chancellor
(b) The Pro-Chancellor
(c) The Vice-Chancellor
(d) The Pro-Vice-Chancellor
(e) Other officers (Treasurer, Registrar, Provosts, Proctor and Librarian) appointed according to the Statutes of the Act to the officers of the university.

The Act made provision for the Chancellor who was to be elected by the Court. Naturally, he held an honourary position.

The Chancellor was to preside over the convocations and meetings of the Court.[42] The tenure of the Chancellor was fixed for three years. Similarly, the position of the Pro-Chancellor was honourary who was to hold office for three years after being elected by the Court.[43] In the absence of the Chancellor, the Pro-Chancellor was to exercise the function of the Chancellor.[44]

The Vice-Chancellor was also to be elected by the Court, and every election was subject to the approval of Governor General in Council and eligible for re-election. Vice-Chancellor was appointed for a period of four years. He was to preside meetings of the Court in the absence of the Chancellor and Pro-Chancellor and was an ex-officio Chairman of the Executive Council and Academic Council. He was also the sole medium of communication between the university and the government.[45]

The Pro-Vice Chancellor was appointed by the Court for a period of five years and was re-eligible for appointment. He was the principal academic officer of the university. He was the ex-officio member of the Executive Council and Academic Council. In the absence of the Vice-Chancellor, he presided over the meetings of the Academic Council. He has also the power to convene meetings of the Academic Council.[46]

The fifth category of officers included Treasurer, Registrar, Provosts, Proctor and Librarian. The Treasurer was appointed by the Court. He was to exercise general supervision over the funds of the university and give advice with regard to its financial policy.[47]

The Registrar was also appointed by the Court for five years. He was the custodian of the records, the seal and other such property of the university, keep and maintain the register of the registered graduates. He was also to attend the Academic and Executive Councils as their Secretary.[48] The Provosts were the boarding house officers. The Proctor was to look after the discipline of the students. The Librarian was in-charge of university library.[49]

Foundation of the Jamia Millia Islamia

After the termination of the First World War, the British attitude towards Khilafat and Turkey frustrated the entire Muslim community in India. Naturally, it also affected a radical section of the Muslim intelligentsia at Aligarh. In the reaction of the British policies against Turkey and Khalifa, the Aligarh National Muslim intelligentsia decided to set-up an independent national university at Aligarh as a national platform for the Muslim youths. Mahatma Gandhi and many other Congress leaders extended their full support to the Aligarh Muslim intellectuals.

The Aligarh national Muslim intellectuals wanted to upgrade the existing MAO College into a national university. However, the great hurdle in this regard was the domination of the loyalists in the MAO College. They opposed every anti-government activity in the college campus. However, the visit of Mahatma Gandhi in Aligarh on 12th October, 1920, while campaigning for Khilafat and Non-Cooperation movements, created a group of national volunteers among the college students. Mahatma Gandhi and Ali brothers requested the college authorities to give up the government aid. Failing to reach any agreement with the college authorities, they decided to establish a national university for the students who had decided to leave the college for the national cause.

On 28th October, 1920, a meeting was held on the steps of the Aligarh Jama Masjid at the Upper Kot. Many national leaders attended the meeting and Ali brothers were the main figure. In that meeting, it was decided to invite both the Hindus and Muslims to attend the inaugural meeting of the National Muslim University which was going to be held on 29th October, 1920 in the MAO College Mosque. [50]

On 29th October, 1920, about 2000 persons were present in the MAO College Mosque. The gathering comprised of the members of each and every community. Such a strong gathering invited the jealousy of the *Aligarh Institute Gazette* which published a rather partisan report as the people came to "Gandhi's Darshan" because it was the rumour that the latter was also one of the invitees.[51] Shaikhul Hind Maulana Mahmudul Hasan along with Maulana Husain Ahmad Madani, Mufti Kifayatullah and Maulana Shabbir Ahmad participated in the meeting on the invitation of Maulana Mohammad Ali.[52]

After Friday's prayer, on 29th October, Shaikhul Hind Maulana Mahmudul Hasan laid the foundation of the Jamia Millia Islamia. While addressing the gathering Maulana Mohammad Ali criticised the British Government as a *Shaitan* (devil) and said that those cooperating with that government were their associates or *Shaitan*. While indicating the teaching of the national university in the MAO College buildings, Maulana Mohammad Ali said, "if the college was closed then there would be no problem, we would resume teaching on the mats. If there was no arrangement of *Safai-wala* (sweeper), I will clean toilet. The education of science was not in any way better than the education of God." Maulana Hasrat Mohani in his speech declared that those Trustees who were against Non-Cooperation should be regarded expelled from Islam.[53]

The other national leaders Hakim Ajmal Khan and Haji Moosa Khan also addressed the meeting. Maulana Mahmudul Hasan started to read his presidential address, but he could not do so because he was keeping a very bad health. His associate Maulana Shabbir Ahmad of Deoband completed his address.[54]

Maulana Mahmudul Hasan's address strongly criticised the pattern of the modern education imparted in Aligarh, making the Muslims devoted and loyal to the British Raj. He thus urged the Muslims to think of the evil consequences of such a system and requested to give heed to Mahatma Gandhi's call.[55] Maulana Mahmudul Hasan also expressed the hope that the National Muslim University (Jamia Millia) would reconcile the English education of Aligarh and religious education of Deoband.[56]

At the same historic meeting of 29th October, 1920, the name of the National Muslim University was changed to Jamia Millia Islamia, and it began to run with immediate effect in the MAO College buildings. Maulana Mohammad Ali was designated as the first Vice-Chancellor. Later on, he was succeeded by Abdul Majid Khwaja.[57]

Foundation of the Jamia Millia University was the big jolt to the loyalist Muslims of the MAO College as it hampered the smooth college teachings in the campus. MAO College Trustees and the Old Boys requested the nationalists to leave the college premises.[58] However, the adamant attitude of Maulana Mohammad Ali and his associates could not heed to their request. Ultimately, the attitude of the nationalists annoyed the Trustees and the Honourary Secretary of the college. Consequently, Syed Mohammad Ali, the Honourary Secretary of the MAO College wrote to Maulana Mohammad Ali,

"In exercise of power vested in me under Section 90 of the rule ....not to hold any kind of meeting not to address the students within the boundaries of the college ground, after receipt of this notice."[59]

Responding to the notice of the Honourary Secretary, Maulana Mohammad Ali wrote, "The work which has brought me here is God's work, I am acting in obedience to His Commandment, I cannot therefore carry out your request which intervenes these Commandments."[60]

The Principal of the MAO College Dr. Ziauddin Ahmad also wrote to Maulana Mohammad Ali that he was staying in the college without the permission of the appropriate authority. He also levelled charges against him for opening and using some of the locked rooms of the *Pakka Barrack*, which was against the peaceful withdrawal of which repeated assurances had been given. He urged upon Maulana Mohammad Ali to leave the college precincts immediately and withdraw all students who were under his influence.[61]

As usual, Maulana Mohammad Ali replied by refuting the allegations that he was not responsible for breaking locks of rooms of the *Pakka Barrack*. He also repudiated that he had given any assurances to the college authorities for his peaceful withdrawal. He thus requested to comply with the request contained in his letter.[62]

In the evening of 30th October, 1920, a deputation of 40 people including, old boys and trustees met Maulana Mohammad Ali and requested him to vacate the college. However, he said that without police or forcible eviction, he would not leave the college.[63]

The management of the MAO College thus could not succeed to persuade Maulana Mohammad Ali for leaving the college buildings and campus. Ultimately, Honourary Secretary of the college requested the District Magistrate Mr. Campbell for the assistance in this affair.[64] As a result of this request, the District Magistrate of Aligarh arrived in the college in the morning of 31st October. Maulana Mohammad Ali was virtually ordered under Section 144, Criminal Procedure Code to vacate the Old Boys Lodge along with his followers, including Maulana Abdul Majid. Maulana Mohammad Ali avoiding further confrontation finally decided to vacate the college.[65]

In a process of peaceful withdrawal, Maulana Mohammad Ali and his associates, along with a caravan of 110 to 150 students, left the college to whom they considered much dearer than their home. In the front, a student led a green flag on which *Kalma Tayyaba* was written.[66]

Maulana Mohammad Ali and students and staff took their baggage to "Krishna Kothi" hired by Khwaja Abdul Majid. Some more private buildings were also hired for the stay of the students.[67] A number of students from the Islamia College Lahore and Peshawar also arrived at Aligarh for admission to the National Muslim University.[68] As the number of students increased, two thatched buildings were raised and a hall with the same material was constructed and called 'Mohammad Ali Hall.'[69]

Further arrangements were made to receive the incoming students seeking admission to the newly set-up university at the Aligarh railway station.[70] Maulana Mohammad Ali prepared a syllabus and himself started teaching English language and the Modern History.[71] Some senior students with good academic career were also appointed Lecturers, including, Zakir Husain, Noorullah, Saiyed Mohammad, Rauf Pasha and others. Maulana Aslam, Maulana Rashid Ahmed, Hafiz Faiyaz Ahmad, Abdul Karim Faruqi also joined as the teachers.[72]

On Maulana Mohammad Ali's request, Mr. Gopalacharya, the Secretary of the Non-Cooperation Movement in Madras sent three of their best workers as Professors in the newly established National Muslim University. Among them, Mr. Kripanidhi was appointed as Professor in National Muslim University and Mr. Rama[73] was appointed Professor of Science. Maulana Abdul Hai of Gurudaspur was appointed as Professor of Theology.[74] In order to attract experienced and highly qualified teachers to serve the National Muslim University, the authorities offered them very handsome salaries. Professor Hadi Hasan, a great teacher of the Muslim University, who was at home in English and Persian literature, also joined the National Muslim University.[75]

The newly established National Muslim University or the Jamia Millia Islamia started fully functioning at Aligarh, but it had to face a legal problem as it could neither award degrees nor assure to provide jobs to its students. The students of this university were trained much for political purposes than academic. The Jamia, however, gave much emphasis on character building rather than academic improvement.[76] The students were provided the religious education and trained for the struggle of the freedom movement. They were also engaged in collecting funds for the institutions.[77]

Thus in Aligarh, two institutions were functioning in December 1920. One the AMU, held by the loyalists with full government support and the other the Jamia Millia Islamia against the government. Both the students and the staff of Jamia Millia Islamia campaigned to woo the students to join their university. They went Ghaziabad, Delhi and Tundla stations to meet the incoming students in order to induce them either to go back or to join the Jamia Millia Islamia. They organised deputations to meet the students at Aligarh station, and they also tried to induce the coolies and *Ekka* drivers not to carry the luggage of the students intending to join the AMU. They arranged Motor Lorries and coolies to bring the students from Aligarh railway station.[78]

Although, there were two universities at Aligarh with two different ideologies and the management of the loyalist group was trying to maintain a strict vigil but students of both the universities continued to maintain cordial relations by visiting each other's places. This was soon taken up seriously by the loyalists. Thus, the Muslim University authorities wrote to Maulana Mohammad Ali, "My dear Maulana Sahib, some of your students have been visiting the boarding houses attached to this institution....you kindly warn all your students and prohibit them from entering the premises of this institution to avoid a friction."[79]

Some of the AMU authorities were deadly opposed to students of the Jamia coming to offer even prayers at the university mosque. They alleged that these students were creating disturbances in the university mosque during the prayer time.[80]

The Muslim University Act was to come into force from 1st December, 1920. According to the provisions of the Act, Sultan Jahan Begum of Bhopal became first Chancellor, Raja of Mahmudabad Mohammad Ali Khan became first Vice-Chancellor, and Dr. Ziauddin Ahmad became the first Pro-Vice Chancellor. When the college was opened on 1st December, 1920, it was in the form of a university.

On 15th December, 1920, the inaugural ceremony of the Aligarh Muslim University was scheduled to be held. The designated

Vice-Chancellor Raja of Mahmudabad though a loyalist extended invitation to Maulana Mohammad Ali to participate in the ceremony but the latter declined the offer.[81]

The Muslim University, so founded, had a complete domination of the loyalists who took all care to ensure that the institution was free from the nationalist students. In a well-thought-out plan the students were divided into three sections:

(i) Non-cooperators,
(ii) Doubtful, and
(iii) Cooperators.

Admission cards were first sent to those students who had cooperated with the college authorities during the crisis. The cases of doubtful students were considered about Xmas holidays, and they were also called for admissions. However, no non-cooperating students were admitted without a written guarantee from the parents.[82] After a proper scrutiny about 325 admission cards were issued.[83]

The strict policy of the Muslim University authorities caused considerable anxieties among the parents of the non-cooperator students. They wrote a number of letters denying connections of their wards with the Non-Cooperation. They made a lot of excuses and condemned the non-cooperators. Even the students, in order to save their future, also wrote to the Muslim University authorities and felt sorry for their past behaviour.

It seems that many students who had taken part in the Non-Cooperation also gave way under the pressure of their parents. The cases of such few students are cited here by way of illustrations. A student Nurul Hasan wrote to the Principal, "Now I am fully convinced that I am wrong in adopting the Non-Cooperation. I hope, you will be kind enough to consider my case favourably."[84]

A student Abdur Rahman of Faridkot writes, "I never joined National College, I am very sorry of my past behaviour and promise that in future I would not behave in a similar way. My life is being spoiled and I am on your mercy."[85]

Another student Rashid Ahmad of Hyderabad wrote, "I was forced to adopt the role of so-called non-cooperator.... Kindly inform at an early date to the exact date by which I should return to Aligarh".[86]

K.B. Mohammad Abdul Hamid Khan Kundi, a Divisional and Session Judge wrote, "My son Abdul Hamid Khan Kundi is a 3rd year student of your college, I request you to kindly forgive and allow him to continue his studies in your college."[87]

Jamia Millia Islamia and Aligarh Muslim University both started functioning in the same city, but their ideologies were different. The authorities of both the universities were deadly against each other but the students due to the unique culture and fraternity of Aligarh could not separate from each other. It also seemed difficult to run the two universities in a small city like Aligarh. Ultimately, after five years successfully running their university at Aligarh, the authorities of Jamia Millia Islamia decided to shift from Aligarh to Delhi in 1925.

NOTES

1. Hali, Altaf Husain, *Hayat-i-Javed,* Delhi, 1990, pp. 187-90 and *Naqoosh*, October 1956.
2. Lalyveld, David, *Aligarh First Generation*, New Delhi, 1878, p. 317.
3. Husain, Mir Vilayat, *Aap Biti*, Aligarh, 1970, p. 161.
4. Sherwani, H.K., *The Aligarh Movement*, New Delhi, 1969, p. 43.
5. *Ibid.,* p. 45.
6. *Aligarh Institute Gazette*, 15 October, 1919.
7. *Modern Asian Studies*, Vol. 8, Part-2, 1974, p. 184.
8. Zuberi, Mohammad Amin, *Zia-i-Hayat*, Aligarh, 1970, p. 83 (Hereafter cited as *Zia-i-Hayat*).
9. *Modern Asian Studies*, Vol. 8, Part-2, 1974, pp. 184-185.
10. *Zia-i-Hayat*, p. 83.
11. *Ibid.*
12. *Modern Asian Studies*, Vol. 8, Part-2, 1974, p. 185.
13. *Aligarh Institute Gazette*, 1st September, 1920.
14. *Ibid.,* 8th September, 1920.
15. *Proceedings, Indian Legislative Council*, Vol. LIX, p. 79 (Uttar Pradesh State Library, Lucknow).
16. *Aligarh Institute Gazette*, 15th September, 1920; see also *Aligarh Magazine*, September-October 1920, p. 12.
17. *Ibid.*

18. *Proceedings, Indian Legislative Council,* Vol. LIX, p. 85 (Uttar Pradesh State Library, Lucknow).
19. *Ibid.*, p. 89.
20. *AMU Act of 1920*, p. 8.
21. *Ibid.*
22. *Ibid.*, pp. 8-9.
23. *Ibid.*, p. 9.
24. *Ibid.*, pp. 10-11.
25. *Ibid.*
26. *Ibid.*, pp. 20-21.
27. *Ibid.*, pp. 8-9.
28. *Ibid.*, pp. 22-23.
29. *Ibid.*, p. 15.
30. *Ibid.*
31. *Ibid.*, pp. 28-29.
32. *Ibid.*, see also *Aligarh Institute Gazette*, 31st March, 1926; and *AMU Calendar, 1921-25*, Aligarh, 1926, pp. 74-76.
33. *Ibid.*, p. 30.
34. *Ibid.*
35. *Ibid.*, see also *Aligarh Institute Gazette,* 31st March, 1926.
36. *Ibid.*, pp. 30-31; see also *Aligarh Institute Gazette,* 31st March, 1926.
37. *Ibid.*, p. 32.
38. *Ibid.*, pp. 11-12; see also *Aligarh Institute Gazette,* 31st March, 1926.
39. *Ibid.*, pp. 23-24.
40. *Ibid.*, p.14.
41. *Ibid.*, pp.12-13.
42. *Ibid.*, p.13.
43. *Ibid.*, pp.13-14.
44. *Ibid.*, p.14.
45. *Ibid.*, p. 24; see also *Aligarh Institute Gazette,* 31st March, 1926.
46. *Ibid.*
47. *Ibid.*, pp. 24-25.
48. *Ibid.*
49. *Ibid.*, pp. 25-26.
50. *Aligarh Institute Gazette,* 30th October, 1920; see also *Zia-i-Hayat*, p. 73.
51. *Ibid.*
52. Hadi, Syed Mohammad, *Ali Biradran Aur Unka Zamana*, New Delhi, 1978, p. 107 (hereafter cited as "*Ali Biradran*").
53. *Aligarh Institute Gazette,* 30th October, 1920.
54. *The Leader*, 1st November, 1920.
55. *Aligarh Magazine, 1953-54-55,* pp. 272-273; see also *Ali Biradran*, p. 102; Rizvi, Khursid Mustafa, *Hayat-i-Zakir Husain*, Delhi, 1994, pp. 66-68.
56. *Modern Asian Studies,* Vol. 8, Part-2, 1974, pp. 187-188.
57. *Hayat-i-Zakir Husain*, Delhi, 1994, p. 68.

58. *Aligarh Institute Gazette,* 1st November, 1920.
59. *The Leader*, 4th November, 1920.
60. *Ibid.*
61. *Ibid.*
62. *Ibid.*
63. *Zia-i-Hayat*, pp. 74-75.
64. Mohsini, Shamsur Rehman, *Hayat-i-Abdullah*, Aligarh, (ND), pp. 105-106.
65. *The Tribune*, 3rd November, 1920.
66. Mudholi, Abdul Ghaffar, *Jamia Ki Kahani*, New Delhi, 1984, p. 25.
67. They also occupied a three or four roomed building which was named as 'Mahmud Court' by the students. Nawab Ismail Khan of Meerut hired few tents which were placed in front of the 'Mahmud Court' *Ali Biradran*, pp. 104-106; *Hayat-i-Abdullah*, p. 106; *Jamia-Ki-Kahani*, p. 25; *Zia-i-Hayat*, p. 75.
68. *Confidential Files, Home-Political, Coll. 210-216 & KW, Dec-A*, 1920, (National Archives, New Delhi); see also *Ali Biradran*, p. 108.
69. *Ali Biradran*, p. 108.
70. *The Tribune*, 3rd November, 1920.
71. *Hayat-i-Zakir Husain,* p. 66.
72. *Jamia-Ki-Kahani*, p. 26.
73. In a report of Dr. Ziauddin Ahmad, it is said that Mr. Rama was the chief lieutenant of Dayal Singh, who was sentenced some years ago for smuggling pistols.
74. *File No. 15, 1920-21* (AMU Archives).
75. *Ali Biradran*, pp. 113-114.
76. *Aligarh Magazine, 1953-54 and 1954-55*, p. 274.
77. Minault, Gail, *Khilafat Movement*, Delhi, 1982, p. 118 (Hereafter quoted as 'Gail Minault').
78. *File No. 15, 1920-21* (AMU Archives).
79. *File No. XX/45, 1920-21* (AMU Archives).
80. *Ibid.*
81. Muhammad, Shan, *Unpublished Letters of the Ali Brothers*, Delhi, 1979, pp. 217-21 (hereafter quoted as '*Unpublished Letters*').
82. *File No. XX/42, 1920-21* (AMU Archives).
83. *Zia-i-Hayat*, p. 75.
84. *File No. 1, 1920-21* (AMU Archives).
85. *Ibid.*
86. *Ibid.*
87. *Ibid.*

3
Educational Activities in AMU, 1920-1928

After elevation of MAO College to the AMU, a new phase of educational development started in the educational history of the Muslim society. In the educational field, Indian Muslims were far behind than the other communities of India. That's why in the race of advancement and development they were also far behind than their Hindu brethren. The Indian Muslim community was so orthodox and not ready to accept even a minor change in their social set-up. They were living in the changed atmosphere but not ready to get adjusted in it not even in the light of their religion. They thought that English education or the education suitable according to the need of time would lead them astray from Islam, and it would bring them into Christian influence.[1]

It was general opinion of the Indian Muslim community that the Christian influence or western education would convert them into Christianity. In these days when the Muslims were so backward due to lack of modem education, Sir Syed Ahmad Khan founded MAO College at Aligarh. According to him, the western education was must along with the Islamic education. It was the only way to insure a position for the Muslims in the Indian society.

In order to encourage the western education among Muslims, a 'Duty Society' was founded by Sahibzada Aftab Ahamd Khan in 1890, with the active cooperation of Mr. T.W. Arnald, Miss. E.J. Beck, Maulvi Tufail Ahamd and others. Its object was (i) to impress upon Musalmans the advantage of western education; (ii) to explain both by precept and personal example the benefits which the

Muslim community was deriving from Aligarh; (iii) to collect money for *Wazaif* (scholarships) and loans for poor students and other university purposes.[2]

Not only the college or university authorities but it was the moral duty of all the students of Aligarh, who were either in the college or outside to preach the values of modern education among the Muslim community. To continue the mission and movement of Sir Syed Ahmad Khan, the old boys had formed an association called the MAO Old Boys Association, the members of which contributed 1 per cent of their income to the aid of their Alma Mater. After the elevation of the college to university status in 1920, the Old Boys Association was re-formed in 1923.[3]

Educational Pattern

The old boys and the students of Aligarh Muslim University developed a unique culture and traditions which gave a distinct identity to the institution differing from other universities of India. Imparting fraternity and a unique Aligarh culture was also one of the parts of the educational pattern of AMU. Undoubtedly, the curriculum of this university was also better and more practical according to the need of the time.

In the first convocation of Aligarh Muslim University in 1922, the Chancellor of the university Nawab Sultan Jahan Begum of Bhopal addressed to the students:[4]

> "Our viewpoint always should be that we protect honour and fame of our university by maintaining high standard of education. Because only those universities survive and attract good students which excel in education and not by merely awarding cheap degrees." Advising the students she said, "You are the future of the community (nation) and it is hoped from you to maintain the reputation of the degrees of your university in every way. By your hard work you would serve as examples for fulfilling the objective of university for which it had been established."

In the AMU convocation of 1935, Girja Shanker Bajpai,

Member, Department of Education, Health and Lands, Government of India addressed the students, "Education is first and foremost national service which enters vitally into most aspects of national advancement."[5]

The education imparted in Aligarh was the education for the cultural and moral advancement. It was free from the bonds of caste, creed and religion. During those days, national movement was going on in India and naturally every student of Aligarh was affected by one way or the other, by the political atmosphere of the country. The students were faced with question, whether they should take part in politics or not? Regarding this question H.H. Nawab Hamidullah Khan Bahadur, ruler of Bhopal addressed the Aligarh students on the occasion of Muslim University convocation held on 16th December, 1939. He said:[6]

> "I think it is very desirable that they (students) should study and discuss political question. But I am strongly of the opinion that in student's life, the difference in political views should not assume a form which may tend to subvert the discipline of university or disturb even the tenure of its academic life. The university is not political institution and there is no justification for making it the arena of political strife." He advised to students, "After leaving the university you should not think that you have learnt all that was knowable and anything which you do not know is not worth knowing. You should act on the principle of 'live and learn' and keep your mind open to receive new ideas and impression from any or every source."

The Aligarh Muslim University was imparting education to the students in various courses of Arts and Science subjects. The authorities remained agile in evolving the pattern of education, even suggesting for oriented education for the benefit of the students. Sir Shah Muhammad Sulaiman, while addressing the convocation of 1934 advised that the system of education should be remodelled so as to find new fields of occupation in increasing number.[7]

He said, "In the existing institutions, mere general education must be transformed into semi-vocational education so as to benefit the students. The aim should be to have industrial and craft school in all the important towns where young men and girls may be trained to earn their livelihood by taking to small industries not requiring much capital. Vocational training should be made compulsory to the schools." He continued, "On the other hand the values of higher education should be judged both from the external and utilitarian point of view. The universities mould themselves so as to be in a position to find employment for their graduates in industries, trade and commerce just as much as in the service. The universities should readopt themselves to the needs of the time and must adjust their teaching to the requirement of the various professions, services and industries."[8]

The Aligarh University adopted the suggestions, but practically it was not possible to start the scheme immediately. No doubt it was the period when unemployment was widespread, and the Aligarh University tried its best to introduce many new professional courses slowly and gradually.

Dr. Ziauddin Ahmad, a reputed educationist and administrator of the Aligarh Muslim University started many job oriented departments and courses in the university. The details of these departments are in the succeeding chapter. His more stress was on making the same pattern of education in Aligarh as prevalent in European and American universities. In 1947, Dr. Ziauddin Ahmad undertook a tour of America and Europe for studying the pattern and system of education then prevalent. His second aim of the tour was to establish a Medical Collage on the model of the Medical Colleges in England. However, unfortunately, while going from Paris to London, he left the world forever on 23rd December, 1947.[9]

Medium of Instructions

In any university or educational institution, the medium of instruction plays the main role. It helps in evaluating the standard of the institution. In Aligarh Muslim University, the medium of instruction was English because it was the requirement of the time and was also in order to compete with the students of other universities. As it was a fact that Muslims were so backward in terms of English education, and it was the responsibility of Aligarh University to impart its education through.

However, the medium of English was confined to the education and university functioning only. Its atmosphere was fully coloured with a national language, Hindustani or "Urdu." The Hindustani language was in vogue in the Aligarh University. The Aligarh people thought that how English language could keep alive to those Indian thoughts and traditions which constituted their culture and, which were part and parcel of their national heritage. Such an object could be served by a language of the people of India.

Honourable Nawab Mirza Yar Jang Bahadur (Mr. Samiullah Beg) addressed AMU Convocation in December 1938. He said, "I feel humiliated when once a Japanese of boardship who had no idea of surroundings and circumstances under which we received our education, expressed his surprise to me on seeing that even among ourselves, we talked oftener in English than in our own mother tongue Urdu means a camp where people of all nationalities can meet. It is not the language of any Islamic country....as far as this university is concerned it should immediately make Urdu its medium of instruction, especially when it happens to be the mother tongue of this province."[10]

Whatever suggestions given by the honourable guests of AMU time to time were discussed thoroughly, but it was decided that only English medium can solve the unemployment problems of the Muslim youths and through this medium only the students of AMU could compete the students of other universities of India.

Spiritual Teachings

It was the dream of the founder of the institution Sir Syed Ahmad Khan that its students would hold Science in one hand and the Holy *Quran* in another. This dream was rightly fulfilled in the succeeding years in the university. The Aligarh students studied modern education, but they were permanently inspired by religious and spiritual teachings through personalities of the Islamic community.

Mirza Yar Jung Bahadur while addressing the students during AMU Convocation in December 1938 said that a religious and spiritual life would greatly help the formation of character. He further said, "if in Cambridge University, attendance at church service and reading of a few verses from the Bible in the dining hall every day before taking lunch have been considered necessary for the formation of the character of its students, no reason is seen why the saying of the daily prayers or attendance in Friday sermons should not be enforced as strictly for the Muslim students as attendance at regular classes. For daily and Friday sermons preachers of the right type will have to be employed."[11]

Nationalism

The AMU students were always taught practical education along with culture and nationalism. They were advised both for the national cause and career building. The students of AMU were very lucky in getting the advice of many eminent personalities. The visitors always reminded them of their culture, traditions and nationalism. Mirza Yar Jung Bahadur during AMU Convocation in December 1938 taught the lesson of nationalism to the Aligarh students by saying, "Love Indian." He said, "I love those who live on this soil irrespective of caste or creed; respect every culture and religion....Yours is the country of rainbow cultures and creeds. Your different culture, if properly mixed, may add to the beauty of the whole, therefore, remain cheerful and optimistic up to the last moment."[12]

It was clear that the aims and objectives of the university were to educate the people, particularly Muslims on the line of Oxford and Cambridge University, but in the light of Islam and nationalism. This institution insisted development of sound judgement, good manners, commonsense and self-sacrifice as essential elements of good education. AMU received ample help and assistance from its non-Muslim friends, and its door were open to persons of all religious classes and creeds.

His Highness Agha Khan, the Pro-Chancellor of AMU in 1936 said, "this university must be cherished by the whole of India as their common trust, their jewel and their child. From Madras to Peshawar we must remember that this university occupies the same position in matters of culture and educational ideals as Delhi do in matters of politics."[13]

Communal Harmony

Sir Syed Ahmad Khan was of the opinion that India is a beautiful bride and Hindus and Muslims are her two eyes. This feeling of fraternity and harmony was always maintained in Aligarh Muslim University. In the admissions of various courses, the non-Muslims were taken without any discriminations.

In Aligarh Muslim University, college and schools, the students came from U.P., Punjab, Hyderabad, Deccan, Madras, Sindh, Delhi, Kashmir, Mysore, South Africa, Ceylon, Persia and Muscat. Besides the Muslim students, this university and its allied institutions had many Hindu and Christian students who represent different parts of the country. As regards the Hindus, it is important to observe that besides the regular students a large number of private candidates appeared in its examinations every year. Thus, while it is true that its main purpose was to provide for Muslim educational needs, this university has always served the educational cause of the country as a whole.[14]

For the session of 1922-23 at least half a dozen Hindu students applied to be admitted as boarders coming from distant places. The university felt the responsibility to make permanent arrangements for these boarders, their kitchens and other requirements. Later on, they were accommodated into S.M. Court, but it was felt that for their permanent boarding old school building would be arranged, if their number increased.[15]

In 1924, many students from Baroda State applied for admission in AMU. However, the problem before this university was about their dining arrangements. This problem was solved when a letter from Captain of Baroda State reached Aligarh. I think this work will be incomplete if that letter is not quoted. The letter was as follows:[16]

> "As regards the feeding arrangements for the Maratha Sardars' boys, there would not be any difficulty. They will and they are quite used to dining with their Muslim brethren. In fact Baroda is very advanced in that way, Marathas, Gujaratis, Brahmans, Europeans, Parsis and Mohammadans always dine at one table and take food

> cooked by Mohammadan cooks. All are non-vegetarian. You will be surprised to learn that almost 75 per cent of the officers and Sardars have been to Europe. The real idea of these parents in sending their sons to Aligarh is that the boys may imbibe and inculcate that spirit which is not found in other colleges of India, Banaras University included."

Captain of Baroda State continued in his letter, "In January last I had gone to Banaras with His Highness the Maharaja Sahib for the convocation meeting. My eyes were keenly comparing the Aligarh spirit with that of Banaras one and to please myself, I can say that my Aligarh is quite different and incomparable...."

The AMU had a good reputation all-over India in all communities and had no prejudice against any caste or creed of India. Unfortunately, some students of Banaras Hindu University, who had been in Aligarh for some time, spread the rumour that in Aligarh no attention was paid to the interests of the Hindu students and no provision was made for the holidays of the Hindu festivals. Nevertheless, these were mere allegations whose fallacy could be proved by the list of AMU holidays, which had been attached in the appendices.[17]

Aligarh University never betrayed any bias against any particular community. Regular convocations were held and students were filled with national feelings, communal harmony and love for their country and countrymen. In the convocation of Muslim University 1940 Sir Sultan Ahmad addressed the students, "racially and politically Hindus and Muslims are Indians and breate in the same atmosphere. No doubt there are differences, but the foundations of life are the same. Political and social salvation can only lie in both, Hindus and Muslims pooling their energies together for reconstruction of a better India." Sir Sultan Ahmad further said, "I conjure you earnestly all young men both Hindus and Muslims to remember this hard sane and incontrovertible fact when you enter a larger sphere of life. You must try to promote mutual understanding, mutual trust and mutual love and to remember your mutual obligation."[18] He warned that any other road would lead India to chaos, anarchy bloodshed and perpetual subjection.[19]

Culture and Traditions

Aligarh Muslim University was one of the best universities of India in its education and professional teachings. However, its unique culture and traditions made it one of the best universities of the world, next to the Oxford and Cambridge. It provided a different character of fraternity oneness, which were almost absent in the other universities in India. Of course, it could not be acquired in the classrooms but as believed to the alumni, it is the special gift of its founder Sir Syed Ahmad Khan.

The culture and traditions of AMU were neither purely Islamic nor belonging to the Hindu or Christian religions. It's the synthesis of all good things of different civilizations of the World. To some extent, due to the Muslim Majority of the students, Islamic character was dominating, but it did not hamper the freedom of non-Muslim students in the university campus. Even the non-Muslim students of AMU were proud of calling themselves as "Alig" and lifelong followed these culture and traditions in their lives.

The common uniform for all students and its discipline constituted main part of the culture and traditions of the university. This particular type of culture and tradition distinguished the university students from other students of India and the world. The university uniform consisted black Turkish coat[20], white trousers or *paijamas* of Aligarh cut, fez, boots or shoes with socks. This uniform was worn by students at lectures, in the dining hall, at the time of inviting on any university officer, visiting the town or railway station and also on such occasions as the Pro-Vice Chancellor directed.[21]

Nevertheless, the research students might be exempted from that provision at the discretion of PVC and on the recommendation of chairman of their respective departments. During the hot weather, i.e. from 15th April or from the date fixed by Pro-Vice Chancellor or the beginning of the long vacations students wore white or light brown Turkish coat, *sherwanis* or *achkans*. Members of the teaching staff wore gowns at invigilation and all university functions. They wore gowns of the universities at which they had graduated. Those members of teaching staff who did not possess a degree recognized by the university were entitled to wear graduate gowns of the university. The observance of this rule during the hot weather was left on discretion of the members of the staff. Graduate students of the university were required to wear gowns on the convocation day.[22]

The uniform was very important for residential university, and every residential institution had its own uniform. It helped the authorities to distinguish the students from those who did not belong to the institution. Another important part of this university was its Proctorial system, which was introduced by Theodore Beck and Sir Theodore Morison in the college days. This system continued when Muslim University was established and afterwards. Here the students were under the eyes of Proctor and Sub Proctor, who looked after the discipline and conduct, at the same time, they were themselves allowed to take part in maintaining order.[23]

The Aligarh University was also very strict regarding of religious side. During the month of *Ramdhan*, Head of the departments, Proctors, Headmasters and Provosts were empowered to formulate some regulations about the Muslim students to show due regard to the sacred traditions of *Ramdhan*. During the days of *Ramdhan* smoking, chewing and use of *Pan* during the daytime was avoided at all public places. There was no singing, playing musical instruments or any other kind of disturbances during the prayer time, including the time of *Taravih*. No parties were given either by students or the members of the staff during daytime. No meals were issued from the dining hall except for the non-Muslims and there was no cooking done in student's rooms during the daytime.[24]

Special arrangements were made for *Taravih* prayers, and these were regularly attended by the students concerned. The Wardens were requested to set that the foregoing instructions were duly observed by the students, and any breach was reported to the Provost concern for action. No students were permitted by the Provosts during this month to visit cinema halls. All the restaurants within university area were closed during the daytime.[25]

AMU while building the career of the students, always remain one of the sources of guidelines for all the minority institutions of India. The AMU authorities gave their instructions to form regulations for other Muslim schools and colleges in India. Brayne Meo High School of Mewat was one of the examples, which was given the guidelines by the AMU. The Secretary of the Brayne Meo High School sent an invitation to the Pro-Vice Chancellor Dr. Ziauddin Ahmad for consultation regarding many problems about the Meo community and the school.[26]

Actually, the AMU was not merely an institution but a movement to educate the people of India, particularly the Muslims. It included the students from all the communities of India but the Muslim students were major part of its strength. On the occasion when H.E.H. Nizam accepted the Chancellorship of the Muslims University in October 1935, many meetings of the Musalmans at many places in India were held and conveyed their sincere and respectful gratitude. These places were Gorakhpur, Allahabad, Saharanpur, Jhansi, Partapgarh, Marehara (Etah), Basti, Sherkot (Bijnor), Dehradun, Hamirpur, Moradabad, Gurgaon, Kanpur, Jaunpur, Banaras, Agra, Buland Shahar, Peshawar, Kohat, Qadian (Punjab), Burhanpur (Central Province), Baghpat Estate (Meerut), Shikohabad, Jaipur, Ambala, Sikandrabad, etc.[27]

All the Aligarh students or old boys popularly known as 'Alig' had much moral interaction among them and always convened meetings and send suggestions, their respect and allegiance to the Aligarh Muslim University.

Raja Mohammad Ali Mohammad Khan of Mahmudabad (17th December, 1920–28th February, 1923)

His Highness, Sir Mohammad Ali Mohammad Khan of Mahmudabad, popularly known as Raja Mahmudabad, was the founding Vice-Chancellor of the Aligarh Muslim University. He worked as the first Vice-Chancellor from 17th December, 1920 to 28th February, 1923. Raja Mahmudabad put extra efforts to give a shape to the newly established University. He donated rupees one lakh to AMU in 1920, just after his appointment as Vice-Chancellor. He also instituted scholarships to the AMU students every year. The period of Raja of Mahmudabad as Vice-Chancellor was most challenging due to the Non-Cooperation Movement. The student's strength of the university decreased from 838 to 512. However, Raja of Mahmudabad took the matter seriously and started the work along with his team.[28]

When Raja of Mahmudabad joined as Vice-Chancellor, many new departments were opened, and many were upgraded, according to the AMU Act of 1920, in order to maintain a standard of education. At the beginning, the AMU had 15 departments of studies, i.e. (1) English, (2) History & Political Science, (3) Economics, (4) Philosophy and Psychology, (5) Physics, (6) Chemistry, (7) Mathematics and Astronomy, (8) Geography, (9) Sunni Theology, (10) Shia Theology, (11) Islamic Studies, (12) Arabic Language and Literature, (13) Persian, (14) Urdu, and (15) Law.[29]

A few departments were not fully functioning and were only on paper such as Islamic Studies, where no teaching arrangements were existed. By the efforts of Raja of Mahmudabad, the Department of Islamic Studies was made functional by providing a syllabus and teachers. There were, however, still some departments functioning in the same way as they did at the time of MAO College.

The Vice-Chancellor, Raja Mahmudabad resigned with effect from 1st March, 1923 due to pressure of his official duties as Home Minister in UP Government. He is also said to have developed personal differences with the first Pro-Vice Chancellor Dr. Ziauddin Ahmad. Even after resigning from AMU as its Vice-Chancellor, he was always associated with the Aligarh Muslim University.[30]

Nawab Mohammad Muzammilullah Khan Sherwani (1st March, 1923–31st December, 1923)

Nawab Mohammad Muzammilullah Khan Sherwani became the Acting Vice-Chancellor from 1st March, 1923 to 31st December, 1923. He was the Nawab of Bhikampur, a small principality in Aligarh District. During this period, the AMU made considerable progress, four new departments namely Sanskrit, Botany, Zoology and Education were created. For the department of Education, a Teachers Training College was also established and placed under the charge of Mr. N.K. Mukerji.[31]

From 1923 onwards, there was a tremendous increase in the strength of the students, particularly private candidates in the university examinations.[32]

Sahibzada Aftab Ahmad Khan (1st January, 1924–31st December, 1926)

On 24th December, 1923, Sahibzada Aftab Ahmad Khan was formally elected as the new Vice-Chancellor of the AMU, but he joined the office on 1st January, 1924. Prior to this, he was the Vice-President and the Secretary of the State's Council for the last seven years which was also known as India Council. On being elected as the Vice-Chancellor of AMU, he decided to devote himself to the work of promotion of Muslim education on the lines of Sir Syed Ahmad Khan. Commenting on his Vice-Chancellorship of AMU, the newspaper "The Times" wrote, "he will be titular as well as the actual leader of the Mohammadan educational efforts."[33]

When Sahibzaba Aftab Ahmad Khan assumed the charge as Vice-Chancellor, he found that the offices and departments of the university were in complete disarray. The office staff, including the *Imams* and the *Muazzins* of the mosque, was unpunctual; the dining halls and the kitchens were full of filth and a threat to the health. The tea stalls hotels added more filth. The wards of Health Centre presented no better look. Such a state of affairs greatly shocked Sahibzada Aftab Ahmad Khan. He resolved to introduce reforms and set an example by his punctuality and hard work.[34]

Here it is worth mentioning that when Sahibzada Aftab Ahmad Khan began to work as the Vice-Chancellor of AMU, political tensions had almost ceased in the campus. The politics of young Aligarh nationalist students for the support of the Khilafat and Non-Cooperation had come to almost an end, especially because the National Muslim University (Jamia Millia Islamia) was shifted to Delhi in 1925.[35]

Though Sahibzada Aftab Ahmad Khan had no immediate political issues to deal with, he faced challenging situation to promote the educational atmosphere in the AMU. In his convocation address of February 1924, he gave more emphasis on the need of technical training to the students to face the economic problems and promote the industrial progress of India.[36]

He also complained that the AMU library was the only library which did not receive any grant from the government while those of Banaras, Allahabad and Lucknow were being regularly provided grants by the government. A good library was essential to the mental and intellectual development for researches.[37]

Referring to the teachings in Theology, he said that admittedly it was a compulsory subject according to the statutes, and the examinations were also being conducted but only the teaching and examination were not enough. He stressed that instead of asking students to read theology books it was essential that a religious atmosphere be created in institution, which demanded appointments of such *Ulema*, who had a reputation for their piety and knowledge. He further elaborated that such *Ulema* should be allowed so much time so that they could meet teachers and students and impress them with their piety, courtesy and knowledge resulting in the emergence of religious atmosphere.[38]

During another speech, Sahibzada Aftab Ahmad Khan made it clear that the financial position of the university was sound to meet the expenses. Hence, he appealed to the well-wishers to give donations generously to the university. He also appealed to the government to extend grant to meet the requirement of AMU.[39]

He saw that the condition of the Training College was hopeless. The students of the Training College were also allowed to attend the classes of M.A. and LL.B., which was not permissible in any Government Training College. So that Director of Education of UP made a policy not to appoint any teacher coming from the AMU Training College. Sahibzada Aftab Ahmad Khan tried to reform the system and succeeded in appointing one Reader and two Lecturers in the Training College. Consequently, a diploma course was introduced in the Training College.[40]

The department of Geography was almost non-functional. Sahibzada Aftab Ahmad Khan took keen interest and soon regenerated it. The condition of the department of Arabic was also not very satisfactory. Efforts were made to obtain the services of the learned persons through inviting applications from India and abroad. Sahibzada Sahib thus secured the services of Allama Abdul Aziz Memon to manage this department. Soon the department improved under the care of Maulana Memon.[41]

Sahibzada Aftab Ahmad Khan also came across the irritating facts that most of the teachers were not punctual and some of them even abstained from their duties to attend their personal works. A majority of students also became irregular in attending the classes. He, therefore, took the matter seriously and after confiding with the Pro-Vice Chancellor Dr. Ziauddin Ahmad, he informed the parents about the carelessness of their wards. His appropriate action worked in restoring the discipline among the students.[42]

Sahibzada Aftab Ahmad Khan made it a regular feature to meet the teachers of the departments and to enquire about their needs. In such meetings, he chanced to meet Maulana Sulaiman Ashraf, the Chairman of the department of Islamic Studies and urged upon him to activate the Department of Islamic Studies.[43]

Sahibzada Aftab Ahmad Khan also improved the working of the administration through several reforms. He inspected the dining hall and set-up a committee for improving its functioning. In the light of that committee's recommendations, the old dining hall contractors were replaced by new contractors. The dining hall functioned for about one year under the new arrangements.[44]

However, as complained by the Vice-Chancellor, the reforms were shortlived partly because of the non-cooperation from Dr. Ziauddin Ahmad, who was the Pro-Vice Chancellor at that time. Consequently, the expelled contractors re-entered. One of the major hurdles in the success of the reforms was the fact that the contractors who supplied the material for the dining hall were also the suppliers of daily needs to the supervisors and keepers of the dining hall. Added to this problem was the fact that some of the employees of the university also functioned as contractors of the dining halls and boarding houses.[45]

Apart from looking into the details of food cooked and supplied to the students, Sahibzada Aftab Ahmad Khan like Sir Syed took the interest in fitness and maintaining good health of the students. He began a Scouting and Drill Society. He also improved the working of Riding School by adding ten horses to the existing four. He also promoted other games such as Hockey, Cricket, Football, Tennis, etc.[46]

For the Intermediate College, Sahibzada Aftab Ahmad Khan appointed a Principal Abdul Majeed Qureshi and eight more teachers. Improvements were also made in the College library and College building. He appointed Bashir Husain Zaidi as Head Master of the university school and granted Rs. 3000/- for furniture of teachers and students. He also gave money for Geography and Science equipment and added new buildings for university school.[47]

He formulated the idea to set-up a school for the blinds under university's care. The idea of opening the school for blinds was not new. Earlier, the move for establishing a school for the blinds was started by Ghulam Ahmad Ahmadi to which Sahibzada gave a practical shape. The foundation stone of the blind school was laid on 14th January, 1925, by Hakim Abdul Wahab Ansari (Hakim Nabina), the elder brother of famous nationalist leader Dr. Mukhtar Ahmad Ansari.[48]

The school building was completed within two years and half. Sahibzada himself, his elder brother Sultan Ahmad Khan and his wife Bilqis donated a handsome amount for this purpose. On 29th November, 1927 the school, was inaugurated by Sir William Marris, the Governor of UP. The school was named as Ahmadi School after the name of its pioneer. At that time, Nawab Sir Muzammilullah Khan Sherwani was the Vice-Chancellor of the university, and he donated to the school a sum of rupees ten thousand in the memory of his elder brother Haji Mohammad Ahmad Sayeed Khan, who became a blind in his advanced age.[49]

In order to meet the growing needs of the university, Sahibzada Ahmad Khan invited the Governor-General Lord Reading to visit the Aligarh. He expected great favour from him. The Viceroy visited Aligarh on 25th January, 1925 and announced the enhancement of the annual grant from rupees one lakh to one lakh and twenty five thousands. He also announced the additional amount of rupees five lakhs for the construction of new buildings.[50]

Dr. Ziauddin Ahmad as Pro-Vice Chancellor (26th March, 1921–27th April, 1928)

The works and achievements of Dr. Ziauddin Ahmad as Pro-Vice Chancellor of AMU were as remarkable as the Vice-Chancellorship of many other renowned persons. In his Pro-Vice Chancellorship, which he served from 26th March, 1921 to 27th April, 1928, he did many developmental works of AMU.

For the development of the university, Dr. Ziauddin Ahmad, the Pro-Vice Chancellor, was also working shoulder to shoulder with the Vice-Chancellor Sahibzada Aftab Ahmad Khan. Dr. Ziauddin Ahmad had faced the eventful years of the university from 1920 to 1925. As far as admission policy of the university was concerned, Dr. Ziauddin Ahmad showed some softness. The session of AMU used to begin from the month of October, it was two months late than other universities and there was also no fixed last date for admissions. His soft views on the admissions were in order to increase the number of students.[51]

Though ideologically Sahibzada Aftab Ahmad Khan and Dr. Ziauddin Ahmad have differences but for the progress of the AMU, they worked together and cooperated with each other as the future events indicate. Like Aftab Ahmad Khan, Dr. Ziauddin Ahmad also believed in the expansion of scientific and technical educations in AMU. In 1922, in the function of Duty Society (*Anjuman-i-Farz*) he presented ten-years plan, stressing the need of technical education for which he fixed a target to raise rupees fifty lakh.[52]

Dr. Ziauddin Ahmad also explained why technical education needed so urgently. He believed that in the existing educational system, every student cannot secure government jobs, so he must get the technical education. The government jobs, due to its scarcity, are now not as much attractive as a few years earlier.[53]

Dr. Ziauddin Ahmad also secured a donation of rupees one lakh from the Nawab of Bhopal added to it in the donations received in the Jubilee Celebrations of 1925. He received the funds for the establishment of the Engineering College. He also purchased necessary equipment for the Applied Physics and Applied Chemistry. The government, however, delayed granting permission while it had already allowed Agra and Allahabad universities to start engineering classes.[54]

Dr. Ziauddin Ahmad also considered that education to the AMU students in modern Medical Sciences was necessary. Hence, he started medical group in the Intermediate Science group, so that the students might obtain knowledge for the admission to the Sub Assistant Surgeon in the Medical College.[55]

In AMU, the Theology and Urdu were made compulsory subjects. These were extra subjects unlike in other universities. Dr. Ziauddin Ahmad started an examination called 'part one' which was to be cleared by the students during the years of their course. He also started coaching for competitive examinations in 1922, but this was not very regular, even then in 1923 two candidates were selected in Roorkee and Shahpur Engineering Colleges, four students selected in Lucknow Medical College. In 1924, three students were selected for provincial services and one in the Indian Civil Services.[56]

Dr. Ziauddin Ahmad started the policy of holding private examinations. Actually poor students from distant areas could not take admission in AMU, and the university had no provision for affiliating schools and colleges out of Aligarh district. So a new system of private examination was started, and many students benefitted from that system.[57]

Until 1924, eight students were sent to Europe for research purposes, and this number increased later on. Three teachers also got the loan from the university for that purpose. For the improvement of education in the university, many societies of departments were started. Until the resignation of Dr. Ziauddin Ahmad in 1928, there were seven literary societies in the university, some of them started journals, some established libraries, some other sent their members for enquiry informative tours.[58]

Golden Jubilee Celebration

On the completion of 50 years from the foundation of this institution, the Vice-Chancellor Sahibzada Aftab Ahmad Khan and Pro-Vice Chancellor Dr. Ziauddin Ahmad decided for a Golden Jubilee Celebration. It was a process to draw the attention of the Muslims towards the educational movement of Aligarh, which got distracted owing to political climate of the country.[59] In this regard Sahibzada Aftab Ahmad Khan said before the Court, "As I desired the celebration of the jubilee to be truly national in scope and character, I started preparation soon after the decision was taken."[60]

A full preparation was made by Sahibzada Aftab Ahmad Khan, but unfortunately his doctors advised him for the complete rest for at least six weeks as his illness reached its zenith. He handed over his work to Dr. Ziauddin Ahmad and left for Agra and then for Delhi for two months.[61]

Dr. Ziauddin Ahmad was busy with his academic works, but he took the responsibility seriously and did his work competently.

He toured some places, met prominent persons and sought their cooperation. Her Highness the Chancellor (Begum of Bhopal) ordered the related officers of her state to provide a high-class *Pandal* and tents for guests. Invitation letters were released from the side of Her Highness Chancellor and Vice-Chancellor to the honourable post holders of Provincial and Central Governments. Education Minister of Afghanistan with other members of the ministry; the representatives of the Oxford and Indian universities and representatives of different states participated in the Jubilee Celebration. His Highness Maharaja of Alwar also arrived in Aligarh and granted Rs. 60,000/- and one scholarship for studies in any foreign country. The Viceroy, the Governors of the provinces and Vice-Chancellors of the universities also sent their messages of good wishes.[62]

The Jubilee Celebration began on 25th December and continued until 31st December, 1925. About 7,000 guests came from far-off places to participate the celebration. The occasion was utilized for holding meetings of important Muslim organizations such as those of All India Mohammadan Educational Conference, All India Muslim League, *Tanzeem*, Muslim Rajput Conference, All India Urdu Conference, etc. The university convocation was also held during the same week.[63]

Besides public meetings and lectures, the programme of jubilee included elocution contests in English and Urdu. A series of games and tournaments was also held, which drew players and sportsmen from different universities and colleges.[64] Rs. 17,600/- in cash were received as donations on the occasion and Rs. 3,00,000/- were promised to be donated. Dr. Ziauddin Ahmad specified this money for engineering and scientific education.[65]

Soon after the Jubilee Celebration, the 5th Convocation was held in 1926. Maharaja of Alwar in his address emphasised the need to strengthen the department of Theology. He said, "Department of Theology is not less important than the establishment of the school of technology, as religious education of high standard is equally essential for the progress of the Muslims. It is unfortunate that despite the provision in ordinances for awarding the degree of Bachelor and Master in Theology, no sufficient staff has been provided for its teaching and conducting examinations for these degrees." Maharaja of Alwar offered to the Vice-Chancellor a donation of Rs. 8,000/- per annum for founding a chair in Theology for five years.[66]

Her Highness the Begum of Bhopal thanked His Highness the Maharaja of Alwar for extending his generous support to the cause of Muslim education. Her Highness expressed her satisfaction with the pace and progress made in the university and establishing new departments. A donation of two lakh rupees was generously announced by her son while laying the foundation stone of Science College.[67] Dr. Ziauddin Ahmad requested the Government of India to open a signaller class on the same condition as it had opened in several schools in India and United Provinces.[68]

AMU in Crisis

During the first decade of its foundation, the Aligarh Muslim University, notwithstanding its profound development, faced a fatal crisis, which led to establishment of the inquiry commissions and consequently, the resignation from the Pro-Vice Chancellorship by Dr. Ziauddin Ahmad. These were due to personal differences among the top-level authorities or more accurately between Vice-Chancellor and Pro-Vice Chancellor of Aligarh Muslim University.

The AMU Act of 1920 made the Pro-Vice Chancellor as the principal academic officer, but the relations between Vice-Chancellor and Pro-Vice Chancellor were not clearly defined. As a result, it caused a lot of practical difficulties in the day to day working and created undue misunderstanding between them. It was for this reason that the relations between the first Vice-Chancellor Raja of Mahmudabad and Pro-Vice Chancellor Dr. Ziauddin Ahmad, got strained.

The Raja of Mahmudabad, during his tenure of Vice-Chancellorship (two years and two months), had his stay at Aligarh for less than two weeks. He attended only nine meetings of the Executive Council out of 28. In such a situation, the Pro-Vice Chancellor, Dr. Ziauddin Ahmad had to carry all the burden of responsibilities. Even then the relations were far from cordial. Besides, Raja of Mahmudabad was not able to work as a regular Vice-Chancellor because he was too busy with his Home

Membership of United Provinces, so he resigned from the post of Vice Chancellorship in February 1923.[69]

In December 1923, Sahibzada Aftab Ahamd Khan was elected unopposed as Vice-Chancellor. The new Vice-Chancellor's appointment also could not improve the equation between the Vice-Chancellor and the Pro-Vice Chancellor. Consequently, in April 1925, Dr. Ziauddin Ahmad tendered his resignation, but it was not accepted. Dr. Ziauddin Ahmad was requested to continue to work in the interest of the university. Actually, the bitterness of the relations was not due to only Raja of Mahmudabad and Sahibzada Aftab Ahmad Khan, but Dr. Ziauddin Ahmad was also equally responsible for it. The Pro-Vice Chancellor had formed a group of his followers from among the university staff and actively participated in Indian politics.[70]

Although he was a full time Pro-Vice Chancellor, he was also a member in the Central Assembly and was permanently appointed member of many different committees. For that purpose, he spent most of his time for their work and went to different places like Bangalore, Decca, Calcutta, Lucknow, Karachi, etc. In this situation, the other office bearers of the university could not pay much attention to the university functioning.[71] Dr. Ziauddin Ahmad's liberal policy of admission and the scheme of private examination, and the system of supplementary and compartmental examination was another subject of much controversy.[72]

At that time, a similar propaganda was being made against the university by certain hostile elements. First among them was the Governor of United Provinces Sir William Marris.[73] The other was Mr. Meekenzie[74], the Director of Education in United Provinces. Third was the English daily "*Leader*" of Allahabad. Added to it, there were the group politics of the university itself. All these hostile elements alleged that under the present authority, the rules and regulations of the university were being openly violated, and the standard of the university was going down.[75]

No doubt the university was going through a dark phase. The authorities instead of improving the standard of the university engaged themselves in setting their personal differences. Another dispute between the Vice-Chancellor and the Pro-Vice Chancellor arose when the former asked to check the functioning of the examination. The Pro-Vice Chancellor did not allow him to interfere.[76] It infuriated the Vice-Chancellor against the Pro-Vice Chancellor Dr. Ziauddin Ahmad. All these differences encouraged government authorities to pay attention towards the university.

Abdullah Enquiry Committee

Shaikh Abdullah, the founder of the Girls School, went to Lucknow for some purposes and heard the rumour that government was about to appoint a commission of enquiry to investigate the university affairs. Shaikh Abdullah returned to Aligarh and informed the university authorities and suggested that the university itself could appoint an enquiry committee immediately to prove before the government that the university authorities were not unaware of university conditions. Dr. Ziauddin Ahmad opposed the idea but in spite of his opposition, an enquiry committee was formed. Shaikh Abdullah became the president of this committee, and the other four members were from among the university staff. This committee came to be known as "Abdullah Committee."[77]

Just after its formation, Sahibzada Aftab Ahamd Khan went to Mussoorie due to his ailment. Twenty two members of the AMU Court and most of the staff members, including Dr. Ziauddin gave their statements regarding the functioning of the university. Finally, a report was written, which came to be known as "Abdullah Committee Report." One of its copies was sent to Sahibzada Aftab Ahamd Khan in Mussoorie on September 4, 1926.[78]

In this report, among all the recommendations, the recommendation about the admission of students was quite considerable. It was said that the admission of the students should be started from the month of October and closed in November, and no student should be admitted after that. The students were requested 75 per cent attendance for appearing in the examinations. However as far as foreign students were concerned, they might be given certain concessions and be admitted until the end of the first term of the university.[79]

The second thing, which the committee had paid attention, was about the result of the university examinations, because many students were admitted without solving their residential problems.

They were bound to hire rooms in the city outside the university campus. By following Abdullah Committee Report, Sahibzada Aftab Ahmad Khan wrote a review of 39 pages on the report and sent it to the Pro-Vice Chancellor Dr. Ziauddin Ahmad on 21st September, 1926.[80]

To sum up, of the review it was urged that there should not be any laxity in the matters of law even at the time of necessity, and the laws should take precedence over necessity.[81] Sahibzada Aftab Ahmad Khan also gave an instruction about the admission of the students, and the date of admission was fixed. The same was ordered for immediate implementation. He wrote, "you consider Acts and Ordinances without caring for the Regulations."[82]

Sahibzada Aftab Ahmad Khan also accepted that the Regulations which were against the Acts and Ordinances were being prepared by Dr. Ziauddin Ahmad and placed before the Academic Council. Sahibzada Aftab Ahmad Khan said that as a Vice-Chancellor, he had the right to veto those Regulations, but he did not do so, that's why he was also responsible for mismanagement. Nevertheless, now there was an urgent need not to repeat such mistakes.[83]

Dr. Ziauddin Ahmad gave a very harsh reply to the criticism of Sahibzada Aftab Ahmad Khan, a few sentences were as follows:[84]

> "Unfortunately this time you have been in ailment for whole year and due to heart disease and paralysis you are unaware of the details of the university affairs. This point shows that you have made so many improper objections in your letter. Among all of your orders, most of them are being implemented."

Dr. Ziauddin Ahmad further said, "I remind you that in my absence when I was in England you had dropped the Regulations prepared by me and formed a committee to prepare the Regulations again. Before my returning from England, the Academic Council presided by you had accepted most of the Regulations. They were accepted completely by June 1925 and you had announced that by October 1925 they would be implemented."

Dr. Ziauddin Ahmad finally said, "In winter 1925, the practical life of the university was paralyzed due to jubilee celebrations. I am working on certain proposals which need to be implemented, rest of the proposals shall be placed before the concerned departments."

Sahibzada Aftab Ahmad Khan returned from Mussoorie to Aligarh on 6th October, 1926 at the time of opening of the university. His term of Vice-Chancellorship was about to end in December 1926. He decided to be one of the candidates for the election of the Vice-Chancellor which was going to be held in December 1926. Sir William Marris, Governor of U.P. suggested the name of Nawab Mohammad Muzammilullah Khan as one of the candidates for the Vice-Chancellor in opposition to Sahibzada Aftab Ahmad Khan. Nawab Mohammad Muzammilullah Khan had solid support in the Court and Dr. Ziauddin Ahmad was also one of his supporters.[85]

The supporters of Nawab Mohammad Muzammilullah Khan tried every bit to defame Sahibzada Aftab Ahmad Khan. In order to defame Sahibzada Aftab Ahmad Khan, the supporters of Nawab Mohammad Muzammilullah Khan wrote four letters and distributed among the Court members and got them published in the newspapers. These letters included different questions related to different matters of the university and demanded answers from Sahibzada Aftab Ahmad Khan. One of the letters was very ridiculous. After an enquiry two letters duly signed by Haji Maulvi Muqtada Khan Sherwani, Manager University Press, were found. Sahibzada Aftab Ahamd Khan placed the matter before Executive Council, but no action was taken against the convict except rebuking.[86]

Considering that the university atmosphere is unfavourable for him, Sahibzada Aftab Ahmad Khan decided to withdraw his name from the candidature of the Vice Chancellorship. In December 1926, Sahibzada Aftab Ahmad Khan formally announced that he was no more a candidate for the Vice-Chancellorship.[87]

Nawab Mohammad Muzammilullah Khan Sherwani (1st January, 1927–8th February, 1929)

The term of Sahibzada Aftab Ahmad Khan completed and in December 1926, Nawab Sir Muzammilullah Khan Sherwani became the next Vice-Chancellor. However, this followed the confusion in the university and personal differences among the university authorities, which led to the setting of a committee of enquiry against the working of Dr. Ziauddin Ahmad. This Committee report led to the resignation of Dr. Ziauddin Ahmad and in his place, Prof. M.M. Ashraf was appointed as PVC on 2nd May, 1928.[88]

On 24th December, 1926, Nawab Muzammilullah Khan Sherwani was elected by the Court for the post of Vice-Chancellorship, who started his work from 1st January, 1927.[89] In between Sahibzada Aftab Ahmad Khan secretly published huge pamphlet on 28th December, 1926 from the university funds. Copies of the pamphlet were given to Sir William Marris, Members of the Court, and its Urdu translation "*Muslim University Ke Maujuda Halat*" was also published on large scale.[90]

According to the most of the Aligarh men, this pamphlet necessitated the intervention of the government in the university affairs. However, it should not be forgotten that before the propaganda made by the pamphlet of Sahibzada Aftab Ahmad Khan, the government was fully aware of the situation in Aligarh Muslim University. This fact is proved from a statement of Sahibzada Aftab Ahmad Khan given below:[91]

> "In August and September 1926, I was in Mussoorie Hills, I returned to Aligarh on 6th October and learnt that Government of India wanted to enquire about the standard of examination in the Muslim University. So as to know the real facts I met Education Commissioner Mr. Richi in Delhi on October 23, 1926. Mr. Richi said that he had asked Dr. Ziauddin Ahmad that government was not satisfied with the results of university examinations and Dr. Ziauddin Ahmad replied that he would place the proposal of enquiry before the University Council. So, the government was waiting for the answer from Dr. Ziauddin Ahmad."

Some members of the Executive Council wanted that government itself should enquire but some others wanted that the university authorities should take its responsibility. However, as the Abdullah Enquiry Committee Report was not fully implemented, most of the members were of the opinion that the government should set-up the enquiry committee. So, it could clearly be said that the pamphlet of Sahibzada Aftab Ahmad Khan was not fully responsible for setting up the enquiry committee, but it made the way easier.

Before discussing the details of the enquiry committee, we must go through the pamphlet of Sahibzada Aftab Ahmad Khan. No doubt it was the direct attack upon Dr. Ziauddin Ahmad, and it was his moral responsibility to answer the allegations. The present Vice-Chancellor Nawab Muzammilullah also demanded an explanation from Dr. Ziauddin Ahmad and other staff members against whom the accusation was made. Dr. Ziauddin Ahmad gave the statement in 35 pages.[92]

In his explanation, firstly, Dr. Ziauddin expressed about his relations with Sahibzada Aftab Ahmad Khan, which were very cordial in the beginning. It is proved by the fact that in the special meeting of the Court held on 28th February, 1926 for the appointment of Pro-Vice Chancellor, Sahibzada Aftab Ahmad Khan himself moved for Dr. Ziauddin's re-appointment as Pro-Vice Chancellor in the following words:[93]

> "The present Pro-Vice Chancellor's term of office will expire on the 2nd March, 1926. I, therefore, propose that Dr. Ziauddin Ahmad be re-appointed as Pro-Vice Chancellor of the Muslim University for another term. The university is still young and is in the process of growth and expansion. It needs the guidance and experience of Dr. Ziauddin, who had great reputation in the educational world. It needs a Pro-Vice Chancellor who knows the special requirements of the community as well as the educational system, which is in the vogue in the country. And our Pro-Vice Chancellor should also be in direct touch with the parents of students in different parts of the country. Dr. Ziauddin fulfils all these conditions. I therefore, recommend his appointment to the members of the Court."

It was surprising that Sahibzada Aftab Ahmad Khan who supported Dr. Ziauddin Ahmad for giving him second term as Pro-Vice Chancellor, after eight months he wrote against him in his pamphlet. It says, "I tried my best to work with him but bitter experiences has opened my eyes as it has shown me the other side of his personality. After having served for three years as Vice-Chancellor, I am of the opinion that the most vital interests of the university are at stake and that its chief characteristics are in jeopardy."[94]

From all the above facts, it becomes clear that the relations between Sahibzada Aftab Ahmad Khan and Dr. Ziauddin Ahmad became extremely bitter in the last months of Sahibzada's Vice-Chancellorship, which adversely affected their working relationship. Sahibzada Aftab Ahmad Khan complained about the non-existence of the Regulations at the time of his assuming the office. About that Dr. Ziauddin Ahmad said that the AMU Act itself provided that at first Ordinances of the university were to be framed under the direction of Governor General in Council. These Ordinances were received by the university in 1923. They did not provide details of the conduct of examinations nor the standard of marks for the classification of successful candidates in various divisions.[95]

The framing of Regulations began soon after that and completed in June 1924. The Regulations were to come into force from October 1924, but during the absence of the Pro-Vice Chancellor while he was in England in October 1924, Sahibzada Aftab Ahmad Khan declared that the Regulations previously made should be treated as null and void, and he appointed his own committee, which took more than a year to frame the new Regulations which came into operation from January 1926.[96]

Another accusation of Sahibzada Aftab Ahmad Khan was that of "singling out Maulana Sulaiman Ashraf[97] and Lt. M. Hamiduddin Khan[98] for extraordinary promotion." Dr. Ziauddin Ahmad refuted that charge and said that the procedure in every such case was that the promotion was, firstly, introduced by Pro-Vice Chancellor whose suggestions were scrutinized by the Finance Committee. The recommendations of the Finance Committee were laid before the Executive Council for final approval. Dr. Ziauddin further said that not only two abovementioned persons were singled out, but a number of teachers had been promoted following that procedure.[99]

As regards Sahibzada's complaint about the non-existence of Islamic Studies, Dr. Ziauddin Ahmad said that much stress was given on framing the syllabi. Actually, the term Islamic Studies was at first used by Mr. Nathan in the report of Decca University. Islamic Studies as understood by Mr. Nathan included the study of Arabic language, Muslim Religion and Muslim Theology. In the Muslim University, Theology was a mere distinct subject, and Arabic was also a separate subject. The process designing courses in a new subject presenting peculiar phases must necessarily be slow. The university, under the guidance of Maulana Sulaiman Ashraf, framed courses in Islamic Studies more than two years ago, and the teaching had been started for the last two years, and students would be examined in Islamic Studies in April 1927.[100]

Regarding Dr. Ataullah Butt, it was mentioned in the pamphlet of Sahibzada Aftab Ahmad Khan that (i) Dr. Ziauddin appointed Dr. Ataullah Butt an Honourary Reader of Zoology without any reference to the Vice-Chancellor. (ii) Dr. Ataullah Butt maintained Chemist's shop and had a consulting room in the city. Dr. Ziauddin Ahmad gave the clarification that in the meeting of the Academic Council held on 20th June, 1925, presided over by Sahibzada Aftab Ahmad Khan, it was recommended that Dr. Ataullah Butt be appointed an Honourary Reader in Zoology. About the second point, a meeting of the Executive Council held on 14th December, 1926, in which Khan Bahadur Syed Zainuddin formally put forward a proposal to this effect. "Dr. Butt be given a Professor's grade and also permitted to practice but he should not keep a consulting room in the city." That reasonable proposal was ruled out of order by Sahibzada Aftab Ahmad Khan.[101]

Sahibzada Aftab Ahmad Khan's allegations that the Readers may not be Chairman of the departments, Dr. Ziauddin Ahmad explained that Readers were appointed Chairman in preference to Professors only in cases where Professors were temporary or teaching in more than one department or engaged in other executive works.[102]

By attacking on Sahibzada Aftab Ahmad Khan, Dr. Ziauddin Ahmad said that he had given very incorrect picture of extension lectures and of literary societies in this institution. Weekly lectures were arranged and many societies like English Society, Persian Society, Arabic Society, Anjuman Urdu-i-Mualla, Philosophical Society, Historical Society, Mathematical Society, Physical Society, Scientific Society, Economic Society, Curzon Geographical Society,

Poetical Society, Educational Society and Law Society were functioning efficiently.[103]

As for the objections regarding admission, Dr. Ziauddin Ahmad cleared that it was impossible to fix a date in the Muslim University. It could only be done in the institutes which draw their students from a limited area living under uniform conditions, where there was no such diversity. Hence in the Muslim University, the Intermediate College and the school drew students from all parts of India and even from abroad. The examinations of different universities were held at different times of the year. A supplementary list of successful candidates in some universities published as late as December and January. The Admission Committee had to consider all these circumstances.[104]

Sahibzada Aftab Ahmad Khan's claim about the number of students also did not seem to be correct according to Dr. Ziauddin Ahmad. He said, "the total strength of the students is 850 and those of teachers, excluding the student demonstrators are 51, so, the number of students per teacher is 17. Out of 850 students, 672 reside in hostels and remaining 178, i.e. 21 per cent reside with their parents and bona fide guardians. This percentage is within the number prescribed by the clause 2 chapter II of the ordinances where it is laid down that the number of non-resident students should not exceed 25 per cent. A member of the staff is being appointed as a Warden of day scholars once a month. On account of the Jubilee Celebrations in October 1925, it was not possible to scrutinize thoroughly the application of day scholars, whose number suddenly increased that year on account of the breakdown of national institution and the students had rent houses for themselves. They were asked not to rent the houses at the beginning of the new session."[105]

Sahibzada Aftab Ahmad Khan also raised objections regarding staff member's election for the Councils. Dr. Ziauddin Ahmad explained that this matter was raised many times in the court. In the Court meeting of December 1923, this question was raised and passed the following resolution:[106]

> "Resolved that no paid servant of the university shall seek election to the Provincial Legislative Council, Legislative

> Assembly or Council of State, except with the previous sanction of the Executive Council. Further resolved that the decision will not have the retrospective effect."

This question was again raised in the meeting of the Court on 25th December, 1926. Syed Nisar Husain moved that the members of the court would not permit the members of the staff to seek elections. It was seconded by Maulvi Habibullah Khan, but was lost by an almost absolute unanimity. Only three persons out of forty voted in favour of resolution.[107]

Dr. Ziauddin Ahmad also gave the suitable explanations regarding the religious matters of the university, Dining Hall, efficiency of the staff, election of members of the Court and members of the staff in the Executive Council, standard of the examination, etc.

Rahmatullah Enquiry Committee

The pamphlet of Sahibzada Aftab Ahmad Khan was laid before the AMU Court with the explanations of the officers at its meeting held on the 18th March, 1927, and the Court passed a vote of confidence in the Vice-Chancellor and Pro-Vice Chancellor.[108] On the other side, the Governor of United Provinces, Sir William Marris persuaded Governor-General (Lord Rector) to set-up an Enquiry Committee to enquire the functioning of the Aligarh Muslim University. Responding to the request of the Governor, Governor-General as a Lord Rector Ordered Her Highness, the Begum of Bhopal (Chancellor) to appoint such a committee of inquiry into certain matters indicated in the pamphlet.[109]

Following the order of the Governor-General, the Chancellor of the university appointed an enquiry committee. The committee was consisting of Sir Ibrahim Rahmatullah (Chairman), Sir Philip Hartog and Sir George Anderson (Members) with Mr. A.F. Rahman as Secretary. The enquiry Committee was known as Rahmatullah Enquiry Committee due to its Chairman Sir Ibrahim Rahmatullah.[110]

At first the members of the committee met at Bhopal on 8th December, 1927, where they were honoured by an interview with

Her Highness, Begum of Bhopal. They assembled at Aligarh on 11th October, 1927, and then had frequent meetings. The invitations were sent through the medium of leading newspapers to all those interested in the welfare of the Aligarh Muslim University. They were requested to send their names to the Secretary in order to give their evidence. The committee also examined the present and past Vice-Chancellors, the Pro-Vice Chancellors, and Treasurers, Registrars, old boys, members of the Court and many staff members of the university and its allied institutions. The valuable suggestions and helpful advices of Sahibzada Aftab Ahmad Khan were also received.[111]

Sahibzada Aftab Ahmad Khan, by enquiring into all the papers, documents, files, books or registers, submitted a detailed written statement of 127 pages to the Enquiry Committee.[112]

After a thorough enquiry of all the documents, papers and interviews, the Enquiry Committee gave a detailed report. At first the Committee said about the Aligarh, "Aligarh is sacred trust of the whole Mussalman community in India. It is a national, and not merely a local institution. Mussalmans throughout India and from outside India have given generous support to Aligarh. They have entrusted their sons to its care, they have shown love and devotion to the place and to its traditions." Regarding Abdullah Committee the new committee opined, "In January 1926, Mr. Aftab Ahmad, the then Vice-Chancellor, appointed a committee of four members of the teaching staff under the Chairmanship of Shaikh Abdullah, the Treasurer, to enquire to the discipline, teaching and other matters connected with the university. The committee submitted its report in September of the same year, and we desire to add that the report had been of great assistance to us during the course of our enquiry."[113]

The Rahmatullah Enquiry Committee found about the admission of the students that in 1926 the Regulations came into force which provided that at the beginning of each year, the Admission Committee would frame rules for the admission of students, and the Pro-Vice Chancellor was authorised to admit all such students fulfilling the conditions. The Pro-Vice Chancellor was permitted by Regulations (Chapter 12, Section 4) to refuse admission to a student on his own authority and without giving any reason. The Pro-Vice Chancellor, therefore, became responsible for all admissions and except in the special cases referred to the committee for all refusals to admit. Not even a list of students thus admitted by him was forwarded to the Admission Committee. The Enquiry Report recommended that the Admission Committee should function in the future as required by the Act and Ordinances.[114]

The report admitted that the statutes 20, which prescribed that appointment of the teaching staff would be made from a list of persons recommended by a special committee of appointment in each case. First list furnished to the Enquiry Committee signed by the Registrar showed that out of 40 appointments on the list 19 had been without committee of appointment. In the second list only a small number of such appointments were shown. A number of appointments were made by promotion confirmed in a meeting of the Executive Council without previous consideration as to whether the higher post was required or not, without definition of the conditions of post, without advertisement and without a committee of appointment to consider qualifications of the persons promoted. The Enquiry Committee recommended that this practice should be discontinued.[115]

The Enquiry Committee registered strong objection to the appointment of Honourary Readers without taking experts' advice upon the qualification in the subject of their Readership. The committee thought that advertisement could almost invariably be resorted to before any permanent teaching post was filled.[116]

According to the Enquiry Committee, a salaried officer and teacher must be appointed on a written contract according to section 36 of the Act. A Reader should not be appointed as Head if there was a Professor in the department. The Enquiry Committee Report also said that the department should not be started if the university was not able to afford to appoint at least a Reader. Honourary Readers should not be eligible to act as Head of the departments.[117]

About attendance and discipline, the Enquiry Committee Report warned that the leave to the staff should only be granted when suitable arrangements had been made. About the attendance of the students, the report clarified that attendance of a student must be 75 per cent of the prescribed lectures. The margin of

25 per cent provided by the Ordinances should be ample to meet all ordinary cases. The Pro-Vice Chancellor should sign the attendance register each month.[118]

The Report further said that the enrolment of the students had advanced from 261 in 1921 to 1174 in 1927, and this large increase had imposed an excessive strain on the resources of the university. It became impossible for a single provost to carry out the duty of supervising the needs of as many as 739 resident students. Moreover, there had been serious overcrowding in the hostels especially in those additional hostels, which had been rented by the university to accommodate a large overflow of the students. The committee was not satisfied over the provision for supervision, which had been made in these additional hostels. The present Vice-Chancellor was in agreement with the committee and had already taken some steps to remove these defects.[119]

It was also found that the present Medical Officer in addition to his duties in that capacity was also Chairman of the department of Zoology and had been recently appointed as Principle of the Tibbiya College. The committee recommended that in order to discharge efficiently his duties, Medical Officer of the university would be a whole time officer. He should not merely be concerned with the students when they actually fell ill but should take steps to improve the health of the students by making proposals for better sanitation and for other preventive measures. He should report to the appropriate authority every month on the general health of the students and should be responsible for the inspection of the university area.[120]

Regarding dining hall, many complaints were made, which did not appear to the committee to be without justification. The Enquiry Committee recommended, therefore, that an enquiry should immediately be made for its management and supervision of the dining hall.[121]

The Enquiry Committee Report also opined about the department of studies that there was a tendency to initiate new departments without firstly taking into account the staff and the demand for such departments. So, the committee advised that before creating a new department, care should also be taken to ascertain that there was demand for the subject and the necessary staff was available. The general working of these new departments and expenditure to be incurred on them should he carefully scrutinised by appropriate authorities.[122]

The problem about the standard of examination was extremely complex before Enquiry Committee. Yet the Committee had given certain important suggestions. The Committee suggested to improve the number of external examiners, and the suggestions made in their report should be carefully considered by the Academic Council. The percentage of marks both for pass and for the different classes and divisions should be embodied in the Ordinances relating to all degrees of the courses. The Registrar should make all arrangements for the appointment of invigilators, subject to the approval of the Pro-Vice Chancellor acting on behalf of the Academic Council. At each examination centre, a superintendent or head invigilator should be appointed with a necessary authority to take prompt action where candidates were detected in using unfair means. In case when the candidate was detected in copying in the examination room and in other similar cases, he must be suspended for two years instead of one. The question of suspension in all cases should be decided by the Academic Council.[123]

Special examination (taking examination for the same degree course in later date than prescribed by the Academic council) should only be allowed in very exceptional circumstances and with the previous sanction of the Academic Council. The Enquiry Committee was not satisfied with the way the students were allowed to appear in the university examinations and even to receive the degrees without paying dues. The Enquiry Committee regarded it as unjustified. In certain cases, the results of degree examinations were withheld until the fees due had been paid. No hall ticket should be issued to him until that was certified.[124]

The report also threw light upon the examination of private candidates. The right of appearing as a private candidate for the degree examinations was limited by the Act to teachers in several categories. The right for the intermediate examinations was limited under certain conditions to the teachers and also to such persons as had been certified as suitable by the Inspector of School appointed in this behalf by the Local Government. There was no Ordinance in regulating the admission of private candidates to the High School examination. Undoubtedly, a liberal policy had been adopted as it was clear from the figure that 237 students appeared for private candidates in 1925 and 402 in 1926. The report suggested that those who were enrolled in a recognised school not have been admitted either as regular or as a private candidate except those enrolled in school maintained or affiliated by the university in accordance with section 12 (ii) of the Act. For those who had ceased to be enrolled in recognized school for a period of seven months, special care should be taken to admit them. The report also recommended that it must be stated on each certificate, whether the successful candidate passed the examination as regular or a private candidate.[125]

Another problem before the Enquiry Committee was contesting of staff members for election to a Legislature and taking part in it. In 1923, Dr. Ziauddin the Pro-Vice Chancellor and Dr. Hyder Professor of Economics were elected to the Legislative Council and to the Legislative Assembly respectively. Mr. Habib, Professor of History was also elected a member of the Provincial Legislative Council. Dr. Ziauddin did not stand for re-election. The committee recommended that the university teachers should not be permitted to stand for election to the Legislature. If the Legislature allowed a seat to the university on its own, there would be no objection to a teacher of the university to standing for that seat.[126]

The Enquiry Committee Report also suggested about the allied institution of the university like Intermediate College, Training College and Muslim University School. About them, the Enquiry Committee Report directed as follows:[127]

1. College and school should be regarded as separate institution.
2. The Managing Committee should be vested with responsible powers and duties.
3. A suitable grant should be provided annually by the university.
4. Subject to the provision of that grant all the arrangements for the management of the college and school should be made by a committee.

5. The university should be represented on the committee of the management and should exercise the right of auditing and inspection. It also advised that number of students in Intermediate College should be curtailed, and more trained teachers be appointed in Training College.

About the finances of the university, Enquiry Committee Report said that the expenditure needed more checking in detail than was exercised. It further said that Building Department could be over-hauled by a competent Architect or Engineer, who would be asked to advise on its future organization.[128]

The Enquiry Committee Report recommended about the Court that written votes should be permissible in the election of the members of the Court. The financial year should begin from 1st October every year. The meeting of the Court should be held in April for consideration of the budget and second meeting in December for supplementary budget. It also said that no salaried officer or teacher of the university should be elected to the Court by any other body except the Academic Council.[129]

Regarding Executive Council, the Enquiry Committee Report opined that the number of the representatives of the Academic Council should be reduced from six to two. Members of the Executive Council living outside Aligarh should receive travelling expenses on a moderate scale. Not more than seven of the members elected by Court should be resident outside the U.P., Punjab and Delhi.[130]

About Academic Council, the Enquiry Committee Report suggested that the Provost also could be the member along with the Professors. The other new includes should be that one person not engaged in teaching to be co-opted by the Academic Council, two members of the teaching staff lower in rank than a Professor to be elected annually by members of the staff other than Academic Council.[131]

The Enquiry Committee Report recommended about the Vice-Chancellor that if any emergency arose, which called for an urgent action, the Vice-Chancellor would take it. He would report within seven days to the officer, authority having practical experience, and they would inform on record about the action so taken.[132]

As far as the duties of the Registrar were concerned, the Enquiry Committee Report said that the Registrar could see that the resolutions of Academic and Executive Council were complied with. He should assist the Vice-Chancellor in enforcing the Act, Statutes, Ordinances and Regulations.[133]

The post of Treasurer was also very important. The Enquiry Committee Report thought that each cheque drawn on the university funds should have two signatures, one of which should be that of the Treasurer, so long as he was available and the other signature should be that of one of the three officers—the Vice-Chancellor, the Pro-Vice Chancellor or the Registrar. In the absence of the Treasurer, the signature of two of the other three officers should be provided for.[134]

The report further said that the main trouble laid in the division of powers between Vice-Chancellor and Pro-Vice Chancellor. Under the present system, the Vice-Chancellor was an executive head, and the Pro-Vice Chancellor was the academic head of the university. The supreme authorities except in matters of emergency were not the Vice-Chancellor or the Pro-Vice Chancellor but the Court, the Executive Council and the Academic Council. It should be the aim of both officers to be loyal to the AMU and to ensure that the quality of its staff and the opportunities given to the students would be second to none in India. Acting loyally in accordance with the constitution of the university they would set an example of loyalty and discipline among the staff and students.[135]

The committee also wrote about Dr. Ziauddin Ahmad, "We favour Dr. Ziauddin's educational ability, his long services in the college and thereafter university and deep passion of love with Aligarh, but we are sorry to say that in recent difficulties in view of his near relations, his continued service in the university shall be contrary to the new spirit of good management and progress, which is necessary for subsequent success of university. Most probably this shall be the better way for Dr. Ziauddin that he takes leave before retirement."[136]

After completing the enquiry the committee submitted its report to Her Highness, the Chancellor on 9th November, 1927, who very graciously wrote memorandum and got both issued to the members of the Court towards the end of March 1928. Immediate steps were taken by university bodies to give effect to as many recommendations as could be done without delay.[137]

Government of India was also satisfied that the university authorities were making sincere and earnest efforts to remedy the defects in the functioning of AMU as revealed by the Report of the Enquiry Committee.[138]

Dr. Ziauddin Ahmad's Resignation

To give effect to the recommendations of the Enquiry Committee Report, Dr. Ziauddin Ahmad submitted his resignation to the Vice-Chancellor on 26th March, 1928, and it became effective from 27th April, 1928.[139]

The Pro-Vice Chancellor, Dr. Ziauddin Ahmad's resignation was as follows:[140]

> "My dear Nawab Sahib... For the few years of the existence of the university we had no Ordinances and no Regulations..... The Ordinances of the AMU were not received till June 1923 and during the first 18 months of its existence, the Vice-Chancellor was invested by Government of India with power to frame any Ordinance or Regulation or to set aside any section of the Act or Statutes, in the universities it is the first occasion when a single individual, not on the spot, has been invested with autocratic powers extended for such a long time. It is a miracle that we did not succumb altogether during this interval."

"During my term of office I unfortunately have to face three special difficulties:

(i) Honourary Secretary and Vice-Chancellor did not give me sufficient support and, at times, they deliberately created rival party in the staff.
(ii) I never had a complete office.

(iii) Some members of the staff never cooperated with me and they formed a solid group in the Academic Council. On assuming the charge of your office, you made honest effort to restore solidarity among the staff and you know yourself how your efforts were defeated."

"The Pro-Vice Chancellor according to the present constitution has got responsibilities for running the entire institution, but he has no power even to stop the ordinary increment of an insufficient and negligent member of staff. Everything depends on the will of the Vice-Chancellor, who may or may not place the suggestion of the Pro-Vice Chancellor before the Executive Council. The late Vice-Chancellor Raja of Mahmudabad gave orders in writing that the Pro-Vice Chancellor had no right to send any suggestion direct to Executive Council. This practice has since been followed. His position is just opposite to that of the dictator."

"I wish better luck to my successor, but I feel that the institution is faced with crucial difficulty. The Pro-Vice Chancellor has got all the responsibilities without power and Vice-Chancellor has got power without the responsibilities. Ever since 1925, I have been attempting to resign my post as Pro-Vice Chancellor. On the 27th April, 1925, after completing 30 years' service, I requested the late Vice-Chancellor to relieve me of my duties as Pro-Vice Chancellor from October 1925, but he in his letter dated 1st May, 1925 induced me not to resign in the interest of the university. A year later in 1926 he proposed my re-appointment."

"After the retirement of the Sahibzada Aftab Ahmad Khan, I requested you in May 1927, to relieve me from my present duties, you verbally told me to wait till the committee of enquiry had submitted its report. I also add that during my stay in Aligarh, I had offers of several posts in various departments. But I declined them all in order to be true to the promise which I had made at the time of my appointment."

"I am now convinced that I can do better service to the

> institution by withdrawing my formal connection with university and I most readily do the service by submitting my resignation which I request you to accept at an early date in manner that may be acceptable to you and Executive Council."

When the resignation of Dr. Ziauddin Ahmad was accepted, many farewell parties were given by different personalities, societies and departments. Curzon Geographical Society, during the farewell said, "Sir you have devoted 33 long years of your precious life to the cause of education and the service of this great national institution ... you have always remain true to your national institution, in spite of so many temptations, your services have been unraveled and invaluable."[141]

Scientific Society[142], Economic Society[143], members of the Math's department[144], gave many impressive addresses during the farewell to Dr. Ziauddin Ahmad. Dr. L.K. Hyder, Prof. of Economics and member of Royal Agricultural Commission also made a memorable speech at the time of Dr. Ziauddin's farewell.[145] Mohammad Imamullah Khan, a brilliant student of M.A made a cordial speech during his farewell.[146]

NOTES

1. *Hayat-ul-Bashir*, p. 89.
2. *AMU Calendar, 1921-25*, p. 513.
3. *Ibid.*
4. *Fikr-o-Nazar*, Vol. II, p. 288.
5. *Indian Annual Register*, Vol. II, 1935, p. 440.
6. *Ibid.*, Vol. II, 1939, p. 488.
7. *Ibid.*, Vol. II, 1934, pp. 540-41.
8. *Ibid.*, pp. 540-42.
9. *Fikr-o-Nazar*, Vol. II, p. 160.
10. *Indian Annual Register*, Vol. II, 1938, pp. 482-84.
11. *Ibid.*, p. 407.
12. *Ibid.*, p. 490.
13. Hasan, Abul, *AMU Aligarh, Addresses and Speeches*, Aligarh, 1987, p. 53 (Hereafter cited as '*Addresses and Speeches*').
14. *Ibid.*, p. 8.

15. *File No. II/7, 1922-23* (AMU Archive).
16. *File No. XV/2, 1923-24* (AMU Archive).
17. *File No. 4 (1), 1930-31* (AMU Archive).
18. *Indian Annual Register*, Vol. II, 1938, p. 480.
19. *Ibid.*
20. The word Turkish coat is a misnomer. There is nothing Turkish about it. It is really a coat designed at Aligarh and it should more appropriately be called a coat of Aligarh cut. (*Aligarh Institute Gazette*, 14th November, 1935).
21. *AMU Calendar, 1932*, pp. 297-298 (AMU Archive) and *File No. IV/1, 1924* (AMU Archive).
22. *Ibid.*
23. *Aligarh Institute Gazette*, 14th November, 1935.
24. *Ibid.*, 12th December, 1935.
25. *Ibid.*
26. *File No. XV/2, 1923-24* (AMU Archive).
27. *Aligarh Institute Gazette*, 10th December, 1935.
28. *Fikr-o-Nazar*, Vol. II, p. 304.
29. *AMU Calendar, 1921-25*, pp. 104-107.
30. *Zia-i-Hayat*, pp. 87-90; see also *Fikr-o-Nazar*, Vol. II, p. 304.
31. *File No. 51, 1923-24* (AMU Archive).
32. Vice-Chancellor's Report to the AMU Court meeting held on 24th December, 1923, *File No. 51, 1923-24* (AMU Archive).
33. *The Times*, London, 8th August, 1924; *File No. 4/2 (I), 1924* (AMU Archive).
34. Khan, Habibullah, *Hayat-i-Aftab*, Allahabad, 1947, pp. 306-9 (Hereafter Cited as '*Hayat-i-Aftab*').
35. *Zia-i-Hayat*, pp. 90-91.
36. *Ibid.*
37. *Ibid.*
38. *Ibid.*
39. Lucknow Rs. 493720, Allahabad Rs. 6,66,750, BHU Rs. 12,30,000, AMU Rs. 43,308 (*Zia-i-Hayat*, pp. 90-91).
40. *Hayat-i-Aftab,* pp. 310-11; see also *Zia-i-Hayat*, p. 111. In *Zia-i-Hayat*, Aftab Ahmad is said to have praised the working and organization of training college.
41. *Ibid.*, p. 311.
42. *Ibid.*, pp. 312-13.
43. *Ibid.*, pp. 320 and 324.
44. *Ibid.*, pp. 313-14.
45. *Ibid.*
46. *Ibid.*, p. 327.
47. *Ibid.*, pp. 328-29.

48. *Fikr-o-Nazar*, Vol. II, pp. 76-77; see also Qureshi, Ishrat Ali, *Aligarh Past and Present*, Aligarh, 1992, p. 98 (Hereafter quoted as '*Aligarh Past and Present*').
49. *Ibid.;* see also *Aligarh Past and Present*, p. 98.
50. *Hayat-i-Aftab*, p. 342.
51. In 1920, when the AMU came into existence, there were 261 students. Gradually, the number went on increasing. However, many students got their admissions transferred to the National Muslim University during the eventful years of 1920-22. This naturally led to the decline in the number of students in the AMU. Dr. Ziauddin Ahmad as PVC made vigorous efforts not only to maintain the interest of the students but also in increasing the number of students through fresh admissions. In March 1924, he instituted ten rewards to the students to encourage fresh admissions to the university. There were other social and charitable organizations in the campus which through their generous contributions to the needy students helped in increasing the number of students (*Zia-i-Hayat*, p. 109).
52. *Ibid.*, p. 109.
53. *Ibid.*, pp. 111-112.
54. *Ibid.*
55. *Ibid.*
56. *Ibid.*, pp. 113-114.
57. *Ibid.*
58. *Ibid.*, p.117.
59. *Zia-i-Hayat*, p. 109.
60. *Court Minutes of AMU*, 1926, p. 7.
61. *Hayat-i-Aftab*, pp. 346 and 352.
62. *Zia-i-Hayat*, p. 96.
63. *File No. 51, 1926-27* (AMU Archive).
64. *Aligarh Past and Present*, p. 98.
65. *Zia-i-Hayat*, p. 98.
66. *Aligarh Institute Gazette*, 7th March, 1926.
67. *File No. IV/I, 1926-27* (AMU Archive).
68. *File No. XV/3, 1925-26* (AMU Archive).
69. *Fikr-o-Nazar*, Vol. II, p. 155.
70. *Ibid.*
71. *Hayat-i-Abdullah*, pp. 349-50.
72. *Aligarh Past and Present*, p. 97.
73. He has been the collector in Aligarh and had bitter discord with Viqarul Mulk in which he was insulted. He had also written articles against the MAO College in 1914-15 in newspapers in England (*Fikr-o-Nazar*, Vol. II, p. 157).
74. He was having personal commotion not only with the Aligarh Muslim University but Dr. Ziauddin Ahmad. He was the first person who tried

to defame the university by talking about the standard of examination (*Fikr-o-Nazar*, Vol. II, p. 157).

75. *Zia-i-Hayat*, p. 99.
76. *File No. 78/3, 1927-28* (AMU Archive).
77. Shaikh Abdullah said, "Dr. Ziauddin came to see me at my residence and said that he would not oppose the committee if he was also included in the committee. Then I told him that this committee was for the inspection of your work. Would it be right to make you to judge your own work?" (*Hayat-i-Abdullah*, p. 327).
78. *Hayat-i-Abdullah*, p. 328.
79. *Hayat-i-Aftab*, pp. 358-59.
80. *Ibid.*
81. *Zia-i-Hayat*, p. 99.
82. *Ibid.*
83. *Ibid.*, p. 100.
84. *Ibid.*, see also *Hayat-i-Aftab*, pp. 359-60.
85. *Zia-i-Hayat*, p. 103; see also *Fikr-o-Nazar*, Vol. II, p. 157.
86. *Hayat-i-Aftab*, pp. 362-63.
87. *Ibid.*, p. 364.
88. *Aligarh Magazine*, *October-December, 1929*, p. (K).
89. *Hayat-i-Aftab*, p. 364.
90. *Zia-i-Hayat*, p. 103; see also *Fikr-o-Nazar*, Vol. II, p. 78.
91. *Hayat-i-Aftab*, pp. 366-67.
92. *Zia-i-Hayat*, pp. 103-104.
93. *Explanation of Dr. Ziauddin Ahmad*, Vilayat Manzil, Aligarh, 1928, p. 2 (hereafter quoted as "*Explanation*").
94. *Ibid.*
95. *Ibid.*, pp. 4-5.
96. *Ibid.*
97. He was appointed in the year 1909 by the late Nawab Viqarul Mulk in the Department of Theology. The grade as Assistant Professor was given to him a year later at the time of his confirmation. Not only Theology but he had also been given teaching classes in Arabic and Persian to the post-graduate level. Since the inception of the university Maulana Sulaiman Ashraf had the sole charge of teaching Sunni Theology (*Explanation*, p. 6).
98. Mr. Hamiduddin Khan rendered valuable services during Non-Cooperation crisis. As a teacher of Persian Mr. Hamiduddin Khan incomparable with any Professor of Persian in any other University. (*Explanation*, p. 6).
99. Messrs. Inamullah Khan, Allah Baksh, F.D. Murad and A.M. Qureishy were promoted to the ranks of Readers in April 1921. Messrs. Mohammad Habib and A.B.A. Haleem promoted to the rank of Professor, in September 1923. Maulana Abdul Haqqi promoted to the Reader's grade

on 12th December, 1923. Mr. Mukhtar Ahmad Khan's grade was revised on the 17th December, 1923. M. Habibur Rahman's grade was revised on 3rd November, 1924. Mr. Hadi Hasan was appointed Professor on 10th March, 1925 (*Explanation*, pp. 5-6).

100. *Explanation*, pp. 7-8.
101. *Ibid.,* pp. 8-10.
102. *Ibid.,* pp. 10-11.
103. *Ibid.,* pp. 11-12.
104. *Ibid.,* p. 13.
105. *Ibid.,* p. 15.
106. *Ibid.*
107. *Ibid.,* p. 19.
108. *File No. IV/I, 1927-28* (AMU Archive).
109. *Zia-i-Hayat*, p. 123.
110. Sir Ibrahim Rahmatullah was the President of Bombay Legislative Council, Sir Philip Hartog was member in Public Service Commission, Sir George Anderson was Director of Education in Punjab and Mr. A.F Rahman was the Provost of the Muslim Hall in Decca University (*Hayat-i-Aftab*, p. 383; see also *File No. IV/I, 1927-28* (AMU Archive).
111. *Report of the AMU Enquiry Committee*, pp. 1-2 (Hereafter quoted as *Enquiry Report*).
112. *Hayat-i-Aftab*, pp. 385-78; see also *File No. 789/3, 1927-28* (AMU Archive).
113. *Enquiry Report,* pp.7-8.
114. *Ibid.,* pp. 8-9.
115. *Ibid.,* pp. 7-8.
116. *Ibid.*
117. *Ibid.,* pp. 8-9.
118. *Ibid.,* pp. 9-10.
119. *Ibid.,* pp. 10-11.
120. *Ibid.*
121. *Ibid.*
122. *Ibid.,* pp. 11-12.
123. *Ibid.,* pp. 13-14.
124. *Ibid.*
125. *Ibid.,* pp. 15-16; see also *Hayat-i-Aftab*, pp. 396-97.
126. *Enquiry Report,* p. 17; see also *Hayat-i-Aftab*, pp. 397-98.
127. *Enquiry Report,* pp. 19-21.
128. *Ibid.,* p. 21.
129. *Ibid.,* pp. 22-23; see also *Executive Council Report*, 9th April, 1928, pp. 8-9.
130. *Enquiry Report,* p. 24; see also *Executive Council Report*, 9th April, 1928, pp. 6-10.
131. *Ibid.*
132. *Ibid.,* p. 27.
133. *Ibid.,* p. 28; see also *Executive Council Report*, 9th April, 1928, p. 11.

134. *Enquiry Report,* p. 28.
135. *Ibid.*, p. 27.
136. *Zia-i-Hayat*, p. 216.
137. *File No. 78/4, 1929-30* (AMU Archive); see also *Hayat-i-Aftab*, p. 388.
138. *Ibid.*, see also *Hayat-i-Aftab*, p. 388.
139. *Aligarh Past and Present*, p. 98.
140. *Aligarh Magazine*, 1928, pp. iv-v.
141. *Ibid.*
142. *Ibid.*, p. xxiv.
143. *Ibid.*, p. xxv.
144. *Ibid.*, p. xxii.
145. *Ibid.*, p. Li.
146. "*Ilahi Shabe Gham Men Itna To Ho, Koi Jhoot Kah De Sahar Ho Gai*" (*Aligarh Magazine, 1928*, p. xxi).

4
Educational Progress in AMU, 1929-1947

A glorious chapter of Aligarh Muslim University was ended with the resignation of Dr. Ziauddin Ahmad. However, the university recovered the loss by appointing Syed Ross Masood, the grandson of Sir Syed Ahmad Khan, as its Vice-Chancellor. Dr. Ziauddin Ahmad was now given the responsibility of Vice-Chancellor until the fateful years of division of India. They undoubtedly did their level best to improve the position of the university and naturally tried to raise this university as world level institution.

Sir Shah Mohammad Sulaiman (9th February, 1929–19th October, 1929)

After Nawab Muzammilullah Khan, a search for new Vice-Chancellor was started. Through a letter, Mr. Theodore Morison suggested that Mr. Ross Masood (the grandson of Sir Syed Ahmad Khan) should be appointed as Vice Chancellor. Begum of Bhopal, who had arrived at Aligarh, also requested the Court to appoint Syed Ross Masood as Vice-Chancellor. The Court members accepted these suggestions and Syed Ross Masood was appointed as Vice-Chancellor with effect from 9th February, 1929.[1]

Meanwhile a rumour spread that Syed Ross Masood had accepted the post of Political Secretary offered by the Nizam of Hyderabad. Nevertheless, the rumour was not true, no doubt both offers were before him, but he accepted the Vice-Chancellorship of AMU.[2] He said that it was the call of the blood which made him to accept the position of Vice-Chancellor. He felt that he must continue the work which his illustrious grandfather had commenced with the desire of raising the intellectual standard of Muslims in the east. When he was asked to go back to Aligarh, he put in all his energies in search of Professors and Lecturers in Great Britain and in many countries of Europe and tried to raise a large sum of money to build finest chemical laboratories in Aligarh.[3]

As Syed Ross Masood was in England, the temporary charge of Vice-Chancellorship was given to Sir Shah Mohammad Sulaiman, the Chief Justice of the Allahabad High Court. In the absence of Syed Ross Masood, Justice Sulaiman did very hard work to raise the standard of the university because the university had a very bad reputation due to the Enquiry Committee Report. He made many changes in order to formulate the Rahmatullah Enquiry Committee suggestions and satisfied the government. It was by dint of his efforts that government granted Rs. 15,00,000 for the building purpose and also raised its annual grant from Rs. 1,25,000/- to Rs. 3,00,000/-.[4]

Another important work of Sir Shah Mohammad Sulaiman was making the arrangements for coaching the students for competitive examinations. As almost all the services were open to capable young men, and it was essential to train students for these competitions. A central office, where necessary information for all the competitive examination was stored, was opened and all efforts were being made to make it updated. Mr. Mohammad Ishaq was appointed to look after this office and to give students all the necessary information regarding conditions, prospectus, syllabus and examinations.[5]

A complete and exhaustive chart of all the Indian services was prepared and published, and one of its copies was supplied to each university student. Similar charts for the provincial, subordinate and the lower services were in the process of preparations. The following staff members appointed on fixed allowances to teach the students in the subjects noted against their name.[6]

(i)	Dr. M. Nazim	History and Political Science
(ii)	Mr. Abdur Rashid	
(iii)	Dr. A. Mukhtar	Economics
(iv)	Mr. Mukhtar Hamid Ali	English
(v)	Mr. S. Mahmudul Hasan	

(vi) Mr. Abrar Hussain Faruqi } Persian and Arabic
(vii) Mr. Allah Baksh Kamali } Lower Mathematics

It is surprising that all the work he had done was the result of only his few days stay at Aligarh. He spent only two days in a week at Aligarh because of his service constraints in the Allahabad High Court.[7]

Syed Ross Masood (20th October, 1929–April, 1934)

Syed Ross Masood assumed the charge of Vice-Chancellorship on 20th October. On 12th September, 1929, Mr. E.A. Horn was appointed as Pro-Vice Chancellor on the advice of Syed Ross Masood before his arrival. The post of Registrar was vacant because of the resignation of Shaikh Abdullah, and his place was taken by Khan Bahadur Fakhruddin Ahmad from Bengal Educational Service.[8]

The tenure of office of Syed Ross Masood was from October 1929 to April 1934. During this period, he faced many challenging difficulties. First was the economic depression from which the whole world had suffered, and it also naturally affected adversely the finance of the university.[9] Second was the problem of Pro-Vice Chancellor because Mr. E.A. Horn died just after his appointment. Mr. Mortin officiated the post for a few months and was succeeded by Mr. B. Ramsbothem, who joined his duties in February 1931. Third was the enhancing the reputation of the university. He faced the problems boldly and worked hard for the betterment of the university. Regarding the AMU, the United Provinces Government observed, "....work of reform was undertaken with the determination of courage and the last few years have been a time of steadily increasing efficiency and the widespread improvement and activity. The university, having set its house in order, can look backward with satisfaction and forward with confidence."[10]

An important work of Syed Ross Masood was the decision to amalgamate the Intermediate College with the university. For that reason Sir Fazl-i-Husain introduced a Bill giving effect to the amendments, suggested by Aligarh University authorities and approved by the Visiting Board, in the University Act. The Bill was introduced in the Legislative Assembly, Shimla in September, 1931.[11]

By this provision, after the amendment, the Intermediate College was amalgamated with the university during the session 1932-33, and MU School was raised to the status of first class high school. MU City School also became high school and the university instead of treating it as an aided school had now included it in the category of institution maintained by it and had thereby become entirely responsible for its maintenance.[12]

Syed Ross Masood laid more stress on Urdu. The medium of instruction in VI, VII, and VIII classes of the school was changed to Urdu. Urdu and Commerce were added to the list of optional subjects for Intermediate examinations, and later on Urdu was included as a subject for M.A. and Honours classes. In 1934, Mr. Rashid Ahmad Siddiqui, a senior Lecturer in Urdu was appointed Reader and Chairman of the department.[13]

As far as Geography was concerned, M.A. and M.Sc. classes were opened in 1932.[14] Syed Ross Masood also gave emphasis on Hindi teaching, and its teachings in the school classes were started from 1931.[15] A graduation studies in Theology was also started.[16]

In 1931, the electrification of the entire university area was completed, and all cost of electrification was met by Her Highness Sultan Jahan Begum. As far as the drainage system was concerned, much spade work was done.[17] Syed Ross Masood instituted the Vice-Chancellor's Fund for the poor and needy students. With the handsome amount of donations from His Highness the Maharaja Sir Tukoji Rao Holker of Indore and Captain Nawab Dr. Sir Mohammad Ahmad Said Khan Chhatari, a spacious gymnasium was built opposite to the swimming bath. The equipments were also purchased for that purpose.[18]

During the Vice-Chancellorship of Syed Ross Masood, many well-known personalities visited Aligarh Muslim University. Most important among them being the great historian Sir Jadunath Sarkar, the world famous scientist Sir C.V. Raman, and the world famous poet Dr. Sir Mohammad Iqbal, who delivered the interesting lectures on their respective subjects.[19]

The university started a coaching class preparing students to appear in the entrance examination to Indian Military Academy. The class was limited to 10 each year, and each applicant had to undergo a selection board before he was admitted to the class.[20]

The most important and highly appreciable work of Syed Ross Masood was the establishment of a Science College. Until then science education was provided in a casual manner without having necessary paraphernalia. Neither there was building nor laboratory or research provision. Syed Ross Masood persuaded the government to sanction Rs. 15,00,000/- and Rs. 1,00,000/- were received from State of Hyderabad for the above purpose. He founded laboratories for Zoology, Botany, Physics and Chemistry and equipped them with latest instruments. He started the research provision, appointed able staff for their guidance and made provision for scholarships for the needy students. He also encouraged research work in Arts subjects. In 1934, the university conferred its first Ph.D. degree in chemistry on Dr. Omar Farooq, and second Ph.D. degree was awarded to Dr. Zakiuddin in Physics in the same year.[21]

He also took care of Training College, which was running into the office of Muslim Educational Conference. He spent an amount of one lakh rupees over the construction of the new building, instruments and library of the Training College. He also increased the strength of the teaching staff to improve the teaching in the Training College. During the academic year 1930-31, the department of Public Instruction had accorded formal recognition to the B.T. Degree of this university and Director of Public Instruction began to select the trained teachers from this university.[22]

He also did much work for Engineering and Tibbiya College. Meanwhile, unfortunately, a section of Aligarh did not appreciate his work and started opposing his developmental policies. Syed Ross Masood, by nature, was very sentimental, and he used to get nervous when someone opposed him and that too when the opposition came from his own friends. In this frustration, Syed Ross Masood tendered his resignation to the AMU Court in April 1934 and left for Europe. Nawab Mohammad Ismail Khan, the Treasurer, was appointed as Acting Vice-Chancellor in April 1934.[23]

In 1935, a new Act known as Government of India Act was passed. The provisions of this Act divided all educational activities into two categories Federal (central) and State (provincial). Aligarh Muslim University fell in the Federal subjects.[24]

Aligarh Muslim University also faced many changes in 1935. In August 1935, His Exalted Highness the Nizam of Hyderabad accepted the post of Chancellor of the university. On 9th April, 1935 Dr. Ziauddin Ahmad was elected Vice-Chancellor by the Court of AMU. K.B. Obaidur Rahman Khan Sherwani was elected Honourary Treasurer, and Mr. Azmat Ilahi was appointed as Registrar. His Highness Sultan Mohammad Agha Khan was elected as Pro-Chancellor of the university on 17th November, 1935, by the AMU Court. Mr. Abu Bakar became the Pro-Vice Chancellor in March 1935.[25]

Dr. Ziauddin Ahmad (9th April, 1935–29th April, 1938 and 24th April, 1941–7th August, 1947)

In March 1935, Sir Fazl-i-Husain introduced a Bill in the Council of State to amend the AMU Act whereby the post of Pro-Vice Chancellor would be voluntary and not obligatory. The Council passed the Bill amending the AMU Act. It enabled the university to fill the post of Pro-Vice Chancellor at the time when it was found desirable.[26]

With this amendment, the dispute regarding Pro-Vice Chancellor came to an end. In this peaceful situation, Dr. Ziauddin Ahmad took the charge of Vice-Chancellorship. Due to his past services to the institution, the alumni and staff had much hope with Dr. Ziauddin Ahmad. He took the challenges facing to the university and tried his level best to improve its standard.

In the first step of improving the standard of the university, Dr. Ziauddin Ahmad, as Vice-Chancellor of the Aligarh Muslim University, invited many important personalities to visit the university during the session of 1935-36. Prominent among them were Honourable Sir Nripendra Nath Sircar, Law Member of Government of India; Honourable Sir Girija Shanker Bajpai, Education Member of Government of India; Honourable Mr. Raghunath Rao, Home Member of the Central Provinces Government; His Excellency the Viceroy and Lord Rector of the university and His Exalted Highness the Chancellor.[27]

The Viceroy Lord Wellington conveyed to the AMU Court on 22nd March, 1936, "Since 1932 (due to World Depression) the recurring grant of the university had been reduced by 10 per cent.... I am glad to announce that we have decided to make this restoration for each of the three universities Aligarh, Banaras and Delhi."[28]

For the development of the university, there was a need of some more lands to start other important courses. For that purpose, Dr. Ziauddin Ahmad appealed to the government to give the Aligarh Fort and its adjoining areas. The Archaeological Department of the Government of India transferred the Aligarh Fort and its grounds to the university. The university intended to open a course in animal husbandry in the fort area.[29]

In 1943, Dr. Ziauddin Ahmad intended to start a scheme for research in fisheries and applied to the Government of UP. The Director of Fisheries, United Provinces approved the scheme accordingly. The ditches of the Aligarh Fort were an ideal place for breeding fishes not only for experimental purposes but also as a means to large-scale fish supply to Aligarh and neighbouring districts. Dr. Ziauddin Ahmad sought permission of the Government of India to use the ditches and to carry on some necessary masonry work for the said purpose.[30]

The Government of India responded favourably over the masonry work in the Fort and by approving the scheme informed the university authorities, "...university may occupy and repair two modern bungalows in the fort for the use of officers of the university. The university shall have the free use of the land attached to the fort for agricultural purpose including maintenance of the cattle. The Government of India reserves to themselves the right to take into its control the Fort premises at any time with one year's notice."[31] So, the Aligarh Fort was granted to the Aligarh Muslim University and the university was free to use the Fort according to its wishes.

Many new departments and courses were opened in the Aligarh Muslim University during the Vice-Chancellorship of Sir Shah Mohammad Sulaiman and Khan Bahadur Obaidur Rahman Khan Sherwani from 1938-1943. The classes of Journalism were opened in 1938 on an experimental basis. It attracted a fairly large number of students.[32] Military Drill was made compulsory in 1939 for the students of 1st year and 2nd year classes and in 1940, it was extended to the 3rd and 4th year classes as well.[33]

Regular classes were started in Agriculture as optional subject for the Intermediate examination. In 1944, an Agricultural College was opened for which the university had received a grant of

Rs. 20,000 from Government of India. A regular Commerce course was also introduced as optional subject for Intermediate examination. In 1944, this department was raised after receiving a donation of Rs. 50,000 from Haji Mohammad Sahab Siddiqui.[34] In 1946, a regular Commerce Department was established and reorganised by Mr. S.M. Shafi.[35]

The Geology course was also started in 1944, and it was hoped that this department would develop into a regular Department of Geology as soon as class room accommodation would be available.[36] By the efforts of Dr. Ziauddin Ahmad, Aligarh Muslim University became the centre for conducting the examination of City and Guilds of London Institute of which Registrar was the Local Secretary.[37] In 1944, supplementary and compartmental examinations were introduced in the university as recommended by the Central Advisory Board of Education.[38]

In the Aligarh Muslim University, many radical changes were introduced in 1944. It was the starting of Faculty system in the university. The Deans were appointed as head of the Faculties. Nawab Sadar Yar Jang Bahadur was appointed as Dean of Theology, Dr. S. Zafrul Hasan of Arts, Dr. M. Babar Mirza of Science and K.B. Abdur Rahman of Engineering.[39] In the same year, the work of Pro-Vice Chancellor was distributed among the Deans and Provosts (head of the residential halls).[40]

When the Second World War was started in 1939, the Aligarh Muslim University got an opportunity of introducing some courses as well as placing the students into the government jobs. It opened many new departments with an excuse of helping the Emergency Commission. Several hundred students were sent out for Emergency Commission and more than a thousand war technicians were trained. Ever since the war broke out in September 1939, the Vice-Chancellor of AMU, made 'Military Drill' compulsory for all students of university. Five staff members were sent to Dehradun for the training in military course.[41]

On the representation of the Vice-Chancellor, the Governor of UP appointed special Provincial Selection Board for Aligarh students and also sanctioned Rs. 700/- per month for the appointment of a special officer to train candidates for Emergency Commission. Handsome grants of Rs. 1500/- as prompt payment and Rs. 10,000/- annually, along with the grant of UP Governor, enabled the university to organise a regular Department of Military Training in 1942 on the lines of the pre-cadet school of Bombay and Madras. This department was put under the charge of Mr. W.C. Qauyle, Ex-Professor of Physics in the University of Rangoon and an Air Pilot.[42]

In 1941, as per requirements of the war, arrangements were made for education and training of the technicians. The government gave grants for that purpose and appointed an experienced officer to train the technicians. The Labour Department of Government of India also granted Rs. 27,000/- for the residential purpose of technical students. Dr. Ambedkar, the then Labour Minister laid the foundation stone of the hostel building. On the representation of the Muslim members of the Central Assembly, Aligarh was included as a centre in a scheme of training to war technicians. The centre was located in the Engineering College of the university. To this course, mostly poor students were admitted. After completing their training, they got jobs in different factories in India.[43]

In 1939, a Flying Club was established and Prince of Berar laid the foundation of an Aerodrome. However, due to the war, the scheme remained in abeyance. In 1943, the dream was fulfilled and a special school for 'Indian Air Training Corps' was started in AMU. By this, the Aligarh Muslim University got the distinction of being the first university to start such a school. The opening ceremony was performed by Air Vice-Marshall A.B.C. Collier on 13th February, 1943. Total 50 students were admitted to this course. They were given a scholarship of Rs. 207/- per month along with one and half rupees by way of holiday pocket money. At the same time, they were allowed to continue their education in the university.[44]

At the suggestions of High Commander Majumdar and other representatives of the Air Headquarters, the Managing Committee of the Engineering College introduced course of instruction in 'Aeronautic Engineering' in November 1943, as an alternative subject in the curriculum. Five planes were received from Air Headquarters for instructional purposes, but a workshop fitted with hangers was yet to be built. However, the temporary rooms of the university were used for that purpose. Among all the Military Departments, the Navy could not become successful in Aligarh as the place was far away from the sea. The theory classes, however, were regularly conducted.[45]

As the war wave was on, everything possible and conceivable was done and achieved in the university. In view of the war emergency, the duration of course was reduced on the recommendation of the Managing Committee of Engineering College.[46]

Fortunately when the office of the 2nd U.T.C. Battalion shifted to Aligarh, the strength of U.T.C., at Aligarh was doubled. This U.T.C. Battalion helped very much in imparting military training to the university students related to that course. Services of Science Department of AMU were placed at the disposal of the Government of India for the preparation of articles needed for the war purposes.[47] For the development of the different branches of defence in AMU, a Military Science Institute was started in November 1944. It was known as Aken Luck Institute of Military Science.[48]

These departments were sometimes inspected by the government officers. In March 1944, Commander in Chief General Aken Luck visited Aligarh and after inspection of all branches of defence education at AMU expressed great satisfaction.[49]

At the beginning of the Second World War, the Aligarh Muslim University faced a legal problem in opening the different defence branches. However, on 27th February, 1943, problem was solved when the Central Assembly passed Mr. J.D. Tyson's (Secretary of Education, Health and Land) Bill to amend the AMU Act. Mr. Tyson's Bill sought to enable the university to modify its ordinances expeditiously and provide special course of study for the interested students.[50]

The university authorities were perhaps hypnotized by the continuous friendly policies of the British Government. The university authorities also showed their loyalties time to time. Sometimes they celebrated the British victories in the Second World War. On 21st May, 1943, while celebrating the British victories, the Vice-Chancellor of AMU Dr. Ziauddin Ahmad delivered a touching speech. He said, "We have assembled here today to celebrate the victory of Allied Forces in the first stage of the war. The Musalmans felt greatly relieved at the termination of Italian hold in North Africa.... The university has sent out about 700 students in

Emergency Commission and they have all gone with the firm resolve that they would take Burma back from Japan and will release our countrymen.... I now give a small contribution of Rs. 5,000/- towards the war efforts and hand over the cheque to the Chairman."[51]

In the midway, when the development measures were being undertaken, Dr. Ziauddin Ahmad resigned from the post of Vice-Chancellorship in 1947 due to some disturbances. Nawab Mohammad Ismail Khan took over as Vice-Chancellor on 20th October, 1947.[52] He was a renowned politician and a well-wisher of the community.

Medical College

The moment the MAO College was elevated to the status of the university, the Muslim community had been urging to establish a Medical College for the benefit of students interested in medical line. In 1923, Mr. Nur Mohammad of Bhera wrote to Pro-Vice Chancellor, Dr. Ziauddin Ahmad and requested him to make all efforts for starting a Medical College in AMU. Ziauddin Ahmad too thought that it would provide good career for young men as only small fraction of them could get admission in the existing Medical Colleges of India.[53]

The old boys from each corner of India too appealed to the AMU authorities to open a Medical College.[54] But the efforts to establish Medical College were slow due to the paucity of funds. It required a huge amount of money for its establishment. When Dr. Ziauddin Ahamd became Vice-Chancellor second time in 1941, Sir Agha Khan donated a sum of one lakh rupees for establishing a Medical College.[55] By 1944, an amount of thirty lakh rupees was collected for that purpose.[56]

Under the guidance of Dr. Ziauddin Ahmad, many delegations consisting of students and teachers toured the country and Dr. Ziauddin Ahmad himself visited big cities like Bombay and Calcutta to collect donations for the Medical College.[57] The Muslim community responded generously to the appeal for funds and by the end of 1946 a sum of 44 lakh of rupees was collected, which included the donation of 10 lakhs rupees given by the Nizam of

Hyderabad.[58] Until the end of 1947 over 50 lakhs of rupees were collected for the purpose of establishing Medical College. Consequently, a plan for the faculty of Medicine was submitted to the Government of India for its approval.[59]

Engineering College

Like the Medical College, there was a lot of hue and cry in the Muslim community for establishment of a Technical College in Aligarh Muslim University. A student of Dr. Ziauddin Ahmad wrote a letter informing him that in Tata Technological College, students from all the universities were given admission excepting from that of Aligarh University. He, therefore, made an earnest appeal to him to open a Technological College as soon as possible.[60]

In 1924, university had made a provision for the teaching of Technology. Accordingly, the Academic Council approved to open three branches of technology viz. (1) Applied Chemistry, (2) Electro-Technic, and (3) Civil Engineering. In Civil Engineering it was proposed to provide teaching only in diploma course.[61] But the real beginning could be made only in 1935, when a Technical Institute was started in the month of November. Consequently, this institute started two courses, i.e. the Electrician course and Foreman course having 20 students in each course. By 1937, the Technical Institute was having the following courses:[62]

(1) ***Diploma course***: three-year course for Fundation Course in Science (F. Sc.), boys.
(2) ***Foreman course***: three-year course for matriculates.
(3) ***Electrician course***: two-year course for boys of elementary knowledge of vernacular and arithmetic.
(4) ***Motor Mechanics course***: two-year course for boys of elementary knowledge of Urdu and Mechanic.

Additional part time courses in Telegraph, Signalling and Driving of motor cars were also started.[63] In 1938, Sir Agha Khan arrived at Aligarh along with Nawab of Rampur. Sir Agha Khan donated one lakh rupees for Engineering College. Nizam Hyderabad also donated same amount and Nawab of Rampur donated one lakh and two thousand rupees.[64]

The College of Technology made satisfactory progress from the date of its foundation. In 1938, 23 students appeared in the City and Guilds examination of Electrical Engineering, 17 of them became successful.[65] In 1940, the government approved the opening of B.Sc. classes in Electrical and Mechanical Engineering.[66] In 1941, Nawab Kamal Yar Jung inaugurated the Agha Khan workshop.[67] As a result B.Sc. in Civil Engineering was started in the same year.[68] In 1942, the Department of Technology was transformed into the College of Engineering.[69] From then onwards the Engineering College gained the great reputations.

Tibbiya College

In 1925, the UP Government appointed a committee under Mr. Gorakhnath Mishra for establishing institutions of Ayurvedic and Unani system of Medicine in 1925. The committee visited many places in the United Provinces, but unfortunately it did not arrive at Aligarh. When the Pro-Vice Chancellor of the AMU was informed about the proposal, he addressed a letter to the President of the committee and urged that the proposed Tibbiya College should be established at Aligarh.[70]

Fortunately, President of the committee Mr. Gorakhnath Mishra considered the proposal of Pro-Vice Chancellor and requested UP Government to establish a Tibbiya College at Aligarh. In October 1927, the university inaugurated a new Department of Unani Medicine for which UP Government had given a recurring grant of Rs. 50,000/- per year.[71]

It was merely a Department of Unani Medicine maintained by the AMU and was not yet given the status of the college. However, in the meantime it made great progress. A laboratory with X-ray equipment and a collection of pathological specimens enabled the students to receive training in the latest methods of diagnosing diseases. The anatomical museum was organised with a large collection of models from Europe covering all the systems of human Anatomy. The department of Physiology was also well equipped.[72] In order to achieve efficient functioning; Dr. Ataullah Butt (earlier a Medical Officer of the university and incharge of the Department of Unani Medicine also from the time of its establishment) was given exclusive charge of the department.[73] By that change, the Department of Unani Medicine continued to make rapid progress.[74]

In the Department of Unani Medicine in academic session of 1931-32, the syllabi of the Unani Tib was split in the following manner:[75]

Syllabi of the Unani Tib in Department of Unani Medicine

- 1st year—Fundamental Principle of Unani Tib.
- 2nd year—Course on Materia Medica (Unani), particularly the simple drugs.
- 3rd year—General Methodology (Unani), general principle of treatment.
- 4th year—Medicine (Unani) particularly symptomology and treatment of diseases.

Practical Classes Data

Years	*Number of cases examined and treated performed before students*	*Number of minor operation performed before students*	*Number of dead bodies dissected by students*
1929-30	12830	11	1 by 8 students
1930-31	17966	425	1 by 11 students

Examination 1930-31 (Students Examined for Three year Classes)

Class	*Number of students appeared*	*Passed*	*Re-examined*	*Passed*
1st Year	7	6	1	1
2nd Year	7	7	—	—
3rd Year	19	17	—	—

The teaching work was quite satisfactory and practical Pharmacy class, in which compound drugs were prepared under the supervision of Hakim incharge, were regularly held. The examinations were conducted by Board of Indian Medicine.[76]

Strength of the students increased the Department of Unani Medicine and departments expanded accordingly. To meet out the further requirement, the foundation stone of new Tibbiya College

Building was laid on 22nd March, 1936 by Prince Azam Jah Bahadur, heir apparent to the State of Hyderabad.[77]

In 1938, a few changes were made in the syllabi as 4th and 5th year classes were started from that time. Accordingly, the class-wise syllabi was as follows:[78]

- 1st Year—Fundamental Principle of Unani Tib.
- 2nd Year—Mufredate and Qarobadin (simple drugs of Unani Medicine and Unani Pharmaco poeia) became the special subject of this class, apart from the lectures on the subject of preparation of Drugs.
- 3rd Year—General Pathology.
- 4th Year—Symptomology and treatment of diseases.
- 5th Year—Hummyat (subject in which different types of fevers is taught) and Moalijat (Unani Medicine) of Qanun Shaikh (Canon of Medicine, a book of Ibn-e-Sina) were daily taught, which completed the Unani Section of the Tib.

It was a matter of great satisfaction to the students of Unani Tib that in 1939, UP Government took 25 Diploma holder Hakims from Aligarh for rural dispensaries in United Provinces.[79] In 1943, the Department of Tibbiya was granted the status of a College to be maintained by Aligarh Muslim University. Its courses of study and examinations were henceforth regulated and controlled by the Academic Council of the university.[80] After 1944, the status of the college was raised to Degree College.[81]

Medical Department

For the health care of the university students, a first class Medical Department was established under the guidance of the Medical Officer Dr. Ataullah Butt. Dr. Ataullah Butt was also the Head of Tibbiya Department. This naturally affected the efficiency of both the departments. Consequently, the post of Principal was created for Tibbiya Department in 1930, separating Tibbiya College from Medical department. Dr. Ataullah Butt assumed the exclusive charge of the Tibbiya College as Principal and Dr. A.R. Mansoor, M.D.,

D.P.H. became the whole time Medical Officer of the university.[82] From that time, the Medical Department continued to do good work under the direction of Dr. A.R. Mansoor.[83]

Women's College

Shaikh Abdullah may be credited for initiating the work of women's education in Aligarh. He formulated the idea of starting girls' school in 1902, but the actual work of collecting donation was started after the Educational Conference at Lucknow, which was held in 1903. Shaikh Abdullah started a journal "*Khatoon*" in 1904 in Aligarh, propagating for women's education, which was so far abhorred. Through this journal, the ladies came out with writing about their social problems.[84]

The journal *Khatoon* carried the message to the ladies of the respected families. This finally led to establishing a lady's school at Aligarh. Her Highness Begum of Bhopal gave handsome donations for establishing a lady's school. Some of the important ladies made a movement and collected funds for the lady's school. Many students of the Mohammadan Anglo Oriental College also responded to the call and joined to collect donations from Kathiawar, Bombay, Hyderabad, etc. Abdur Rahman Siddiqui, Khan Bahadur Buniyad Husain, Zahoor Ahmad, Abdur Rahman Bijnori also participated in these tours for donations. Even Syed Mahmood toured different areas and collected donations for establishing a lady's school in Aligarh.[85]

In June 1906, Shaikh Abdullah sent a letter to Governor of United Provinces informing him about the plan for establishing a lady's school in Aligarh. He appealed to grant money for the same. He also requested to see him with a delegation on 2nd August, 1906 for the meeting. Shaikh Abdullah sent the delegates name of Nawab Mohsinul Mulk, Nawab Mohammad Faiyaz Khan, Maharaja Mahmudabad, Raja Tasadduq Rasul Khan, Nawab Muzammilullah Khan, Sahibzada Aftab Ahamd Khan, Raja Naushad Ali Khan, Maulvi Mohammad Nasim Advocate and Khwaja Ghulamussaqlain to the Governor. However, on the appointed day only three persons namely Raja Naushad Ali Khan, Maulvi Mohammad Nasim Advocate and Khwaja Ghulamussaqlain reached with Shaikh

Abdullah. With reference to Begum of Bhopal, Shaikh Abdullah said that Her Highness had granted donations and desired to get the assistance from the government. The Governor permitted to start the school but asserted that monetary grant would be released only after a satisfactory inquiry by the government.[86]

From 1907, a regular school for girls was started. Its first lady teacher was Akhtari Begum Abdullah Waheed Jahan and her two sisters Sikandar Jahan and Sayeed Jahan also started teaching in that school. Sedans were arranged to carry veiled girl students from nearby areas. Within three months from the inception of the school, 50 students were enrolled. A Government Inspector came for an enquiry and gave a satisfactory report to the Governor of UP. The Governor in order to fulfil the promise granted Rs. 17,000/- for building purpose and Rs. 250/- monthly for school.[87]

The government grant raised the hope of Shaikh Abdullah, and he became sure that this primary school would be raised to a college in the near future. However, undoubtedly, it was not an easy task. Shaikh Abdullah faced many difficulties in persuading the people to send their daughters for his school. At this juncture, Begum Abdullah played key role in convincing the mothers of the girls. On the other side, those who were against the girl's education started creating problems in the works of Shaikh Abdullah. They condemned the girl's education and committed absurdities in order to harass Shaikh Abdullah.[88]

However, notwithstanding all the difficulties, Shaikh Abdullah continued to work towards his goal without caring the criticism. Shaikh Abdullah purchased a land of 14 Bigha from Nanak Rai by paying a meager amount of Rs. 1,950/-. It was a very big garden and Shaikh Abdullah sold only woods worth of Rs. 5,100/- and for this money, he purchased another surrounding land for the school. In a very few year Shaikh Abdullah could secure forty-acre land for the school.[89]

In 1911, when Shaikh Abdullah intended to construct a new permanent building for the school, the opposition created hindrances once again. According to them, the place for the building of girl's school was very near to the MAO College, which would badly affect the college atmosphere. They started back biting Nawab Viqarul Mulk. Nawab Viqarul Mulk enquired all those persons, who were opposing Shaikh Abdullah's planning. The leaders of opposition were Sir Arche Bold, Principal of the MAO College and Dr. Ziauddin Ahmad.[90]

The Principal Sir Arche Bold said to the Nawab Viqarul Mulk, "I shall resign if that school will be built." He further said, "Muslim girls' school near the college would cause depravity for both the institutions. I am sure that for this reason, both the institution will be defamed." Dr. Ziauddin Ahmad seconded the Principal's opinion saying, "I doubt that the people will send their girls in view of the nearness of the college. We shall have no objection if the school be built on the other side of the city."[91]

Regarding these objections, Shaikh Abdullah explained that most of the staff members were living with their families in the college campus, and no difficulty arose out of it, then to what harm it could cause if a boarding house was going to be built one and half miles away from the college. On hearing this argument of Shaikh Abdullah, the opposition became silent and Nawab Viqarul Mulk gave judgement in his favour.[92]

On 11th November 1911, the foundation stone of the Girls School building was laid by Mrs. Porter, the wife of Mr. Porter, the Governor of United Provinces. On this occasion many chiefs, noblemen, Talluqdars, staff of the MAO College, Hindus, Muslims and Christian ladies were present.[93] The work of Shaikh Abdullah was greatly admired and appreciated.

After the success of the foundation stone ceremony, Shaikh Abdullah decided to construct at first the boarding house, because it was the first requirement of the students coming from the very distant areas of the country. Shaikh Abdullah collected forty thousand rupees from the donations. The government also granted twenty thousand rupees for that purpose. From this sixty thousand rupees, the construction of the boarding house completed in 1914.[94]

After completing the boarding house building, Shaikh Abdullah wanted its lavish inauguration. For this purpose Shaikh Abdullah along with Hakim Ajmal Khan and Sahibzada Aftab Ahamd Khan, met to the Begum of Bhopal and requested for inauguration. Begum of Bhopal accepted the request and on 14th February, 1914, the inaugural ceremony was held with great pomp and show.[95]

Shaikh Abdullah faced another difficulty as no parents were ready to lodge their daughters in the boarding of the Girls School. After continuous efforts of Shaikh Abdullah and his family, some parents became ready to lodge their daughters but before lodging their daughters they wanted to be assured about the proper functioning of the boarding house. The parents were also concerned in the observation of *Pardah* system. Shaikh Abdullah said that only gents' water carrier and sweepers (*Bhangi*) would be allowed to enter the boarding house.[96]

On the very first day, only nine girls were admitted in the boarding house. Among these girls, three were the daughters of Shaikh Abdullah, other three were the nieces of Begum Abdullah, one was the daughter of Shaikh Abdullah's friend, and the remaining two were persuaded by Begum Abdullah. Begum Abdullah herself began to live with the boarders in the boarding house. Gradually, the number of boarders started increasing and many parents got their daughters admitted happily in the boarding house.[97] In due course of time, the functioning of the school became very smooth. The number of girls increased. For the first time in 1916-17, three students appeared in the middle class examination.[98]

The girl students further demanded that the arrangements should be made for matric classes. Nevertheless, the resources were too meager to appoint new teachers. Shaikh Abdullah, however, secured the donations from Nizam of Hyderabad, Nawab of Tonk, Nawab of Bahawalpur, Nawab of Jawara, etc. He also requested the government to raise its annual grant. Government immediately raised its grant from three thousand to eight thousand rupees. As the monetary problem was being solved, Shaikh Abdullah appointed qualified teachers. For the first time in 1921, six students appeared in matric examination. The school, then was raised to the status of "Muslims Girls High School."[99]

Shaikh Abdullah, in order to solve the residential problem, requested Nawab Muzammilullah Khan for help. Nawab Muzammilullah donated Rs. 7,000/- to construct the residence of four lady teachers and this building, later on, was denominated after the name of late daughter of Nawab Muzammilullah Khan.[100]

In 1925, during the Golden Jubilee celebrations of the university, after a prolonged debate, girl students were allowed to listen the speeches from behind the curtain. It was the golden time in the history of liberation of Muslim Women in India and Shaikh Abdullah became the pioneer of liberation of Muslim women by virtue of his great efforts.[101] The girl students were also encouraged to participate in extracurricular activities.[102]

In 1926, one girl student of this school appeared in Intermediate examination from UP Board and thereafter many students appeared every year. Later on in 1929, the school was raised to Intermediate College and was recognised by UP Board. Shaikh Abdullah, however, wanted its affiliation with the Muslim University. In order to affiliate the college, university made a provision of Rs. 100/- as annual grant. Hence from 1930, the college got affiliated to the Muslim University.[103]

With the increasing strength of the students, it was felt necessary to start B.A. classes. This could only be done by raising necessary funds and making proper arrangement for teaching.[104] In 1935, the Muslim Educational Conference was held at Rampur. It was presided over by Syed Husain Bilgrami, an eminent officer of Hyderabad State. Shaikh Abdullah also attended the conference and put up his proposal for opening a Degree College for the girls at Aligarh. Many delegates supported the proposal.[105]

However, finally, the proposal of Shaikh Abdullah was not accepted. Shaikh Abdullah unfettered by the conservative attitude of the Muslim intelligentsia continued his efforts. He wrote articles highlighting the need of encouraging higher education among the Muslim girls.[106] When Sir Shah Mohammad Sulaiman became the next Vice Chancellor, Shaikh Abdullah finally succeeded in getting his approval for the Degree College. The university granted Rs. 5,000/- annually for the Girls College in 1938 and B.A. classes were started in the same year.[107]

In 1938, the Education Minister of the UP Government, Mr. Sampurna Nand visited Aligarh. Shaikh Abdullah met him and requested him to visit the Girls College and demanded a grant of Rs. 20,000/- for the Girls College to build the Science laboratory. Mr. Sampurna Nand appreciated the efforts of Shaikh Abdullah in the field of girl's education and approved the grant.[108]

Later on, the university permitted the girl students of Girls College to attend the PG classes in the university and several other improvements followed.[109] To accommodate the Girls College in the university and PG education to the girls in the university, necessary amendments in the university constitution were attempted. On 5th November, Honourable Mr. N.R. Sarkar introduced a Bill to amend the Aligarh Muslim University Act to enable the university:[110]

(i) To admit to its privileges a Degree College for women whom it was proposed to organise at Aligarh; and
(ii) To confer degrees on passing degree examinations from that college.

An autumn session of the Council of States also began in November in New Delhi. In that session speaking on the motion for consideration of the Bill to amend the Aligarh University Act, Sir Mohammad Yaqub and Mr. P.N. Sapru welcomed the proposal to organise Degree College for women, to be affiliated to the university. Pandit Hridaya Nath Kunzru, while not wishing to oppose the Bill said that he would have preferred if girls were to receive education in Aligarh Muslim University in the same way as boys instead of being in a separate college. The establishment of such a college, he felt, would be in contravention of the principle underlying the Aligarh University, which was a unitary teaching university. Finally, the Bill was passed without further discussion.[111]

The Girls College was, undoubtedly, now a first class Degree College managed by the Aligarh Muslim University. However, it faced a monetary problem as it received a meager grant of Rs. 5,000/- per annum from the university. Facing with such a monetary problem, Shaikh Abdullah thought it proper to get it de-affiliated from the university and make up a provincial college to get full grant from UP Government.[112]

In the process of this new planning of Shaikh Abdullah, Dr. Ziauddin Ahmad, who was at that time the member of the Provincial Assembly did lot. He put up the matter before Assembly and empowered the university to cancel the affiliation of the Muslim Girls College. From that time, the Muslim Girls College became a provincial college maintained by the UP Government. Now Shaikh Abdullah made efforts to get much more grants from the UP

Government. In 1944, UP Government sanctioned eighteen thousand and five hundred rupees (Rs 18,500/-) for the Muslim Girls College. A Managing Committee for the college was elected for managing the college, and this system continued until the time of Independence. In 1944, the strength of the college was two hundred and twenty five, but it increased rapidly afterwards.[113]

Until 1944, there was a Women's Hall in AMU for the admission of the women candidate in the M.A., B.T. and other higher classes in the university. However, in 1944, the Women's Hall was abolished and the university empowered the college to give admission to the candidates directly. The Executive Council of the university declared that the postgraduate students for whom provision for the classes was not made in the women's college were allowed to attend lectures in the university under *pardah* arrangements. The Women's College was to pay the tuition fees of such students to the university and no additional fee was charged.[114]

The Girls School started in 1907, became a Degree College and reached its peak in 1947. It was all due to the hard work and efforts of Shaikh Abdullah and Begum Abdullah. Due to their affectionate attitude with students, they were lovingly known as "Papa Miyan" and "Aala Bi."

NOTES

1. *Urdu* (Masood Number), 1937, pp. 837-838; see also *Fikr-o-Nazar*, Vol. II, p. 298.
2. *Aligarh Magazine, January-February, 1929*, pp. 4-5; see also *Urdu* (Masood Number), 1937, p. 836.
3. *Urdu* (Masood Number), 1937, pp. 875-876, 887.
4. *Aligarh Magazine, October-December, 1929*, p. L.
5. *File No. 51, 1928-29* (AMU Archive).
6. *Ibid.*
7. *Aligarh Magazine, October-December, 1929*, p. L.
8. *Fikr-o-Nazar*, Vol. I, p. 298.
9. *AMU Annual Report*, 1931, p. 2.
10. Anderson, Sir George, *Progress of Education in India 1927-32*, Delhi, (ND), p. 73.
11. *Indian Annual Register*, 1931, Vol. II, p. 113.
12. *Ibid.*, see also *File No. 51 (I), 1930-31* (AMU Archive).

13. *File No. V/2, 1931-32* (AMU Archive); see also *AMU Annual Report*, 1933, p. 2.
14. *File No. 51, 1933-34* (AMU Archive).
15. *File No. XVII/2, 1930-31* (AMU Archive).
16. *Past and Present*, p. 99.
17. *AMU Annual Report*, 1931, p. 3.
18. *File No. 51, 1934-35* (AMU Archive).
19. *File No. 51, 1929-30* and *File No. 51, 1931-32* (AMU Archive).
20. *AMU Annual Report*, 1933, p. 20; see also *File No. 51, 1934-35* (AMU Archive).
21. Coatman, J., *India in 1933-34*, Delhi, 1935, p. 179; see also *Aligarh Magazine, December 1932*, p. 3, *File No. IV/2, 1931-32,* p. 7 (AMU Archive); *Urdu*, (Masood Number), pp. 763-765; and *Past & Present*, p. 101.
22. *Urdu*, (Masood Number), pp. 840-41; see also *AMU Annual Report*, 1934, p. 1 (AMU Archive).
23. *Ibid.*
24. Aggarwal, J.C., *Landmarks in the History of Modern Indian Education*, New Delhi, 1984, p. 49.
25. *AMU Annual Report*, 1935, pp. 1, 2, 5; see also *Indian Annual Register*, 1937, Vol. I, p. 411.
26. *Indian Annual Register*, 1935, Vol. II, p. 36.
27. *File No. 51, 1935-36* (AMU Archive).
28. *Addresses and Speeches*, p. 65.
29. *File No. 604/36,* Uttar Pradesh State Archive Lucknow (UPSAL); see also *AMU Annual Report*, 1936.
30. *File No. 62, 1938-44* (AMU Archive).
31. *Ibid.*
32. *File No. 51, 1935-40* (AMU Archive).
33. *AMU Annual Report*, 1940, p. 16.
34. *File No. 51, 1941-42* (AMU Archive); see also *AMU Annual Report*, 1944, pp. 1-2.
35. *Past and Present*, p. 104.
36. *AMU Annual Report*, 1944, p. 2.
37. *Ibid.,* p. 3.
38. *File No. 51, 1945-46* (AMU Archive).
39. *Ibid.*
40. *Past and Present*, p. 103.
41. *Zia-i-Hayat*, p. 177.
42. *Aligarh Institute Gazette,* 15th July, 1943; see also *File No. 51, 1942-43* (AMU Archive); and *Zia-i-Hayat*, p. 179.
43. *Ibid.,* see also *Zia-i-Hayat*, p. 177.
44. *Ibid.,* see also *File No. 51, 1942-43* (AMU Archive); and *Zia-i-Hayat*, p. 180.
45. *Ibid.,* see also *File No. 51, 1942-43* (AMU Archive); and *Zia-i-Hayat*, pp. 180-82.

46. *Ibid.*
47. *Ibid.*
48. *Zia-i-Hayat*, p. 183.
49. *Ibid.*, p. 181.
50. *Indian Annual Register*, 1943, Vol. I, p. 168.
51. *Aligarh Institute Gazette,* 1st June, 1943.
52. *Fikr-o-Nazar*, Vol. II, p. 314.
53. *File No. XV/2, 1923-24* (AMU Archive).
54. *File No. XV/3, 1926-27* (AMU Archive).
55. *Fikr-o-Nazar*, Vol. II, p. 14.
56. *AMU Annual Report*, 1944, p. 1.
57. *Past and Present*, p. 104.
58. *Ibid.*
59. *AMU Annual Report*, 1947, p. 2.
60. *File No. XV/3, 1926-27* (AMU Archive).
61. *File No. 51, 1924-25* (AMU Archive).
62. *File No. 51, 1937-38* (AMU Archive).
63. *Ibid.*
64. *Fikr-o-Nazar*, Vol. II, p. 14.
65. *File No. 51, 1938-39* (AMU Archive).
66. *File No. 51, 1940-41* (AMU Archive).
67. *Past and Present*, p. 102.
68. *File No. 53/4, 1940-41* (AMU Archive).
69. *File No. 51, 1942-43* (AMU Archive).
70. *Aligarh Institute Gazette,* 28th April, 1926.
71. *File No. IV/1, 1927-28* (AMU Archive).
72. Coatman, J., *India in 1929-30*, Calcutta, 1931, p. 347.
73. Coatman, J., *India in 1930-31*, Calcutta, 1932, p. 472.
74. *AMU Annual Report*, 1931, p. 4.
75. *File No. 51, 1931-32* (AMU Archive).
76. *AMU Annual Report*, 1933, p. 161.
77. *File No. 51, 1935-36* (AMU Archive).
78. *Ibid.*, 1938-39.
79. *Ibid.*, 1939-40.
80. *Ibid.*, 1942-43; see also *File No. 51, 1943-44* (AMU Archive).
81. *AMU Annual Report*, 1944, p. 11.
82. Coatman, J., *India in 1930-31*, Calcutta, 1932, p. 472.
83. *AMU Annual Report*, 1931, p. 4.
84. *Muslim University Girls High School Magazine, 1964-65-66*, p. 28; see also *Fikr-o-Nazar*, Vol. III. p. 17.
85. *Hayat-i-Abdullah*, p. 198.
86. *Ibid.*, pp. 198-99.
87. *Hayat-i-Abdullah*, pp. 200-201. In the *Muslim University Girls High School Magazine 1964-65-66*, it is said that (the Governor granted Rs. 7,000.00

for the building purposes (*Muslim University Girls High School Magazine 1964-65-66*, p. 28).

88. Hamid Hasan Tehsildar spread the rumour that once an *Ekkawala*, who was carrying a girl student entered his veiled *Ekka* and came out after a long time, and then he carried her to the school. This rumour created a bad effect upon the school. Shaikh Abdullah went to the school for the further enquiries then he met the Tehsildar. The Tehsildar began to swear and refused to even know this rumour (*Hayat-i-Abdullah,* pp. 202-203).
89. *Hayat-i-Abdullah,* pp. 203-204.
90. *Ibid.,* pp. 205-206.
91. *Ibid.*
92. *Ibid.*
93. *Ibid.,* p. 207.
94. *Ibid.,* p. 208.
95. *Ibid.,* p. 210.
96. *Ibid.,* p. 211.
97. *Ibid.,* p. 212.
98. *Ibid.,* p. 220.
99. *Ibid.,* p. 221.
100. Abdullah, Shaikh Mohammad, *Mushahidat-o-Taassurat,* Delhi, 1969, p. 338.
101. *Ibid.,* p. 334.
102. *Ibid.*
103. *Hayat-i-Abdullah,* pp. 221-22.
104. *Ibid.,* p. 223.
105. *Ibid.*
106. *Ibid.,* p. 224.
107. *Ibid.,* pp. 223-25.
108. *Ibid.,* p. 226.
109. *File No. 41/3, 1939-40* (AMU Archive).
110. *Indian Annual Register*, 1941, Vol. II, p. 121.
111. *Ibid.*
112. *Hayat-i-Abdullah,* p. 225.
113. *Ibid.,* p. 226.
114. *File No. 41/1, 1943-44* (AMU Archive).

5
AMU's Contribution to the National Politics till 1937

It is generally the stereotype raking that Aligarh Muslim University, and its alumni did nothing for the Indian National Movement. Even it is branded as the propagator of the Pakistan Movement. No doubt as an institution AMU has the people of different opinions and naturally, they were free to express their thought, but a majority of them were the nationalists. They took both the issues of nation and community. The so-called loyalists were also of the opinion that without the sound position of the community, there can be no national service. The people generally misunderstand the service of the community and service of the nation and began branding the service of the community as separatist movement or pro-Pakistani leanings. Actually, Aligarh was not a merely institution, but a school of thought, which naturally moulded the destiny of the nation. It also represented the welfare of the Muslims in all-over India.

The political awareness in Aligarh was started with the ideology of Sir Syed Ahmad Khan, who continuously worked for the betterment of the Muslim community after the shocks of 1857. His friends and disciples continued his works after his death. They took the cause of the Muslim community and sought the representation in the Assembly and concessions in the government jobs and administration. The government also became more favourable for the Muslim community as they were leaning towards loyalty after hundred years of animosity.

At the beginning of their rule, the British were very hostile to the Muslim community. They considered that they have seized the power from the Muslims and the Muslims could never be friendly with the British Government. So, they shake their hands with the Hindu community and told them they were suffering from the centuries by the Muslim cruelties. They came here to save them. Slowly, the Hindus became aware of their power and began to demand their share in the power and naturally the British were annoyed with this community. Now, the cunning British turned towards Muslims and told them that they were the minority in India. The British Government only could save their future and provide them the powers in proportion to the Hindus.

The Muslim leaders of that time find it a long-awaited opportunity to get the share in the political power to which the Hindus were enjoying from the decades. On the pattern of the Indian National Congress, they also formed an organization named as Muslim League. It must be remembered that till that time many extremist elements had made their entry in the Congress and ultimately they all had waged a movement of Swadeshi and Boycott against the British Government's decision of Bengal Partition. Naturally, the Muslim League gained much attention and favour from the British Government. Whatsoever was the work and result of the so-called Muslim favour by the British Government, but it could not be denied that it was a trick of their divide and rule policy which they had launched in India after historic Hindu-Muslim unity of 1857.

Formation of Muslim League

After the death of Sir Syed Ahmad Khan, the duty of nursing the Muslim society fell upon his friends and associates like Nawab Mohsinul Mulk, Nawab Viqarul Mulk, Sahibzada Aftab Ahmad Khan, Dr. Ziauddin, etc. It must not be forgotten that it was the period when the British Government gave more impulse to its policy of divide and rule and started to woo the Muslim intelligentsia by promising them to share in the administrative as well as legislative powers. It created a rift between the Hindus and Muslims and ultimately with the instigation of the British Government, the Muslims founded their own organization called as Muslim League.

In 1905, due to the divide and rule policy of the British Government, Lord Curzon divided the Bengal into two halves, one was dominated by the Muslims and other was Hindu dominated region. This division definitely injured the Indian sentiments, and as a result Swadeshi and Boycott movements were started. A voice of opposition was raised from each and every corner of the country. Almost all the nationalists, particularly Hindus participated in these movements. However, some Muslim leaders felt movement as a danger to the Muslim interest as Lord Curzon had convinced them that the partition of Bengal was only a move to give more powers to the Muslims of Bengal. So, these Muslim leaders decided to meet the Viceroy and put before him certain demands for Muslim's security and interest in India.[1]

At the indication of Nawab Mohsinul Mulk, the other Muslim leaders Nawab Viqarul Mulk and Syed Husain Bilgrami very carefully drafted an address which was to be put before the Viceroy. Nawab Mohsinul Mulk sent its copies to the leading Muslims all-over India to elicit their opinion. On certain issues, many differences arose and to sink these differences Nawab Mohsinul Mulk called a meeting in Lucknow on September 16, 1906 to discuss the draft and get final approval for it. In this meeting, after a long discussion, the draft was given a final shape. This meeting also authorized Nawab Mohsinul Mulk to select the members for deputation to meet the Viceroy.[2]

On October 1, 1906, a deputation of 35 members headed by H.H. Agha Khan, including Nawab Mohsinul Mulk, Nawab Viqarul Mulk, Sahibzada Aftab Ahmad Khan, Nawab Muzammilullah Khan, Hakim Ajmal Khan, Nawab Mohammad Ismail, Sir Ali Imam, Omar Hayat Khan and other prominent Muslim leaders from different parts of the country, reached Shimla to present their address to the Viceroy Lord Minto. This deputation is popularly known as Shimla Deputation.[3]

In their address, they drew the Viceroy's attention to their political importance and the value of the contribution they made to the protection of the Empire. The inadequate Muslim participation in the judiciary, local bodies and university bodies was highlighted. The existing method of election was also criticised for the insufficiency of Muslim representation of local self-government institutions and Legislative Council. The address asked the Viceroy to provide Muslim community the right to select their representatives by electorates confined exclusively to their community. The address also demanded that Muslim representation should be proportionate not merely to their numerical strength but should reflect the significance of their community as an important factor.[4]

The Viceroy Lord Minto very cautiously replied, "you have addressed me, gentlemen, at a time when a political atmosphere is full of change. We all feel it... your address, as I understand it, is a claim that in any system of representation... in which it is proposed to introduce or increase an electoral organisation, the Mohammadan community should be represented as a community and you justly claim that your position should be estimated not merely on your numerical strength but in respect to the political importance of your community and the service it has rendered to the empire.... I am entirely in accord with you.... I am as firmly convinced as I believed you to be, that any electoral representation in India would be doomed to mischievous failure which aimed at granting a personal enfranchisement regardless the beliefs and traditions of the communities composing the deputation of this continent."[5]

Lord Minto also assured the deputation that their political rights and interests would be safeguarded in administration with which he was concerned.[6] The Viceroy fully encouraged the Shimla deputation, so these prominent Muslim leaders began to think to unite the Muslims in the form of an association.

The first step in regard of forming an association was taken by Nawab Salimullah of Decca. When the Muhammadan Educational Conference was over on December 30, 1906 at Decca, Nawab Salimullah Khan convened a meeting to discuss the scheme of a Muslim organization. Nawab Viqarul Mulk was voted to the chair, and he addressed that time and circumstances made it necessary for Mohammadans to unite in an association to make their voice heard above the din of other vociferous parties in India across the wide sea to England.[7]

Nawab Viqarul Mulk clarified the position of Indian National Congress that it served the country, but he also regretted its revolutionary methods of attaining the objects, their harsh and ill worded speeches against the British.[8] Nawab Salimullah Khan while introducing his scheme said that there was a special need for increasing political activity on the part of Muslim community as only those who cried loudest had a chance of being heard.[9] The resolution put before the assembly for the vote was as follows:[10]

> "Resolved that this meeting composed of Musalmans from all parts of India assembled at Decca decided that a political association be formed, styled All-India Muslim League for furtherance of the following objects—
>
> (a) To promote, among the Musalmans of India, feelings of loyalty to the British Government and to remove any misconception that may arise as to the intention of the government with regard to any of its measures.
>
> (b) To protect and advance the political rights and interests of the Musalmans of India, and to respectfully represent their needs and aspirations to the government.
>
> (c) To prevent the rise, among the Muslims of India, of any feelings of hostility towards other objects of the League."

The resolution was supported by Hakim Ajmal Khan, Maulana Zafar Ali Khan, Shaikh Abdullah and Maulana Mohammad Ali along with a number of other Muslim delegates, and the All India Muslim League was founded accordingly.[11]

The work of the Muslim League was to unite to Muslims all-over India, to demand and get share in the power and remain loyal to the British Government. The Act of 1909 was the reward of the Muslim League in which they got the historic separate electorate.

Responses over Tripoli and Balkan Wars

The Tripoli War, which was started in 1911, caused great concern among Indian Muslims. The Muslim League passed a resolution appealing the British Government to put a stop to this brutal war. The *Aligrah Institute Gazette* reproduced the resolution passed by the Muslim League. This was the proof of their being the traditional supporter of Turkey.[12] Aligarh students, responding to the call of the Muslim League, contributed to the funds raised for Tripoli victims. They also began to boycott the Italian goods. Even the petty shopkeepers and servants followed the same.[13]

Maulana Abul Kalam Azad also had a very critical attitude towards Italy. He encouraged the Indian Muslims to extend hope in favour of Turkey. In his paper *Al-Hilal*, he said that Muslims could keep in mind the fact that the European powers were making an attempt to oust Islam from Europe through their formidable influence. He reminded that the same ambition was not new to Islam because it had been facing these ambitions for the last thirteen hundred years. Although almost everything in the world has undergone the drastic change but God remains the same, totally unchanged and even today He can perform miracles.[14]

The Tripoli war thus had a great impact on the educated Muslims, especially of Aligarh. Most of the Aligarh Muslims had very much expectation from England, and they thought that the British Government would certainly favour the sentiments of the Muslims. However, the British Government's announcement of neutrality in the war, and its directives to the subjects to remain neutral and warning them to desist from its violation, was an eye-opener to the Muslims of Aligarh.[15]

In this Tripoli War, the Turkey was finally defeated but the British Government did not help the Turkey on the repeated requests of the Indian Muslims. It frustrated the Indian Muslims, particularly Aligarh Muslims, because they had much expectation from the British Government.

Soon after the Tripoli War, Balkan War began from October 1912. During the progress of this war, anti-British feelings gained ground among educated young Muslims, especially at Aligarh.[16] On 17th October, 1912, after the Friday prayer at the MAO College mosque, the Muslims prayed for Turkish betterment. On 27th October, 1912, once again the people gathered at Aligarh. Even non-Muslims also gathered along with their Muslim brethren and expressed their sympathy with Turkey while demanding the release of Bal Gangadhar Tilak.[17] Maulana Shaukat Ali proposed volunteers to fight against Balkans and asked for government's help.[18]

However, in the Balkan War, much against the wishes of the Indian Muslims, the British Government once again pleaded and advised neutrality. The Aligarh Muslims never followed the advice of the British Government. Most of the Aligarh teachers, students and other Muslims felt that the Balkan War was not merely a political but a religious war for the entire Muslim community. This consideration was based upon the fact that the Austrians and Russians were also supporting and helping the Balkan states.[19]

It was interesting that the Balkan issue was not only confined to the men folk of the Indian Muslim community, but for the first time in the history of modern times, the Muslim ladies also came out boldly to condemn the Balkan war. On 29th November, 1912, Mrs. Mahmood Begum arranged a meeting of women in Aligarh and delivered a stirring speech persuading them to donate liberally to the victims of the Balkan war. She argued that it would be the participation by Muslim ladies in the Holy war.[20] Mrs. Mahmood Begum thus succeeded in raising a sum of Rs. 1,358/-.[21]

Maulana Shibli, on the commencement of the Balkan war in October 1912, was very much grieved and wrote a poetry entitled "*Shahr-Ashooh-i-Islam*."[22] In this poem Maulana Shibli described that how Islam is being attacked by combined European forces.

The MAO College students of Aligarh were very much emotional due to the Balkan war and the British diplomacy. In order to raise money for Turkey, they decided not to eat meat and rice.[23] They also demanded to the College management that the total of the fund collected for the establishment of the Muslim University should be given to Turkey. However, trustees of the college ignored this proposal.[24] In order to cure the war victims of Turkey, a medical mission led by Mukhtar Ahmad Ansari accompanied by Chaudhary Khaliquzzaman, Abdur Rahman Siddiqui, Shoaib Peshawari from MAO School was sent to Turkey in December 1912.[25]

The Turkish issue created a chasm among the trustees, teachers and students in Aligarh. Now, the groups of the loyalists and those having anti-British ideology or the nationalists had emerged in Aligarh. By that time, the loyalists were of the view that the establishment of a Muslim University could be only possible if the British Government would provide its approval. They were alluring a section of the Muslim community in favour of the British Government on the pretext of the establishment of a Muslim University. However, the loyalists in Aligarh were in great embarrassment when the India Office refused to approve the Government of India's recommendation to the elevation of MAO College to the status of a university on the terms proposed by the Muslims in 1912.[26]

The nationalists of Aligarh, by taking the advantage of the situation, held a series of secret meetings of students exposing the role of British Government in India and tanned their sentiments by citing the fate of Islam in Morocco, Persia and Turkey. Political agitation in Aligarh thus reached on its peak, causing great concern to the British high officials.[27]

Sir Valentine Chirol remarked that a new generation of young Mohammadans had nevertheless been growing up who knew not Syed Ahmad and regarded his teachings as obsolete.[28] Ali brothers backed by Maulana Abdul Bari of Firangi Mahal organized *Anjuman-i-Khuddam-i-Kaaba* in 1913 to raise funds to protect religious places of Muslims and to provide whatever assistance, they could to Turkey.[29]

Most of the Aligarh Muslims openly advocated pursuance of a policy of joint struggle against the British by joining hands with the Indian National Congress. Following the ongoing international situations now there was a clear shift among the youths of Aligarh and sure departure from Sir Syed's policy.

The manifestation of this attitude was first seen in the seizure of the office of Muslim League at Lucknow in 1912 by the nationalist youths from the loyalists. Wazir Hasan, T.A.K. Sherwani, Ali brothers, Hasrat Mohani, Zafar Ali Khan, Aziz Mirza, Musa Khan, Allama Shibli, etc. were its prominent leaders.[30]

The nationalists at Aligarh propagated their ideology very effectively. They opposed the Muslims who were still loyal to the British. They were impressed considerably with the ideology and policies of the Indian National Congress. By the writings, speeches and regular campaigns of the nationalists of MAO College, a number of students were inclined towards radicalism, and they became very critical of British Government and entertained the anti-British feelings. The Turkish problems in the First World War further strengthened the anti-British feelings among the MAO College students.

Khilafat and Non-Cooperation Movement in Aligarh

After a long time bloodshed and destruction of the properties, the inhuman First World War came to an end on 11th November, 1918. In this war, Turkey was defeated badly by the Allied powers and the Sultan of Turkey (*Khalifa*) became a puppet in their hands. It caused much resentment all-over the Muslim world. In India, the Muslim political leaders supported by the Congress, became very critical to the British Government. The Indian Muslims wanted an assurance to the safeguard of the Holy places of Islam in Mesopotamia and Arabia against Christian Allied powers.[31] The *Ulema* or the Muslim Theologians also supported the Muslim political leaders and assured them to fight for the Khilafat cause.[32]

According to Maulana Mohammad Ali, Khilafat was the most important institution for the entire Muslim world. It was also almost unanimously approved by the *Ulema* as well as the Muslim political leaders of the Congress and the Muslim League.[33]

In this crucial period in December 1918, the annual meeting of the Muslim League was held, and Khilafat issue was the main topic of debate. Dr. M.A. Ansari said that the Muslim holy places should be left intact. The other speakers in this meeting were Qazi Abdul Ghaffar, Mohammad Shoaib, Hasrat Mohani, Maulana Abdul Bari of Firangi Mahal and Maulana Azad Subhani. They all in their speeches repeated the issues raised by Dr. M.A. Ansari.[34]

On 17th October, 1919, on Friday, the first Khilafat Day was observed. Mahatma Gandhi was also one of the invitees by the Khilafat leaders. In his address, Mahatma Gandhi appealed to the Hindus to cooperate with the Muslim brethren at this hour of their grave concern.[35]

Mahatma Gandhi approved the idea, given by the Khilafat leaders, not to participate in the forthcoming peace celebration. On 16th November, 1919, Mahatma Gandhi presided over a meeting of 10,000 persons held at Delhi. In this meeting, an Anti-Peace Celebration Propaganda Committee was formed.[36]

On 23rd November, 1919, an All India Khilafat Conference was held. It was organized by Hakim Ajmal Khan and Dr. M.A. Ansari and presided over by Mahatma Gandhi in which it was officially declared not to participate in the peace celebration and if

Khilafat question was not settled, then it would be the duty of all the Muslims to withdraw cooperation from the British Government.[37]

Between November 1919 and May 1920, the Indian Muslims held a series of meetings under the Khilafat Committee. The Aligarh nationalists group took leading part in all these meetings.[38] Peace terms of the Treaty of Sevres were announced on 16th May, 1920. On the Peace terms of the Treaty of Sevres Mahatma Gandhi showed his reactions. Mahatma Gandhi's reaction to the Treaty of Sevres was spontaneous, sharp and quite clear, "a staggering blow to the Indian Musalmans and non-cooperation is the only effective remedy."[39]

The Treaty of Sevres made Turkey to renounce all rights in her former African possessions as well as Syria, Palestine, Mesopotamia and Arabia.[40] Nothing remained with Turkey except Constantinople and mountainous Anatolia. Meanwhile, the "*Young Turks*" led by Mustafa Kamal established their government at Ankara. They did not accept the Treaty of Sevres and started attacking on Allied occupations. They attacked Gallipoli peninsula, Cilicia and the French occupation. Young Turks won a series of victories against France, Italy and Britain. The Young Turks now set-up a new government under the name of Grand National Assembly.[41]

With the establishment of the new government within Turkey, a new political awakening and national unity were forged. This awakening reduced the hold of the Sultan of Turkey. His position as Khalifa of the Musalmans was also under the serious threat. While in Turkey, a new era had dawned, in India the Indian Muslims, by and large, stuck to their stand to protect the Khalifa and the Caliphate. In the meeting of Central Khilafat Committee at Allahabad in June 1920, Mahatma Gandhi put forward the Non-Cooperation in regard to honourary offices, titles and civil employment under the British Government.[42]

This proposal of the Non-Cooperation was opposed by the loyalist group of Aligarh led by Syed Raza Ali.[43] But the voice of the Aligarh loyalists was too weak against the dominant Aligarh nationalist group led by Maulana Shaukat Ali and supported by Maulana Abdul Bari. In the next meeting of the Khilafat Committee, a resolution of Non-Cooperation and Boycott, including the renunciation of titles, was passed.[44] It was also decided to establish contact with *Ulema* of Darul Uloom of Deoband, Firangi Mahal and Nadwatul Ulema of Lucknow.[45]

Not only in India, the Muslims were mobilizing the people in favour of Khilafat and Turkey, but in England, Sahibzada Aftab Ahmad Khan was making rigorous efforts to mobilize favourable opinion of the protection of Khilafat and Turkey.[46] In Aligarh, a large number of students took the interest in Khilafat Movement and supported Ali brothers and Hasrat Mohani. At this juncture, Mohammad Ali's criticism to the loyalists of Aligarh, like Shaikh Abdullah and Dr. Ziauddin Ahmad, can be easily understood.

Here it may be pointed out that the nationalists in Aligarh were also under constant attack by the loyalists. Shaikh Abdullah and Shaukat Ali during this period developed serious differences of opinion. Especially Shaikh Abdullah and like-minded persons strongly objected to the Shaukat Ali criticism of Sir Syed. Shaikh Abdullah alleged that the Ali brothers were pleading to send the donations raised for the Muslim University fund to Turkey. Mohammad Ali strongly argued that the Khilafat was at stake and what would be the use of a university in such a situation. However, the MAO College authorities could not trust Ali brothers believing that if the money was handed over to the Ali brothers, they would squander it.[47]

In the Lucknow meeting, another appeal was made by the name of the *Khalifa* that his existence was under threat and further declared that with the disappearance of Khilafat the name of Islam would be erased. Shaikh Abdullah bitterly criticized this objectionable argument. To counter the agitation for the Khilafat Movement, the Aligarh loyalists began to circulate pamphlets among the Muslims. One of the pamphlets carried Sir Syed's opposition to the institution of Khilafat. Despite the loyalist's determined efforts to counter the Khilafat propaganda in 1920, Ali brothers came to Aligarh for mobilizing students to join the movement. From Aligarh, they moved to London with a view to convince the government and the public for the Khilafat cause.[48] Mohammad Ali headed the London deputation and Syed Sulaiman Nadvi and Mr. Syed Husain were members of the deputation.[49]

The London deputation under the Ali brothers returned to India without any success. The Khilafat committees in the meantime had been very active in mobilizing general support in India for the Khilafat cause. On 1st August, on the occasion of Khilafat Day, a call for strike was given. Maulana Abul Kalam Azad issued a *Fatwa* (religious decree) declaring that according to the *Shariat* (Islamic Law) the Muslims of India had no choice but to migrate from India.[50] Following Maulana Abul Kalam Azad, a large number of *Ulemas* issued similar *Fatwas* supporting the Khilafat Movement.[51]

Maulana Azad's *Fatwa* and Ali brothers' arguments of *Hijrat* (migration) evoked a mixed reaction among the *Ulema*. Maulana Abdul Bari, an active supporter of the Khilafat, showed his disagreement over the issue of *Hijrat*.[52] Deoband School maintained neutrality over the issue of *Hijrat*. Ironically, Maulana Ashraf Ali Thanvi of Deoband School was also against the venture.[53] Maulvi Ahmad Raza Khan Barelvi, during this period, with a large follower of Sunni Muslims had been generally supporting the government policy and declined to support the Khilafat as well as *Fatwa* of *Hijrat*.[54]

Despite the divided opinion of *Ulema* on the *Hijrat* issue, a large number of Muslims from Punjab, Baluchistan and some from UP and Bihar migrated to Afghanistan as they expected a fair deal from the Amir of Kabul. However, they were disillusioned when the Amir of Afghanistan refused their entry. Consequently, the migrants suffered a setback. Many women and children died in harness.[55]

While thousands of Muslims were migrating from India, the MAO College was reeling under serious conflicting opinions. The government was bargaining with loyalists in Aligarh by promises of raising the status of MAO College to a university.[56] The Aligarh trustees thus were showing great interest in the establishment of a Muslim University rather than the Khilafat issue. This was naturally a great chagrin to Mualana Shaukat Ali and the like-minded old boys of the MAO College.

Mualana Shaukat Ali delivered an emotional speech chastising the trustees, "O Muslims! Remember this that one who has no love for *Khalifa* has no love for Islam.... I repeat *Kalima-e-Tauhid* and declare that in the service of Islam and in the service of *Khalifa*, I offer to sacrifice my life."[57] Mualana Shaukat Ali's pleadings and chastising to the Aligarh loyalists bore no fruit at all. The loyalists thought that the Khilafat propaganda was the nonsense. They struck to Sir Syed's concept and believed that the Khalifa of Turkey was no way their religious head.

On 4th September, 1920, a special session of the Indian National Congress was held at Calcutta and in spite of much opposition, the resolution of Non-Cooperation and Boycott was passed, which was earlier announced on 1st August, 1920. More stress was given in boycotting the councils, government courts and the educational institutions aided or supported by the British Government. The Khilafat Committee, Muslim League and Jamiatul Ulema also followed the same line. In December 1920, at Nagpur, the programme of Non-Cooperation was again adopted enthusiastically in the annual session of the Indian National Congress. Even C.R. Das and Lala Lajpat Rai who had opposed the programme in Calcutta session endorsed the programme.[58]

The anti-British feelings were considerably generated by the Ali brothers and Hasrat Mohani at Aligarh. A large number of students joined the Khilafat and Non-Cooperation Movement much to the displeasure of the trustees of the MAO College. Trustees did not wish to drag the college into the vortex of politics. They were keeping themselves away from the changed conditions and continued to stick to the object and loyalty to the Raj on an obvious endeavour to improve the position of the middle class Muslims.

The general Muslim population was still economically and educationally backward. No concerted effort seems to have been made to wage a crusade against backwardness, poverty and ignorance of the community. The MAO College trustees and other loyalists were unfortunately thrown to narrow politics of opposing the Khilafat and Non-Cooperation Movement. Credit must be given to those nationalist Muslims at Aligarh, who continued their journey on the road of nationalism with determination and resolution without caring acrimonies from the opponents.

Ali brothers and the like-minded students in Aligarh created an atmosphere surcharged with the nationalist activities. The loyalists were perplexed over such developments. To add to their discomfiture, the Ali brothers succeeded in persuading Mahatma Gandhi (Calcutta 4th September, 1920) to visit Aligarh. Responding to the call, Mahatma Gandhi accompanied with Swami Satyadeva,

Maulana Azad Subhani, Jan Mohammad and others, reached Aligarh on 11th October, 1920.[59]

Mahatma Gandhi's presence in Aligarh generated great pressure on the loyalists. Shaikh Abdullah stated the situation and concern of the loyalists in these words, "This caravan reached Aligarh. Gandhiji stayed at the house of Amir Mustafa Khan and Ali brothers stayed at the Old Boys Lodge with their friends. I asked Dr. Ziauddin Sahib the Principal (MAO College) that Ali brothers, Gandhiji and others should not be allowed to enter the college campus because they are coming with the intention to disturb our arrangements. Nevertheless, here Dr. Sahib (Ziauddin) showed weakness. He said, if we do so, the students who are with us would rise against us."[60]

It is notable that Shaikh Abdullah, a loyalist admits that the students on the Non-Cooperation issue were divided in the college campus and majority of them seems to be supporting the nationalist group in joining the Non-Cooperation Movement. Shaikh Abdullah sincerely felt that the students joining the Gandhian way would ruin the college and in turn harm the community.[61]

Shaikh Abdullah's great concern seems to have made him to refer Dr. Ziauddin's meetings with Gandhiji where the former told the latter, "If the students are misled and persuaded to quit the college, it would harm the college and the Muslim community greatly." Mahatma Gandhi replied to Dr. Ziauddin Ahmad, "When there would be our government, we would build a great college. At present we wish to get the college buildings and boarding houses vacated and establish Congress office and lodge Congress volunteers therein."[62]

The whole statement of Shaikh Abdullah does not seem to be correct. Dr. Ziauddin learnt of Ali brothers and Mahatma Gandhi's programme at Lucknow only on 10th October. He immediately reached Aligarh. His position was quite delicate. As a Principal of MAO College, he was under the continuous pressure of the trustees. He, however, met Mahatma Gandhi on the evening of 11th October and reminded him of his promise made in Delhi in March 1920 that he would issue a manifesto to the students not to participate in active politics. Dr. Ziauddin wished to know from Mahatma Gandhi the cause for this changed stand. Mahatma Gandhi replied that the Hunter Commission Report and the terms of the treaty for peace with Turkey had greatly influenced his opinion. Dr. Ziauddin then objected to Mahatma Gandhi's direct appeal to the students without the consent of the trustees, teachers and the Principal. Mahatma Gandhi said that from educational point of view he would not support his attitude, but for higher political reasons, he would reject such educational principles.[63]

The author of *Zia-i-Hayat* admits that Mahatma Gandhi knew that the trustees were not to take any risk for the stoppage of the government grants and the teachers were in general not prepared to take the risk of their jobs, hence Mahatma Gandhi's appeal was with the students.[64] It is noteworthy that Dr. Ziauddin Ahmad does not refer to Mahatma Gandhi's saying of construction of a greater college after the establishment of his government as stated by Shaikh Abdullah in his book *Mushahidat-o-Taassurat*. Moreover, such statements are alien to Mahatma Gandhi's style of politics.

Despite opposition to the loyalists, the nationalists led by Maulana Mohammad Ali organized a meeting in the afternoon of the 12th October, 1920. The nationalist students of the MAO College gave memorable reception to Mahatma Gandhi. He was also given the honourary membership of the Union Club.[65]

On this occasion, Maulana Mohammad Ali delivered an impressive speech. He asserted that Muslims are keen to save Islam, liberate it from the danger and release the *Khalifa* from the slavery. While indicating his aims and objectives Maulana Mohammad Ali asserted that the Muslims should join the Hindus and first secure freedom of the country. Regarding *Jihad,* he agreed with Mahatma Gandhi's view that the Indian Muslims did not possess the enough strength to carry on *Jihad*. Mohmmad Ali, however, agreed that *Hijrat* was permissible. He emphasised that the students of the MAO College should severe all connections with the British.[66]

Addressing the same meeting, Mahatma Gandhi strongly supported Mohammad Ali and exposed the real nature of the British rule and its policy of dividing the Muslims and Hindus on communal lines. The excerpt of his speech is as follows:[67]

> "...The heart of the Muslim brethren have therefore been deeply pained. The next thing is that the actions of the government in the Punjab after passing of the Rowlett Act

> have convinced both Hindus and Muslims that it is impossible to get justice from this government.... they made us Hindus and Muslims quarrel among ourselves. They used to speak very ill of Hindus before Muslims and Muslims before Hindus .... If Islam is in danger today, Hinduism is also in danger, for if it is Islam's turn today, it will be ours tomorrow....both (Hindus and Muslims) have decided that by fighting with the sword they would loose their money, their precious time and they would be enslaved still more as they do not possess guns and ammunitions in such quantities. We have received no such training from the government... we are taught the lessons of slavery in the Aligarh College. We should boycott this slavish education."

Mahatma Gandhi further said, "This is my first lesson ....when thirty crore of men combine and organise with a view not to have government in their midst, it would be impossible for government to remain in India ... we should boycott government educational institutions. It is shame for us that we have not as yet left them as the Non-Cooperation Movement has been in existence for some months. We should give up practicing as their lawyers. We will become mendicant. We will beg. We will subsist on rice and pulse. We will accept bare bread, but will take our liberty also with it. It is then alone we can be counted among the human beings. No one who is not free can engage himself in devotion to God .... we do not want their titles. We regard their titles as badges of slavery and want to return them. We do not want to send a single soldier or labourer in their army. It is our right and no one can use force towards us in this respect ... we are not going to enter their Legislative Councils ....Non-Cooperation is nothing more than sacrifice .... Indian has to pay seven crore of rupees for cloth and therefore Swadeshi Movement has also been included in this. Non-Cooperation with one means cooperation with others. Unless we have mutual regard for each other we cannot become united or organized."

Another speaker of the meeting Swami Satyadev strengthened Mahatma Gandhi's stand on the Non-Cooperation issue. He said that if they had faith in God, they should keep before their mind's eyes to the atrocities committed in the Punjab, and oppression practiced on the Mohammadans. He further said that the doctrine of Non-Cooperation was like a stream of nectar flowing into India and asked them to drink it. Then no one has the power to kill. They should think that they were going to repudiate the kingdom of *Satan* and establish the kingdom of God in the country and in the world.[68]

The speeches of the Non-Cooperation leaders stirred the students and teachers present in the meeting.[69] Undoubtedly, Ali brothers played the key role in mobilizing the students. According to the Intelligence Report on 12th October, 1920, Ali brothers aroused the sentiments of the students and ultimately the whole situation was changed.[70]

Almost all the students present in the Mahatma Gandhi's meeting were agreed to quit MAO College, but they were also keen to continue their studies. They decided to demand for the establishment another parallel college in Aligarh. Zakir Husain was the first student who renounced the scholarship and demanded for an independent college.[71]

Responding to the demand of the students, Ali brothers promised for the independent college and also promised to raise a sum of rupees one crore for that college.[72] On these assurances, seven hundred students decided to leave the MAO College and finally joined the movement.[73] It led to the adverse change in the politics of the MAO College for the loyalists of Aligarh. Some of the trustees of the college also changed their stand under the influence of the nationalists.

The nationalist trustees led by Hakim Ajmal Khan, Mohammad Ismail Khan, H.M. Moosa Khan and Amir Mustafa sent a requisition to the Honourary Secretary, MAO College, "In view of the open hostilities shown by Britain to Islam in Turkey... we, therefore, call upon you and other trustees of the college and members of the Muslim University Association to refuse hence forward to receive any aid from the government or to permit any kind of government interference, whether directly or indirectly through Allahabad University or any other agency in these institutions and we desire to inform all our other colleagues that we are also calling upon the teachers and adult students at Aligarh to withdraw themselves and other students to withdraw their wards from this college and school on 29th October, 1920, in the event of trustee's refusal to comply with these obvious requirements of the Islamic faith. We therefore request you with the earnestness at our command to take the action we recommend at earliest possible date and to treat this matter as of the greatest possible urgency."[74]

The students also passed the similar resolutions on 13th October, 1920:[75]

1. The meeting of the students of the Aligarh College strongly condemns the attitude adopted by British Government towards Turkey.
2. Approves the suggestion by the Khilafat Committee.
3. Strongly urges the trustees to stop receiving aid and disaffiliate the college from the government university.
4. If the trustees do not agree to this by 29th October, students will employ means of their power to turn the college into a national organization under the Khilafat Committee to train young men in Khilafat work and refuse any connection with the government chartered university.
5. Requests all title holders among the staff to renounce titles and resign honourary government posts and call upon the government scholarship holders to refuse to accept the scholarship.

The new uprising in the MAO College turned the table against the loyalists. College Secretary Syed Mohammad Ali was out of Aligarh at that time and Principal Dr. Ziauddin Ahmad was left alone to tackle the situation.[76] The college trustees were undoubtedly divided. A group with a considerable students' support played an important role into the national politics. The other group of the trustees still held its support for the British Government. The students and teachers in majority were now in favour of the Non-Cooperation Movement. Dr. Ziauddin Ahmad, Principal of the MAO College had no alternative but to close the college and break the solidarity of the college students on the Non-Cooperation and Khilafat issue. Closure of the college was followed by letters and telegrams to the parents of the students, "I appeal to you again that in the light of these circumstances, you would consider the situation as extremely grave and come up to Aligarh to take charge of your sons and relatives, as I feel that I cannot alone bear the burden of whole responsibility."[77]

The syndicate of the MAO College dominated by loyalists took strong measures against the nationalists of Aligarh. They prohibited the nationalists in delivering lectures and addressing students without written permission of the Principal.[78] The Honourary Secretary Syed Mohammad Ali also came and shared the problems with the Principal.[79]

To some extent, the syndicate and the Secretary strengthened the position of the Principal. The responses of the Principal's letters and telegrams issued to the parents of the college students seem to have greatly served the purpose. About 60 or 70 parents and guardians came at Aligarh and took their wards back home. Most of the parents send the telegrams and letters disapproving the politics of Ali brothers and Gandhiji in the college.[80]

The college authorities imposed a ban on the entry of Ali brothers and political activities in the campus. It seems that a very organized effort was made to break the solidarity of the nationalists ignoring the ban kept on meeting the students. A very organized effort was made to break the solidarity of the nationalist students. The Pioneer reported that the Bhopal State withdrew all Bhopal students. About 200 telegrams and letters have been received from old boys and friends from Gorakhpur, Mirzapur, Bhera, Loyalpur, Muzaffarnagar and other places expressing strong disapproval of the incident.[81]

Many parents still stayed in Aligarh. On 21st October, they passed a resolution in support of the college administration urging the trustees to take effective measures to stop entry of outsiders to the campus with the object of inciting the students to politics.[82]

On 23rd October, 1920, Mohammad Ali, Hakim Ajmal Khan, Dr. M.A. Ansari, Maulana Abul Kalam Azad, Azad Subhani, Maulvi Abdul Majid of Meerut and Abdul Ghaffar reached Aligarh from Delhi. They were accorded warm reception by the students and despite the ban, they held discussions with the College Khilafat Committee.[83]

After the *Maghrib* (evening) prayers, they declared to lay the foundation of a National University. Maulana Abul Kalam Azad was appointed as the Head of the Religious Instructions of the new institution. A list of the other university staff was also announced. Initially, the name of the new institution was suggested, "National Muslim University", which was to be established on 29th October, 1920. About half of the MAO College students decided to join the National Muslim University where both the collegiate and High School instructions were to be imparted.[84]

Establishment of the National Muslim University at Aligarh evoked the interest in Punjab. Dr. Saifuddin Kitchlew (Amritsar) and Dr. Mohammad Iqbal (Lahore) promised every help to the students. Many other students, like Zafar Husain, Kunwar Muhammad Ashraf were in the forefront on this occasion.[85]

The British Government, in order to weaken the growing nationalist trends, began to lure the talented and promising young students of better employment opportunity.[86] Zakir Husain was thus offered deputy collectorship through Dr. Ziauddin, the Principal of MAO College. Zakir Husain rejecting the offer, stood firm for the National Muslim University and nationalism.[87]

Taking cause from the stand of their seniors many young students courageously wrote to the Principal MAO College expressing that they were prepared to study in his college provided it adopted the creed of nationalism in place of loyalism. Failing they expressed the willingness to face the doom awaiting their non-cooperator brothers.[88]

Some of the students though under double pressure from parents and the college management were bold enough to raise the voice of their conscience defying authorities. Mushirul Hasan quotes a letter from one such student to the Principal, MAO College:[89]

> "My father has forced me to join your college once again, and I have reluctantly bowed to the parental authority. It is a mighty fall indeed, the whole enthusiasm ends in the air, but you cannot realize under what great mental torture I am labouring today."

Contrary to this, there were also the instances when the guardian themselves advised their wards to join the National Muslim University, abandoning the loyalists of the MAO College. The Intelligence Report submitted to the government during the period indicates great concern for the rise of nationalist forces in MAO College campus.[90] In one of its reports, the Intelligence Department expressed satisfaction that the non-cooperators were not much successful in the city though had exaggerated purposely.[91]

It is further said in the Intelligence Report that there was also no instance of great excitement, and the masses were unaffected. In the city, only one constable resigned his pension and a vakil Abdur Rahim announced his intention of retiring from practice. However, the intelligence official was alarmed at the situation in the MAO College as Mohammad Ali had got the signature of 200 students, who promised him their full support to the Non-Cooperation.[92] These 200 students (out of 900) were the firm and dedicated and kept on supporting the nationalists despite all pressure from the college trustees and the Principal.[93]

The situations in the MAO College definitely went out of control of the management. On 27th October, 1920, the trustees were called to hold a meeting at Aligarh to deal with the situation created by Mahatma Gandhi and Ali brothers in the campus. This meeting was held in the house of Nawab Mohammad Muzammilullah Khan. Sixty two trustees from all parts of the country took part in the meeting. There seem to have been the hectic debates. The trustees who favoured joining the main stream of the national movement were defeated after a more than eight hours meeting.[94]

The trustees voted in favour of Non-Cooperation were Hakim Mohammad Ajmal Khan, M.A. Ansari, Moazzam Ali, Zahoor Ahmad, Mohammad Ali, Amir Mustafa Khan, Haji Moosa Khan, A.M. Khwaja, Agha Safdar of Sialkot, Ismail Khan, Syed Nasir Husain, T.A.K. Sherwani, Syed Mohammad Khan, and Quasim Husain of Hyderabad State Services.[95] Forty eight trustees voted against the Non-Cooperation and they passed three resolutions at the meeting. The first resolution rejected the proposal to give up the government grant and to disaffiliate the college. The second resolution emphatically disapproved the action of Shaukat Ali and others in obtaining direct access to the students in defiance of the

Principal. The third resolution confirmed the syndicate. Principal and the staff expressed disapproval of the Non-Cooperation.[96]

The college, which had already been closed by the Principal, was further extended to 30th November by the trustees.[97] However, the nationalists were stood firm on their goal. Even after being defeated on the Khilafat and Non-Cooperation issue by the board of trustees, Ali brothers did not give way. They decided not to leave the college. They also resolved to lay the foundation of a national university at Aligarh on 29th October, 1920, to support the nation's call for boycotting educational institutions run and aided by the British Government.[98]

MAO College loyalist group dominating the syndicate with full government support was determined to take a firm action against Ali brothers. The Honourary Secretary with full support of the syndicate issued a notice to Mohammad Ali asking him to vacate the college premises immediately. He also asked him to withdraw students and supporters and abstain from holding any meeting within the college boundaries.[99]

The Secretary's notice was taken as a challenge by Mohammad Ali and his fellows. They firmly decided not to leave the college, although, a number of old boys also requested him to withdraw peacefully from the college premises. Mohammad Ali, in the meantime had entrenched himself by taking possession of one wing of the boarding house and refused to yield.[100]

In the evening of the 28th October, a massive meeting was held on the steps of Aligarh city Jama Masjid, and about 5,000 people were present in that meeting. While speaking in the meeting, Mohammad Ali condemned the actions of the trustees and their supporters. Mohammad Ali intelligently used his talents and dexterity to win people's sympathies and support. He fully utilized the Khilafat issue, which had already made a large number of Muslims against the government. Exploring the Khilafat sentiments he told the people that they had come with a message of religion, which was met with the vote of censure by the trustees.[101] Emotion ran high and there were loud cries "kill Ziauddin" the Principal of MAO College.[102]

In order to lay the foundation of the National Muslim University, Mohammad Ali issued invitations to attend the inaugural ceremony of the national university on 29th October, 1920.[103]

Now, an open confrontation with the MAO College authorities and the nationalists led by Mohammad Ali was inevitable. Though closure of the college had been officially announced, a number of nationalist students still held ground in the hostel. Until then, the students of MAO School did not join the nationalist students of the college. In order to force all the college and school students, the Principal Dr. Ziauddin, ordered the cutting of electric and water supplies, stoppage of food, forbidding the sweepers from scavenging. He also ordered the locking of hostel rooms. The school students were forced to return home without leave, arbitrarily.[104]

As the idea of Non-Cooperation had become popular about that time, Mahatma Gandhi appealed to the parents of Aligarh students to understand the value of the programme and let they allow freedom to their boys from parental bounds. Mahatma Gandhi also advised them to admit their boys in the national institutions set-up by the religious and charitable Hindu and Muslim funds.[105]

Apart from the known nationalist leaders, there were many student leaders, who were on the forefront of the Non-Cooperation Movement in Aligarh. One of them was Kunwar Mohammad Ashraf, a student of B.A., abandoning his education at MAO College; he joined the National Muslim University. Kunwar Mohammad Ashraf was one of the brilliant students of the MAO College. He opposed the policy of loyalism and was a great preacher of nationalism. He commanded great influence among the students including the Hindus. During the Khilafat and Non-Cooperation Movement in Aligarh, he seized an opportunity to mobilize the opinion in favour of the movement.[106]

On the occasion of the *Eid Milad-un-Nabi*, Kunwar Mohammad Ashraf addressed a 2,000 strong audience comprising of both Hindus and Muslims at the Aligarh city Jama Masjid. In view of the importance of his speech, a portion of it, is being reproduced as follows:[107]

> "The time has now come that the nation, which wants you to sit here in peace and tranquility, may kill you one day with their tyrant hands like thousands of Muslims and other souls massacred by them..... I want to assure you that if you give a slap to the meanest or kick an ordinary Ticket

> Collector, then you lose all estimation in the eyes of the English, but revered *Shaikhul-Islam* is sent to the Malta in chains. It is not necessary to *Jihad* with those accursed (*Mardoods*), who tried to occupy *Haram-e-Kaaba* and those malign, who have occupied Najaf, Baghdad and *Baitul Muqaddas* (Jeruslam) and committed massacre there."

Kunwar Mohammad Ashraf gave the example of Holy *Quran*, "if anyone kills you, and you are innocent, you must take revenge." He further continued his speech, "This is the demand that must be ready for *Jihad* now. We must today be ready and massacre those *Haramzadas*, who are oppressing us ....you help that *Haramzadi* Government... so that your *Khalifa* may be destroyed.... Now is the time when not only your rule, your honour, but even your faith is at stake... your own object is to cause the English to suffer so that their feelings be burnt."

Kunwar Mohammad Ashraf continued his speech, "By the grace of God, the British Empire has become such a destructive that you can have a good opportunity to give them a blow...if you have a sense to unite together you can 'destruct' them very soon... Now, when not your nation alone, but even your religion and Khilafat are at stake, you have no sense of feelings in you....in short the nation which bombarded the Barrusa Mosque, that *Mardood* nation, which massacred 15,000 Turks in Adrianople, is the same nation, which has outraged modesty of wives and women, which had made over our sisters to the Negroes. In short if you cannot bring your revenging power into passion, it is a matter of regret. Brethren, what passion? You must be ready for *Jihad* just at this very moment."

The Khilafat leaders made every effort to arouse religious zeal of the Muslims in favour of *Khalifa*. However, in the meantime Mustafa Kamal Pasha set-up a nationalist government in Ankara. He compelled the Italian troops to quit southern Anatolia and expelled the French troops from Cilicia. He overthrew the recently established Armenian Republic. He also expelled not only the Greek soldiers, but every Greak inhabitant from Asia Minor.[108]

Mustafa Kamal's victory gave a strong moral support to the Khilafat leaders in India. All India Khilafat Conference of Karachi in 1921 congratulated Mustafa Kamal Pasha and his National

Government for his glorious victories. On the occasion, seven leading Khilafat leaders viz. Ali brothers, Maulana Husain Ahmad Madani, Dr. Saifuddin Kitchlew, Pir Ghulam Mujadid, Maulvi Nisar Ahmad and Bharti Krishna Tirathji *alias* Venkataraman delivered speeches asking the Muslims not to join the British army. Responding over their speech, the British Government in India took a serious note on it and criminal proceedings instituted against them.[109]

AMU under the Influence of Congress and Muslim League

When the Khilafat and Non-Cooperation Movements were going on in Aligarh, a section of the Muslim intelligentsia remained loyal to the British Government. They were in the hope of getting the charter of the Aligarh Muslim University. Soon they got the reward and in December 1920, the MAO College was elevated to the status of Aligarh Muslim University. However, as the Jamia Millia Islamia also had been established in Aligarh in the same year, the activities of the Khilafat and Non-Cooperation did not stop and gained momentum day by day.

Most of the non-cooperators, who were admitted in Jamia Millia Islamia had their friends in AMU and utilised a fair chance to convince the students of the AMU. Although, the authorities of the AMU were not in favour of any political movement in Aligarh, but its students driven by their youth hot blood and national feelings had secretly engaged in political activities. They were touch of the national movement, which continued until the suspension of the Non-Cooperation Movement and end of the Caliphate or that of the Khilafat Movement.

The English daily "Englishman" of 17th July, 1924, (published in London), remarked about the meeting of the AMU Association held at the Savoy Hotel. In that meeting Lord Meston made a confession that efforts to induce Indian (AMU) undergraduates not to engage themselves in politics were hopeless.[110]

The first Vice-Chancellor of the AMU was Ali Mohammad Khan, Maharaja of Mahmudabad. He was, although, a loyalist but also had the nationalist feelings and was a staunch supporter of Hindu-Muslim unity.[111] Maharaja of Mahmudabad was a man of

Congress mentality and a good friend of Moti Lal Nehru, Sarojni Naidu and Miss Annie Besant. He also attended the Amritsar session of the Indian National Congress presided over by Motilat Nehru.[112] It was very much natural that during his Vice-Chancellorship, the students would have been affected by nationalist activities and Congress policies.

The second Vice-Chancellor of AMU, Sahibzada Aftab Ahmad Khan, was undoubtedly a loyalist in order to secure the help of British Government for AMU and Muslim community, but he had Congress ideology and character. He was against the political and educational ideas of the other loyalists and had sympathy with the Congress policies.[113] Sahibzada's loyalty and affection to the Congress was evident by the fact that, much against the wishes of the government officials and other loyalists, he performed the duties of Vice-Chancellorship by wearing *Khadi Sherwani*.[114]

In AMU, he admitted the nationalist minded Muslim students, who had taken active part in Non-Cooperation Movement. During the Vice-Chancellorship of Sahibzada Aftab Ahmad Khan, the students also devoted their time and energy to their studies because after the suspension of the Non-Cooperation Movement, the students had diverted their mind to their studies. Even the students of Jamia Millia Islamia fully attracted towards the AMU as the degrees of Jamia had no recognition from government. These newly admitted Jamia students, who were having the nationalist background, created a national atmosphere at the AMU.[115]

Due to the growing nationalism in AMU, not only the Congress but the Congress backed political party named Swaraj Party had also a firm footing in AMU. Many leaders of this party visited Aligarh, they took part in the debates and discussions conducted by the AMU Students Union from time to time. On 15th March, 1925, two distinguished public men Mr. Chaman Lal and Mr. T.C. Goswami (MLA) took part in the debate on the topic, "The scheme of Swaraj Party will hasten the advent of Swaraj in India."[116]

After the failure to the Swaraj Party on the political front, the Congress once again succeeded in acquiring the support of the students of the AMU. In 1927-28, the AMU Students Union declared that "....the Aligarh union heralded that Non-Cooperation Movement for good or for worse. The students have led the most astounding agitations in the late MAO College days and they cannot even today be blamed for their community and the country. The students have led most custodians of their own rights in our university and they should be such even today. Aligarh has ever been proud of the achievement of its boys both present and past."[117]

The Congress leaders deliberately visited the university (AMU Union Club) and gladly accepted membership of the students union. In 1928-29, the leaders, including Mrs. Annie Besant and Dr. Shafaat Ahmad Khan visited Aligarh. Mrs. Annie Besant was made life member of the union.[118] Next year in 1929-30, Mr. M.K. Jayakar and Mahatma Gandhi visited Aligarh and delivered memorable speeches before the students. Mahatma Gandhi became the life member of AMU Students Union.[119] In the Year 1931-32, the members of the union had the privilege of being addressed by the distinguished nationalists like Dr. Shafaat Ahamd Khan, Azad Subhani and Mr. T.A.K. Sherwani.[120]

At the time of Vice-Chancellorship of Sir Ross Masood, the AMU students of Congress mentality had the great fortune of having the chance to meet and listen to the likes of Jawahar Lal Nehru, Dr. Shafaat Ahmad and Sir Tej Bahadur Sapru.[121]

At the beginning of 1937, Sarojini Naidu was invited to AMU. While welcoming her, the Vice-President of the University Union said that Aligarh was welcoming the first lady of the land. He also said that she was made an honourary life member of the union 20 years ago when many of the students were not even born. Mrs. Naidu, addressing the students, said that Indian National Congress under the leadership of her great friend and leader Jawahar Lal was struggling for India's freedom and that she herself was carrying the torch of Indian freedom from one part of India to another. She stressed "some twenty years ago I came here to hand over the torch of freedom but none cared to take it, they want that I should address the sons and daughters of free India and tell them the stories of heroic deeds of those who inhabits in halls and hostels of Aligarh today."[122] She appealed to the students to cultivate an international outlook and make every effort to see India free.[123]

Hayatullah Ansari, a Congress minded nationalist and President of the "Aftab Majlis", had invited Pandit Jawahar Lal Nehru to come to Aligarh and address the students of the AMU. At that time, Sir Ross Masood was the Vice-Chancellor of AMU. Sir Ross Masood was a dynastic friend of Jawahar Lal Nehru, but it was also equally important for him to maintain good relations with the British Government while being the Vice-Chancellor of AMU. When Jawaharlal Nehru arrived at Aligarh, it was a dilemma before Sir Ross Masood as to how tackle the situation.[124]

Sir Ross Masood went to the railway station to receive him and after a grand welcome, he brought Pandit Jawahar Lal Nehru directly to his residence just like a dynastic friend. From there Pt. Nehru and Ross Masood reached Stretchy Hall, where Pandit Jawahar Lal Nehru addressed a large gathering of students, and they listened to him with rapt attention.[125]

Outside the university campus, the Aligarh city was visited by the Congress leaders many times, and there they made a great number of supporters for their activities. On 29th January, 1926, Lala Lajpat Rai visited Aligarh and was given a reception at the railway station. He presided over the Achhutoddhar Conference in the local Arya Samaj Temple. The municipal board presented an address before him and later in his own speech, he appealed for continued Hindu-Muslim unity.[126]

On 26th November, 1927, the United Provinces Political Conference was inaugurated in Aligarh by Pt. Govind Ballabh Pant. Kailash Nath Katju hoisted the Congress flag and explained the importance of Congress flag under which all sections of India should unite. By opening the exhibition of *Khadi*, he explained the economic significance of *Khadi* and Mahatma Gandhi's love for it. Among the presentees were Shiv Prasad Gupta, Sampurnanand, Sita Sahai, Kishan Chand Sharma, T.A.K. Sherwani, Krishna Dutt Paliwal, Deo Narayan, Udai Vir and many others. The conference was attended by nearly 2,000 persons.[127]

Besides Indian National Congress, the All India Muslim League had also made inroads into Aligarh, but it had no firm footing in AMU or Aligarh city until 1936. Although, Mr. Mohammad Ali Jinnah frequently visited Aligarh, he could not succeed in getting any substantial support. Until that time both Congress and the Muslim League had similar political programmes against the British Government.

Until 1936, Muslim League had not adopted any separatists or communal approach, and Congress had also favoured the Muslims in their demand. That's why Muslim League had no firm footing, not only in Aligarh, but anywhere in UP and Congress was very much popular among the Muslims. In UP, the Muslim League was mere a small group, led by Nawab Mohammad Ismail and Chaudhary Khaliquzzaman, rather than a political party. The differences between the Congress and Muslim League arose on the issue of the distribution of portfolios of UP ministry in 1937.

On 31st March, 1925, Mr. Mohammad Ali Jinnah visited Aligarh and took part in the Aligarh Muslim University Union debate on the motion "the time has come that immediate steps be taken to establish a responsible government in India."[128]

Muslim League got the opportunity to express their point of view before the Aligarh students at the time of Jubilee Celebration of AMU in December 1925. On this great occasion, the 7th session of the All India Muslim League was held from 30th December, 1925, to the beginning of the January 1926. Sir Abdur Rahim was the President of the 7th session of the All India Muslim League. Among those presents were Mian Sir Mohammad Shafi, Shaukat Ali, Seth Yaqub Hasan, Dr. Abdur Rahim and Mr. Sorabji Rustamji of the South African delegation. Shaikh Abdullah was the Chairman of the reception committee, who welcomed the League to Aligarh.[129]

Mr. Jinnah in inviting Dr. Abdur Rahim to take chair said that by the cooperation of the assembled people, the League would achieve the results, which would benefit not only the Muslim community but India as a whole. Dr. Abdur Rahim in his Presidential address emphasized the grave conditions of Indian Muslims as a result of communal riots prevailing all-over India. He also refuted the allegations made by their Hindu brethren that Indian Muslims had to lack of patriotism as they were interested in the fate of their coreligionists abroad. He asserted that some Hindus were actively engaged in conspiracies with foreign societies, whose primary object was to cause trouble in India. According to him, such people were a serious challenge to Islam and grave threat to the political status of the Muslims.[130]

On 20th October, 1926, the AMU Students Union, as part of their social and intellectual activates, organised a jubilee debate in which distinguished visitors, including Sir Ali Iman, Sir Abdur Rahim, Mr. Mohammad Ali Jinnah, Sir Mian Mohammad Shafi, Mr. Abdullah, Yusuf Ali, etc. took part. Several *Ulema* were also present.[131]

In the session of 1929-30, prominent leaders of Muslim League like Mr. Mohammad Ali Jinnah and Dr. Sir Mohammad Iqbal visited university and graced the union by addressing it. Dr. Sir Mohammad Iqbal was made the life member of AMU Students Union.[132]

It is a fact that every Muslim League leader, who visited Aligarh had no separatist ideas in his mind but was inspired by nationalist feelings and did his very best to ameliorate the position of the Muslims of India. The AMU became the symbol of advancement for Muslims and the only source of hope for them. Not only the Indian Muslims sympathised with it but their Hindu brethren as has been said earlier had frequently visited Aligarh in order to extend their support to the university and give guidelines to the students.

The other countries outside India were also influenced by the pattern of education in AMU and its emancipation work. His Majesty Ghazi Mohammad Nadir Shah the King of Afghanistan announced the donation of Rs. 3,600/- annually to the AMU and invited two leading educationalists Sir Ross Masood and Dr. Sir Mohammad Iqbal to Kabul to advise him on educational matters.[133]

The mixed influence of the Congress and the Muslim League in Aligarh, particularly AMU created a unique political atmosphere and made the Aligarh students purely secular in their thought, policy and behaviour. One of its result was that Shaikh Abdullah (Alig) formed the Independent Muslim Party in October 1926, and declared that it would prepare to cooperate not only the political party the aim of which may be common good of the country but on occasions, it will be ready to lend its support to the government and throw its weight against any of the parties whose object will be the defeat of the higher national aims through its narrow-minded communalism. The Independent Muslim Party had its goal for attainment of self-government in India by constitutional means. It also declared that it would not tolerate the introduction of any such measure that may not be in consonance with the special interest of the Muslim community.[134]

The nationalism in Aligarh reached its climax, when a group led by Maulana Syed Tufail Ahmad Manglori opposed the separate electorate for the Muslims. It was in sharp contrast with his ideology of the day, when he was a member of the Muslim League. In 1936, he joined the Congress and strengthened his relations with Babu Sampurna Nand and Sir Tej Bahadur Sapru, Dr. Shafaat Ahmad and Dr. Syed Mahmood.[135]

It cannot be ignored that the students had most actively adopted the nationalist flavour of Aligarh politics. It made them more efficient and confident and men of independent thinking. In August 1936, there was a strike in AMU against the injustice meted out to the students. No doubt the immediate cause was the rustication of a student, but the real cause was political awakening of the students and their nationalist feelings. A group led by Kunwar Mohammad Ashraf sided with the students and demanded from the university authorities to call back the rusticated students and not to do any harassment to the students, who were participants in the strike.[136]

On the intervention of Kunwar Mohammad Ashraf, the authorities assured him that the treatment meted out to the strikers would be lenient as was consistent with the maintenance of the university discipline. Even the ring leaders stood a very fair chance of making up the required percentage of attendance for the year 1936-37, if they attended their classes regularly after their return to Aligarh on the dates fixed for them. No student who did not participate in the strike was punished.[137]

The university authorities decided to take a lenient view of conduct for the freshers, who were misguided by the senior students, but it was felt necessary to call explanations from them and give them due warning through their parents and guardians.[138]

The Pro-Vice Chancellor Mr. A.B.A. Haleem explained to the Vice-Chancellor about the strike as follows:[139]

> "There was students' rainy season pastime, locally known as 'mud-riot' in the university in the course of which some students of the V.M. Hall ragged a fresher residing with a warden himself. One of the students was fined Rs. 15/- by the acting Provost. The student whose offence was graver reported to me and on the written recommendation of the Provost, I ordered his rustication. About 60 or 70 students of V.M. Hall came to my house. I told that discussion with

a mob was not possible. To the representatives, who remained with me, I explained that my order must be obeyed, but if the rusticated student left Aligarh and applied for re-admission, his case would be considered."

"The student left Aligarh and applied after a few days. No other representation was made to me by the students verbally or in writing. While the application of the rusticated student was under my consideration, the students of the V.M. Hall went on strike all of a sudden on Tuesday last. They refused to eat their meals in the Dining Hall or to attend their lectures; the gates of the hall were closed and thereafter even the members of the staff were only admitted on sufferance. The acting Provost informed me that he had discussed the matter with the students for several hours but they were not prepared to listen the reasons, their demand being that the rusticated students should be recalled and the warden incharge should be dismissed before they brought the strike to an end."

"After the strike had continued for two days in spite of all possible efforts of the officers in charge, matter was carefully considered by Academic Council on Thursday, August 13, 1936 and it was decided to remove the name of all students of V.M. Hall who did not return to their normal life by 8.00 A.M. on Friday from the rolls of the university, their re-admission, however, was permitted on such conditions as may be deemed fit. The students were addressed by you (Vice-Chancellor) and myself on Friday. We did our very best to assure them that the authorities had the utmost regard for the present convenience and the future careers of all the students, but it was not possible for us either to dismiss university officers or to cancel disciplinary orders at the dictate of the strikers."

"I very much regard to say that in spite of all these efforts, the students of V.M. Hall decided to spread the strike to other Halls. The Academic Council therefore directed the university to be dosed for the autumn vacation immediately, i.e. w.e.f. 15th August, 1936, instead of 13th September, 1936, as had been previously notified. On the evening of

> Friday, August 15, the students of V.M. Hall rushed into S.S. and Aftab Halls, closed the gates, but they failed to enlist the sympathy for more than a handful of the students in either Hall. On Saturday and Sunday the students of these Halls left for their houses in obedience to the order of the authorities with the exception of the few, who are preparing for competitive examinations or came from long distances and have been permitted by me to remain in residence during the autumn vacation."
>
> "The majority of V.M. Hall students also have realised their mistakes and have tendered written and unconditional apology for their behaviour to their Provost Mr. A.M. Qureshy. By Sunday evening all the hostels of V.M. Hall were cleared of their occupants and I am glad to inform you that the strike is quite over...."

It was not only a strike but a fight between nationalism and loyalism. It was, undoubtedly, a brilliant example of the national flavour gaining ground in the AMU. However, from that time for one year, the political activities in Aligarh came to a standstill and resumed only after the election of 1937, and the formation of Congress ministry in UP. The opposition of Muslim League to the Congress ministry again warmed up the political atmosphere in Aligarh.

Efforts of Hindu-Muslim Unity and Role of AMU

In order to promote Hindu-Muslim unity and strengthen nationalist feelings in Muslim community, Shaikh Abdullah formed Independent Muslim Party. This party did not allow narrow minded communalists to join it. Its aim was to cooperate with any political party, the aim of which may be the common good of the country. This party set before it as its goal, the attainment of self-government in India by constitutional means but also supported the special interests of the Muslim community.[140]

The Independent Muslim Party attracted many secular minded Muslims. By its campaign of nationalism, the loyalist group of Aligarh also started favouring the ideology of Shaikh Abdullah. His party played an important role in preventing the communal tensions between two communities by propagating the brotherly feelings and nationalism. He expressed the secular and patriotic ideas in many public meetings.

In 1925, when the session of All India Muslim League was held at Aligarh, Shaikh Abdullah, as Chairman of the Reception Committee gave a remarkable address regarding the communal problem which has been quoted as follows:[141]

> "....the real cause of the Hindu-Muhammadan estrangement and strife in these days is to be found in the notions of false patriotism of certain leaders.... the notion of Swaraj of a single community has unquestionably been sprung from some unhealthy brain and I hope its absurdity will soon be declared by the commonsense of Hindu community itself... the League has got a very clear duty before it in this behalf and it must do something to stop the further growth of the great mischief to the cause of the motherland..."

Shaikh Abdullah further said, "I assure the critics that the generality of the Musalmans, and particularly their educated classes are as good patriots as the Hindu themselves. Of course, the Musalmans of India have got much warmth in their feelings for Musalmans all-over the world, based as they are on the conception of Islamic brotherhood; but at the same time they are not ignoring their duty to their motherland.... telling the whole body of my brethren in faith that the love of our motherland is our permanent duty not on national ground only but on religious ground also. No Musalman should ignore that love of the motherland is one of the articles of our faith and it should be cherished as such."

Unfortunately, after the suspension of the Non-Cooperation Movement, the fierce riots were started all-over the country. Many political leaders and intelligentsia tried their level best to bring to an end the fierce communal riots. A fast was undertaken by Mahatma Gandhi in Delhi when he was in jail. The common people also came to Delhi from different communities to cope with the challenges of communalism. Pandit Moti Lal Nehru presided over the Unity Conference to consider the whole question of communalism. The leaders of both the communities sincerely attempted to bring about unity between the two communities. Even those leaders who had been most opposed to the spirit of Mahatma were loudest in their demand to release Mahatma Gandhi and started to follow the path of Hindu-Muslim unity.[142]

No doubt the single hope of unity and the end of communal riots was Mahatma Gandhi. Nevertheless, this step of Hindu-Muslim unity and national programme of Mahatma Gandhi was not appreciated by some fanatic Hindus and Muslims and they criticised him in their own way. The Hindus said, "you asked the Hindus to make common with the Musalmans on the Khilafat question. That resulted in unifying and awakening the Musalmans and now that the Khilafat is over and the awakened Musalmans have proclaimed a kind of *Jihad* (holy war) against us."[143]

On their part, the Musalmans said, "We simple minded people have been unjustly treated. You by your agitation won over Mohammad Ali to your side and you attacked the famous institution at Aligarh built with patient care by Sir Syed Ahmad. Your boycott of councils prevented our able men from going to the council to fight against the prejudice of the interests of our community."[144] Maulana Mohammad Ali was blamed by Muslims as a Gandhi worshipper.[145]

Most of the Muslim leaders were either the followers of Mahatma Gandhi or members of other secular bodies, and staunchly supported Hindu-Muslim unity. Only a handful of Muslims, who were engaged in counter movements of *Shuddhi* named *Tabligh* and *Tanzeem* opposed the Hindus for their anti-Muslim activities. The Aligarh Muslim University was also a supporter of the Hindu-Muslim unity much against the wishes of British Government. That's why in 1930, Sir Malcolm Haily and Lord Irwin made a diagnosis and told about the Aligarh University that the Muslim community had failed to produce the leaders.[146]

Aligarh remained peaceful throughout the sensitive years of communal riots except in September 1925, a time when the *Ramlila* festival (*Dashehra* festival) was about to be celebrated. This Hindu festival gave rise to acute communal tension in many places of India, including Aligarh. Its celebration was marked by one of the worst riots of the year. In Aligarh, the riot assumed such a dangerous position that the police were compelled to fire to restore order and five persons were killed either by the police or the rioters.[147]

Actually, the disturbance started following the order of the Aligarh Collector Mr. Darvin not allowing the Ramlila Committee to play music before the mosque at all times without the consideration of the time of the Musalman for saying their prayers. The Ramlila Committee protested against the restrictions, and Musalmans demanded that the old and time honoured traditions should be followed, and the stoppage of music before the mosque should be strictly adhered to.[148]

Perhaps this was the only instance of disturbances, which had wounded the secular history of Aligarh; and it was very strange that Aligarh University was untouched by any type of disturbances and communal riot. This is very much proved by the fact that when the whole India was burning in the communal fire, the Aligarh University organised a debate on the occasion of Jubilee Celebration in 1925. The topic of the discussion was "Hindu Muslim unity is the urgent need of today." The debate was attended by many Muslim leaders, including Mr. Ghulamus Saiyadain, Sir Shafaat Ahmad Khan, Sir Ali Imam and Mr. Mohammad Ali Jinnah.[149]

National Programmes and AMU

The Aligarh Muslim University, being the national symbol and the symbol of Hindu Muslim unity, always extended its cooperation to the national leaders in their national programmes. The university maintained the secular credential and national character until Mr. Jinnah's separatistic approach. After launching the Pakistan Movement by Muslim League, its policy had deviated towards the situational trends. Nevertheless, the *alumni* of the *alma mater* always shouted the national goals for the freedom of the country.

Simon Commission

Some days before the general election of 1927, in England, the Conservative Government appointed Indian Statutory Commission in November, 1927 popularly known as Simon Commission after the name of its Chairman Sir John Simon. It was an all-white commission and did not include any Indian in it. The aim of the commission was to enquire the working of the system of government, development of representative institutions and matters connected with the constitutional problems.

All the Indian political leaders decided to boycott the Simon Commission. Maulana Abul Kalam Azad with the help of Dr. M.A. Ansari and Mr. T.A.K Sherwani formed the Muslim Nationalist Party in order to bring the Indian Muslims in the national fold. He created a band of the people for the oppositions of Simon Commission and other objectionable activity of the British Government.[150] Over the issue of opposing the Simon Commission, the Muslim League was divided into two groups—one was led by Mohammad Ali Jinnah, who opposed the commission and the other was led by Shafi and Fazl-i-Husain who supported the Simon Commission.[151] *Jamiatul Ulema*, Khilafat Committee, etc. also opposed the commission. Other prominent Muslim leaders who opposed the commission were Sir Ali Imam, Syed Hasan Imam, Maharaja of Mahmudabad, Sahibzada Aftab Ahmad Khan, Maulana Mohammad Ali and Shaukat Ali, etc.[152]

The Indian nationalists became active, when Simon Commission landed at Bombay on 3rd February, 1928. All the major cities and towns observed a complete *hartal*. Rallies, black flag demonstrations and processions were held. Mohammad Ali Jinnah was the first to raise the protest cry "Simon go back." He declared, "Jallianwala Bagh was the physical butchery, the Simon Commission is the butchery of the soul."[153]

In Lucknow on 28th-30th November, a grand reception was given to the Simon Commission by the talluqdars and Khaliquzzaman floated kites and balloons with 'Go Back Simon' slogans. Jawahar Lal Nehru and Govind Ballabh Pant were beaten up by the police.[154] Raja of Mahmudabad and his men were also meted out the same as Chaudhary Khaliquzzaman from his *kothi*. The police also raided the residence of Raja of Mahmudabad.[155]

Aligarh was also very much affected by the storm of this movement. *Hartal* and demonstrations were very successful. Processions were marched all-over the city waving black flags and banners carrying "go back Simon" slogan.[156] Many prominent leaders of Aligarh like Malkhan Singh and Hanuman Prasad Vakil gave thrilling speeches and motivated public mind against Simon Commission as well as the British Government. The visit of Mahatma Gandhi in Aligarh in November 1929 mobilised the people into action for the national cause.[157] T.A.K. Sherwani, Sahibzada Aftab Ahmad Khan, etc. also left no stone unturned to oppose the Simon Commission.[158]

The involvement of the above leaders might have instigated the students of AMU, but there is no documentary proof of the active participation of Aligarh Muslim University students in the anti-Simon campaign, except a few local people's oral statement. They say that a section of the students was always in the university, which participated in all anti-government campaigns.

Nehru Report

Lord Birkenhead, the Secretary of State for India in the Conservative Government, made a taunt that Indians were quite incapable to formulate a concrete scheme of constitutional reforms, which had the support of wide sections of Indian political opinions. Liberal politicians like Sir Tej Bahadur Sapru and Muslim leaders headed by Mr. Mohammad Ali Jinnah joined hands with the Congress to accept the challenge of the British Government. Nearly all political parties, except Justice Party in Madras and Punjab Unionist, decided to formulate a new Constitution. On 20th March, 1927 in Delhi, Mohammad Ali Jinnah persuaded the Muslim leaders in an informal conference regarding new Constitution. In this conference, it was resolved that the Muslims would accept joint electorate on some conditions.[159]

To cope with the challenge of the Secretary of State, almost all the political parties joined together to form a Constitution. The all party's conference, which met in February, May and August 1928, finalised a report of the Constitution known as Nehru Report after the name of its author Moti Lal Nehru. The report defined the dominion status as a form of government desired by India.[160]

The Nehru Report was ready, but in spite of its acceptance as a Constitution, some of the top-ranking Muslim nationalist leaders like Maulana Mohammad Ali and Shaukat Ali opposed the Nehru Report, as its aim was dominion status for India. They demanded complete Independence as their goal. Mohammad Ali said in the all-party convention of December 23, 1928 at Calcutta, "I do not ask for dominion status under British or Hindus or Musalmans or Turkey or Afghansitan. But I want freedom for myself and my country." He further said, "I ask for no Constitution except one article namely that India shall be free and independent."[161]

Maulana Shaukat Ali, in presiding over UP Muslim's all-party conferences, gave a frustrated statement while rejecting the dominion status. He said, "The dominion status resolution as betraying the slavish mentality of the Hindus. Hindus have been habituated to slavery and they would remain slaves. The Musalmans are a freedom loving people and would not submit to either Hindus or British rule."[162]

By the efforts of Abul Kalam Azad, who had formed Muslim Nationalist Party with the help of Chaudhary Khaliquzzaman and other nationalist Muslims enlisted their support in favour of Nehru Report.[163]

The young and radical nationalists led by Pandit Jawahar Lal Nehru also favoured Ali brother's protest in support of complete Independence and opposed the Nehru Report. They were dissatisfied with the declaration of dominion status and demanded complete Independence.[164]

The Aligarh opinion was also divided over the Nehru Report, as it has already been said that Ali brothers and Khaliquzzaman have their own opinion about Nehru report. A reputed Aligarh nationalist Tufail Ahmad said that due to the political and ideological differences between Hindus and Muslims, the Indian nationalists failed to accept the challenge of Lord Birkenhead. His taunt became true, and both Hindus and Muslims dishonoured India in the eyes of the world.[165]

Notwithstanding, it also could not be ignored that the dispute over the Nehru Report, naturally, gave a new dimension to the freedom movement and further impetus to the freedom of the country. Almost all the nationalist leaders realized that they should move forward beyond the dominion status and try for the complete Independence.

Civil Disobedience Movement

The Civil Disobedience Movement started by Mahatma Gandhi was very strong movement except for a short break due to the Gandhi-Irwin Pact. It was the first effective movement after Khilafat and Non-Cooperation Movement. After a long gap, the people of India got an opportunity to invest their energy for the national cause. All the communities and classes of India actively participated in this movement.

The Muslim political leaders like Maulana Abul Kalam Azad, Dr. Ansari, Dr. Syed Mahmood, T.A.K. Sherwani, Mr. Rafi Ahmad Kidwai, Khan Abdul Ghaffar Khan, etc. became more active. Muslim Nationalist Party, Jamiatul Ulema-i-Hind, Ahraratul Islam, Khudai Khidmatgar gave many sacrifices for the movement without caring for the government policy of trying to keep away the Muslims from the movement.[166]

The Ali brothers, due to their ideological differences with Gandhiji and other Congress leaders, slowly and gradually drifted away from the Congress and warned the Congress that it would be disastrous for the Congress to launch a campaign without Muslim cooperation. Even Dr. M.A. Ansari was afraid of the consequences like other Congress minded Muslims. However, by the efforts of Maulana Abul Kalam Azad most of the Muslim leaders participated in the movement. In 1930, when Maulana Azad was sent to jail, Dr. Ansari became acting President of the Indian National Congress.[167]

The Aligarh Muslims were divided during the Civil Disobedience Movement. One group was taking active part in the movement, and another group was under the influence of government and opposed the movement. They were basically the Muslim traders and shopkeepers, who were misguided that the Civil Disobedience Movement would adversely affect the business of the Muslim community.

On 17th June, 1930, a large number of Muslims gathered in Jama Masjid of Aligarh in order to oppose the movement and organise an anti-picketing party to counteract the picketing of foreign cloth shops of Muslims by the Congress volunteers. In that meeting, many members made vigorous speeches in favour of the role being played by them. They made serious efforts to bring other panics to oppose the movement. Many shopkeepers organised the anti-picketing party in order to counteract the Congress volunteers.[168]

The dividing opinion of the Muslims regarding Congress policy and Civil Disobedience Movement forced the Muslim Congress leaders of Aligarh to think seriously about it. Mr. Nisar Ahmad Sherwani vakil brother of Mr. T.A.K. Sherwani organised the dormant nationalist forces of the Muslims to cooperate with the Congress and its movements. He made a fervent appeal to the Muslims of Aligarh to strengthen the hands of Congress. He sounded a note of warning to Muslims against non-cooperation in the fight for freedom of their motherland.[169]

The British Government made its best efforts to prevent the Muslims as a body from declaring in favour of Civil Disobedience Movement. However, it was unfortunate for the government that in spite of all their efforts, most of the Muslim population took active part in the movement.[170]

In the first phase of the movement, the Aligarh nationalists, including both Hindus and Muslims violated the salt Act. The salt making was started at Koil, Khair and several places of Aligarh districts before a large gathering. When the news of Gandhiji's arrest reached Aligarh, the *hartal* was observed and Congress flag was taken out in procession, and the patriotic songs were sung. The boycott of foreign clothes and picketing of liquor (*Tari*) shops continued unabated at Aligarh.[171] Even temples were being picketed to prevent worshippers wearing foreign clothes from obtaining entrance. Many spinning competitions were also held.[172]

As far as the picketing of foreign cloth shop was concerned, the volunteers arrived in batches from the Ashram and lie down before the shops. Nearly all the Hindu shopkeepers sealed their foreign cloth shops, but Muslims refused to do so and appealed to the government for help. The Congress intended to boycott all foreign goods and the people who were dealing in such stores were nervous and in case of the Musalmans the communal feeling became very bitter. They beat up many volunteers, and it was very interesting that the volunteers were anxious to be beaten up to pose as martyrs.[173]

Despite the picketing, the no rent campaign was also a part of the movement. The tenants refused to pay rent to the landlords or *zamindars*. The police witness that they had never seen such a wild type of speeches as people delivered in Aligarh. They were mainly the boys or irresponsible young men (freedom fighters). They had no hesitation in abusing the King. They preached the doctrine that to loot public money or to rob government servants was no crime.[174]

Navjiwan Bharat Sabha at Aligarh presented an address that embodied the most touching references. The speeches of Sardar Kishan Singh and Satyapal moved even stone hearted persons among the audience who actually shed tears.[175] In the rural areas of Aligarh, the local peasant refused to pay land revenue, and the several arrests were made. This movement continued unabated until Gandhiji withdrew Civil Disobedience Movement in May 1934. During this movement more than 600 persons from Aligarh district were sent to jail and fined.[176]

During the time of Civil Disobedience Movement, the Aligarh Muslim University remained unaffected and there was no disciplinary difficulty for the administration.[177] During the movement Lord Irwin made a speech at Aligarh and appreciated the students for their aloofness from the movement. He said, "The students of Aligarh remained staunch not because of any lack of high spirit or enthusiasm that is one of the best endowment of the youth, but simply because of their own good sense of loyalty to their *alma mater*. They showed that discipline in Aligarh is not merely imposed from the above or from without but something intelligently and deliberately accepted by the student body as a necessary condition of healthy life and work in the university."[178]

Act of 1935

The Act of 1935 passed by the British Parliament provided many powers to the Indian people. However, the Aligarh Muslims were afraid of the Act of 1935 that it would provide more powers to the majority community. On 27th January, 1937, while welcoming the Governor of UP Sir Harry Haig, the AMU Court members expressed their doubt before him. They said, "....the new constitution ....will transfer a large measure of power and responsibility to vote of majority and it is natural for those who are in minority to feel anxious about their future.... Nevertheless, Muslims on their part are prepared to work the new Constitution and cooperate with other communities for the advancement of the country's cause..."[179]

Sir Harry Haig assured the AMU Court members that the position of the Muslims had been safeguarded as much as it was possible to safeguard any community in the democratic constitution.[180]

Election of 1937

According to the provisions of the Act of 1835, the provincial election was due in 1937. Almost all the political parties intended to fight the elections. The Muslim leaders also decided the same. They either joined Congress or Muslim League to fight in the provincial elections. The Congress decided to fight elections and postponed the decision on office acceptance to the post-election period. Congress fought the elections on the issues of agrarian and national programmes.[181]

The political leaders of Indian National Congress toured all-over India for election campaign, Jawahar Lal Nehru along with other political leaders also arrived in Aligarh and Khair, a tehsil of Aligarh district.[182] In his reception, the involvement of the government servants was checked by district authorities and disciplinary action were taken against them.[183]

The election mania had caught all the people of each section or society or religion who were interested in politics. In Aligarh, both the nationalists and loyalists were active in the elections. The Aligarh nationalists were members of the major parties of Congress and Muslim League. Even the Muslim loyalists, the supporter of the British Government, also fought the election. However, most of the Muslim opinion and votes went for national candidates.[184]

After much campaigning and hard work, the elections were held and the result declared. The Congress became victorious in six provinces namely Madras, Bombay, Central Provinces, Orissa, Bihar and United Provinces. In Bengal, Assam and North-West Frontier the Congress was the largest single party. Muslim League faced very bad defeat in all the provinces except very few seats in Muslim majority provinces.[185]

Alumni's Role in National Politics

Most of the Indian Muslim political leaders and other Muslim intelligentsia were directly or indirectly connected with Aligarh and were collectively known as Aligarh brotherhood. However, they were unfortunately not united on one platform due to political, economic, social and religious problems. They were closely attached with almost all political parties in India in order to serve the nation shoulder to shoulder with their co-religionists. There were also some leaders who were neither attached to any political party nor strongly supported the national movement but cooperated with the British Government for the sake of improving the condition of the Muslim community. Broadly speaking, the Indian Muslim political leaders and other Muslim intelligentsia or Aligarh brotherhood was divided into two groups of the nationalists and the loyalists.

Nationalists

In the group of nationalists, the members of the Muslim community associated with the AMU were the top-ranking Congress members. Dr. Zakir Husain was most prominent among them as he had been very much in limelight from 1920 onwards. Among the others were Dr. Syed Mahmood, Rafi Ahmad Kidwai, Hayatullah Ansari, Mohammad Abdur Rahman (Kerala), T.A.K. Sherwani, etc.

Dr. Zakir Husain after finishing his school education from Etawa, admitted in the MAO College and studied up to M.A. He played very active part in Non-Cooperation Movement and in the foundation of Jamia Millia Islamia in 1920 in Aligarh. He went to Berlin for higher studies in 1923 and after his return, he joined the Jamia Millia Islamia as Vice-Chancellor and took the responsibility of preparing Indian youth, particularly Muslims for the national struggle. He became the President of the Hindustan Talimi Sangh Sewagram from 1938-48.[186]

Another leader of the Indian National Congress, Dr. Syed Mahmood was a born leader of India. He was educated in MAO

College Aligarh from 1901-07. During his days as a student in the MAO College, due to his nationalistic ideology, he was popularly known among the students as "nation".[187] He held several spells of imprisonment. He was General Secretary of the Congress in 1923 and again in 1929-36. He was appointed Minister of Education and Industry in the first Congress ministry in Bihar in 1937. He was opposed to the "Quit India" programme but had to 'give in' on account of Gandhiji's insistence. Dr. Mahmood was again appointed Minister of Development and Transport in 1946 in the Congress ministry in Bihar.[188]

Rafi Ahmad Kidwai, a national leader, graduated from the MAO College in 1918, but before completing LL.B., he fell under the spell of Mahatma Gandhi and left the college. He was very active in politics from the time of Non-Cooperation programme. He started to work as Private Secretary to Moti Lal Nehru and virtually became a member of the Nehru family. In 1923, he was elected to the Central Legislative Assembly on Swaraj Party ticket and resigned in 1930 on the call of the Congress. The most reputed post he held was Secretaryship of the reception committee of the Kanpur session of the Indian National Congress in 1925. In the cabinet of UP in 1937, he was appointed as Revenue Minister. His virtual enactment of the UP Tenancy Act created conditions for the abolition of *zamindari* system. In UP cabinet of 1946, he became Home Minister.[189]

Another leader of the national stature in the Congress was Hayatullah Ansari. He graduated from AMU in 1934 and took Gandhi ideology and plunged into freedom movement. In 1937, he started bringing out "*Hindustan*" weekly, an organ of the Indian National Congress. Somehow it was to be closed in 1942. Hayatullah Ansari became the first editor of "*Qaumi Awaz*" which was started in 1945 with the effort of Jawahar Lal Nehru and Rafi Ahmad Kidwai.[190]

The most prominent Alig national leader of the south India was Mohammad Abdur Rahman. He discontinued his studies from Aligarh in 1921 at the call of Mahatma Gandhi and Ali brothers and left for Malabar to carry on the Congress activities. He fought against the "Mopla Outrage Act", the "Inland Emigration Act" etc. When the Kerala Provincial Congress Committee decided to launch salt *stayagraha* in 1930, and a section of the Muslim community backed by the British Government opposed the move, Abdur Rahman along with his friends strongly resisted it and appealed to the Muslim community to join the national movement.[191]

His towering personality and oratory inspired the people, specially the younger generation and students. Later on in 1939, he became the President of the Kerala Provincial Congress Committee and a member of All India Congress Committee. In 1939, he became the President for Forward Block of the Kerala unit after being insured by the ideology of Subhas Chandra Bose. However, after 1945, he again became an active member of the Indian National Congress. During the struggle for freedom, he was sent to jail several times.[192]

In Aligarh itself, the Indian National Congress had a firm footing under the leadership of Tassadduq Ahmad Khan Sherwani (T.A.K. Sherwani). He was educated from MAO College and Cambridge. He was a nationalist from the start and was expelled from the MAO College for his participation in a strike in 1907 but was allowed to return. He was a firm Congressman and a devoted admirer of Moti Lal Nehru. He joined the Swaraj Party in January 1923. He also took part in the Civil Disobedience Movement of 1930 and became the President of the UP Congress Committee in 1931. In 1934, he became a member of the Congress Parliamentary Board and worked closely with Jawahar Lal Nehru throughout his life.[193]

There were many leaders who played an active role in the national movement were also associated with the Muslim League. Among these leaders associated with AMU, Khwaja Nazimuddin was most prominent. Khwaja Nazimuddin after his early education in Decca admitted in the MAO College where he studied for a few years. He was a leader of the Muslim League in Bengal and also a member of the working committee of All India Muslim League during the decisive decade of 1937-47. During the Elections of 1937, Muslim League was in a very weak position in Bengal and commanded little influence over the Muslim masses in the province. In Bengal, A.K. Fazlul Haq with his Krishak Praja Party gained much greater support than Muslim League. When the question of forming the ministry came, Fazlul Haq sought the coalition of the Congress but Congress turned down the proposal. Fazlul Haq then turned towards the Muslim League for coalition and for the four years the coalition government remained in the office. It gave an opportunity to Muslim League strengthening its position in Bengal. Nazimuddin became Home Minister in the province. Under the influence of Mr. M.A. Jinnah, Nazimuddin became the strong supporter of Pakistan in the later years.[194]

Due to the differences between the Indian National Congress and the Muslim League, a new section of Aligarh Muslim leaders came to the fore. This new group was purely national in character. Among the leaders of this group were Maulana Mohammad Ali and Shaukat Ali, Ajmal Khan, Nawab Mohammad Ismail, Chaudhary Khaliquzzman, Syed Wazir Hasan, Mohammad Ibrahim, and Mohammad Ali Khan Raja of Mahmudabad.

Maulana Mohammad Ali and Shaukat Ali popularly known as Ali brothers were prominent among the Aligarh nationalists. In the previous section of this work, their role is very much emphasised, particularly under the topic of Khilafat and Non-Cooperation Movement.

Another leader of this group Hakim Ajmal Khan was a trustee of the MAO College Aligarh until 1920. He played an active role in the Khilafat and Non-Cooperation Movement along with Mahatma Gandhi. However, he joined the Swaraj Party of Moti Lal Nehru in 1923 due to the suspension of the Non-Cooperation Movement. He was also a member of the Muslim League and Khilafat Committee. He strove manfully in 1922-23 to keep alliance between the Congress and various Muslim groups. He retired from politics in 1925 because of ill health.[195]

When Hakim Ajmal Khan died in 1928, Mahatma Gandhi said in his paper "*Young India*" of 1st January, 1928, "In the death of Hakim Ajmal Khan the country has lost one of the trusted servants .... He was a courier patriot .... he was a great Musalman and equally great Indian.... Hindu-Muslim unity was the breath of his nostrils."[196]

The other prominent leader of this group was Nawab Mohammad Ismail Khan. He worked as first Treasurer of AMU and appointed Acting Vice-Chancellor from 1934-35. In 1947, he was appointed full-fledged Vice-Chancellor of AMU. In the early years of his life, he was a member of the Meerut Congress Committee and remained its active member until 1928. His mind started diverting towards the Muslim League when

Swami Shraddhanand started *Shuddhi* and *Sangathana* movements in order to call back the new Muslims into Hindu order. Nawab Mohammad Ismail Khan with the cooperation of Haji Mohammad Syed Husain formed anti-*Shuddhi* League in 1923. From 1930 to 1946, he was a prominent leader of the Muslim League.[197]

In the election of 1937, the Muslim League was in coalition with the Indian National Congress. As an active and responsible member of the Muslim League, Nawab Mohammad Ismail Khan worked hard for his party and even for the Congress in the election campaign in many constituencies, where the Muslim League was not active. However, he got a personal setback when his name was rejected by Congress Parliamentary Board from the ministry in UP. He had the claim of two members in the ministry. Although their coalition with the Congress in UP could not become successful yet he had many friends in Congress and had good relations with the Congressmen. He was President of the UP League Action Committee in 1945-46. In the later years, due to his independent thinking, he faced displeasure of Mr. Mohammad Ali Jinnah. Due to that displeasure, he could not be selected for the membership of the Interim Government of 1946. He became politically inactive after assuming the charge of Vice Chancellor of AMU in 1947.[198]

Chaudhary Khaliquzzaman was also a leader associated with Aligarh. He obtained BA and LL.B. degree from Aligarh and played a great role in the Khilafat and Non-Cooperation Movements. After the suspension of the Non-Cooperation Movement, he joined the Swaraj Party in 1923. After a few years, he loosely associated himself with Muslin League but still had sympathy for the Congresses. As the Muslim league had no firm footing in UP until 1937, Chaudhary Khaliquzzaman and Nawab Mohammad Ismail Khan along with their group decided to support the Congress in UP election of 1937, where the Muslim League was not active.[199]

Thus, he reached with the UP Congress leaders a "gentleman's agreement" that his group would support the Congress candidate in their election campaign and in return the group would be given sufficient representation in the UP cabinet. However, when the Congress candidates returned to the Assembly with the absolute majority, the Congress refused to give Chaudhary's group more than one cabinet seat. He demanded two seats to which the Congress did not agree. The refusal of the Congress compelled Chaudhary Khaliquzzaman to sit in the opposition.[200]

Undoubtedly, it was the political blunder on the part of the Congress that facilitated to give strength to the Muslim League. It may be concluded that it was the Congress which was responsible for the Muslim League to flourish in UP. From 1937 onwards, Chaudhary Khaliquzzaman worked hard to energise the Muslim League in UP. He convinced Muslim intelligentsia to cooperate with Muslim League in his goal. At the time of partition, he was a member of All India Muslim League Working Committee and a lieutenant of Jinnah. He was a staunch supporter of the creation of Pakistan.

The other leader of this group was Syed Wazir Hasan. He completed his B.A. and LL.B. from MAO College Aligarh. He joined the judicial service in 1903. In 1926, he returned to the politics and became President of the All India Muslim League at Bombay. He joined the Congress in 1937 and became close to Moti Lal Nehru. Being of an aggressive nature, he opposed the Gandhian method of politics. He opposed Gandhiji's mixing politics with religion. He was staunchly secular in views and opposed the idea of Pakistan. He remained Congress member until his death in 1947.[201]

Another important leader of this group was Mohammad Ali Khan popularly known as Raja of Mahmudabad. He was a loyalist in the beginning of his life but his deep love for the nation compelled him to fight for the national cause. He was a close friend of Moti Lal Nehru, Sir Ali Imam and Wazir Hasan. From 1920 to 1926, he was the home member of the Governor's Executive Council of UP. During the five years of his membership, he supplied food and other thing needed to the national leaders in Lucknow jail. He made arrangements for better food and lodging to them and got a number of them freed from jail. When his term of home membership was over, he wrote a note to the government that the time had come to give Constitutional rights to the Indians.[202]

Raja of Mahmudabad was a freelance nationalist and staunch supporter of Hindu-Muslim unity. Although, he was associated with the Muslim League, he always supported the programmes launched by the Indian National Congress. He was of the opinion that Hindus and Muslims should collectively press the government to provide them the Constitutional rights.

Another Alig nationalist of this group was Hafiz Mohammad Ibrahim. He studied in MAO College Aligarh from 1908 to 1915. In the 1937 elections of UP, he secured victory on the Muslim League ticket and due to the rift for portfolio between Congress and Muslim League, he jumped to the Congress benches. Mohammad Ibrahim was promptly picked up by the UP Congress as minister in the Congress Government. From that time until his death in 1964, he remained a Congress worker and great nationalist.[203]

Besides this group, a lot of nationalist political leaders and intellectuals belonging to both the Hindu and Muslim communities related to Aligarh associated themselves to various political and independent Muslim parties like Unionist Party, Muslim Conference (Kashmir), Congress and Khilafat Party, Progressive Party, etc. Among these were Sir Sikander Hayat Khan, Chaudhary Mohammad Yasin Khan, Abdul Majid Khwaja, Yaqub Hasan, Maulana Hasrat Mohani, K.M. Ashraf, Khawaja Ahmad Abbas, Jan Nisar Akhtar, Josh Malihabadi, Mohammad Habib, Mushir Hasan Kidwai, Mir Vilayat Husain, Mirza Mohammad Afzal Beg, Shaikh Mohammad Abdullah, Raja Mahendra Pratap, etc. They all played very important role in freedom struggle, educational field and political as well as social development of India.

Sir Sikandar Hayat Khan completed his matriculation from MAO School Aligarh, and he left Aligarh afterwards. He was a Unionist Party member, believed firmly in communal harmony and regarded the communal problems as the biggest misfortune. He remarked about the separate electorate as utter shame. He expected India to become an influential and dominant partner in the British Commonwealth.[204]

Another popular leader was Chaudhary Mohammad Yasin Khan. He admitted in MAO College Aligarh for the LL.B. degree but before completing the course he left Aligarh due to some personal reasons. He was elected as a member of the Punjab Assembly from 1926-46 on the Unionist Party ticket and from 1952-62 on the Congress party ticket. He fought for the problems of the Meos in Mewat, particularly against the Raja's of Alwar and

Bharatpur. At the time of partition in 1947, he prevented the Meo community from migrating to Pakistan.[205]

Abdul Majid Khwaja joined the MAO College Aligarh for his early education, but later on he went for higher studies in Cambridge. He was a leader of Khilafat and Non-Cooperation Movement and Secretary of the Congress Working Committee in 1923. He joined the Swaraj Party and stood against Dr. Ziauddin for Legislative Council but could not succeed. Later on, he became a member of the Muslim Nationalist Party. He was a great advocate of Hindu-Muslim unity. He believed in India attaining Independence and wanted protection of the religious rights of Muslims in preference to a separate homeland for them. He opposed the creation of Pakistan. He advised the Indian Muslims to find out solutions for problems directly concerning their own religion and community.[206]

The next important leader of this group was Yaqub Hasan. He was educated from MAO College Aligarh. At the time of demand of complete Independence, Mr. Yaqub Hasan, a Congress member, opposed it and left the Congress temporarily in 1928. He was elected to the Madras Legislative Council in 1930 on the Muslim Party ticket. In 1937, he successfully contested on the Congress ticket and became the Minister of Public Works, Irrigation and Electricity. With the resignation of the ministry in 1939, his political career also came to an end.[207]

The most important leader of Independent thinking was Maulana Hasrat Mohani. He studied in MAO College Aligarh and being a poet and speaker selected among the students as Secretary of *Urdu-i-Mualla*. He was associated with various political parties like Congress, Muslim League, Khilafat Committee, Jamiatul Ulema-e-Hind and Communist Party. During the Khilafat and Non-Cooperation Movement, he moved a resolution of complete Independence at the annual session of the Indian National Congress at Ahmedabad in 1921, but Mahatma Gandhi opposed it and the resolution lost by a big majority.[208]

After his active participation in the Khilafat and Non-Cooperation Movement, Maulana Hasrat Mohani was imprisoned in 1922. After that he associated himself with the well-known communists. He left the Congress and also resigned from Jamiatul

Ulema-e-Hind in 1929. In 1930, he attached himself with the Civil Disobedience Movement. From 1937, he was a leading worker of All India Muslim League. When the scheme of Pakistan came into its final shape and came before Muslim League for approval, Maulana Hasrat Mohani, the old rebel took exception to it and challenged the leadership of Mr. Jinnah. In the storm of shouts he stood firm to make his voice heard, "Look here, Mr. Jinnah, you are surrounded by political adventurers." He was a member of the Constituent Assembly and was the only one among the fathers of Constitution of India who refused to sign when its draft was complete. His unwillingness was due to partition of India and its membership of the Commonwealth.[209]

Dr. Kunwar Mohammad Ashraf was also a leader of independent thinking. He was the student of graduation in MAO College Aligarh, when Khilafat and Non-Cooperation movements were launched. He was very active in Aligarh politics during Khilafat and Non-Cooperation Movement. In 1928, he actively worked against Simon Commission. He took inspiration from Russian Revolution and social reconstruction of the Soviet Union and became a Communist (Nationalist Marxist). He joined The Congress Socialist Party and later on became an active member of the Communist Party of India. His activities were mostly in the regions of Alwar, Bharatpur, Gurgaon, Mathura, Agra and Aligarh.[210]

A famous writer and thinker, Khwaja Ahmad Abbas, took his higher education from AMU. He graduated in History and Politics in 1933 and Law in 1935. The Progressive Writers Movement (PWM) which began in India in 1936 nurtured him as a writer. It brought him in contact with Communism and Marxism. Later on, he became the Secretary of the PWM and wrote much about the communist ideology. In his writings, he also gave much stress on the Indian Independence and national movement.[211]

Another progressive Urdu poet Jan Nisar Akhtar completed all his educations like B.A., M.A., Ph.D., from AMU. He was full of progressive and communist ideology in AMU. He was also having many friends and teachers of same ideology in AMU like; Ali Sardar Jafri, Majaz, Ahmad Abbas, Sibte Hasan, Akhtar Husain Raipuri, Hayatullah Ansari, Saadat Hasan Manto, Shahid Latif, Jazbi,

Akhtarul Iman, etc. Jan Nisar Akhtar was true Marxist and professed it through his poetry. His poetry was full of nationalistic feelings.[212]

Another national writer Josh Malihabadi admitted in MAO College in 1912 for his school education. However, after a few years, he left Aligarh and completed his education from Lucknow and Agra. He was also a progressive national writer. In 1934, he met Qazi Sir Azizuddin, the Prime Minister of Datia State. The Datia State PM offered him rupees sixteen hundred for editing a pro-British newspaper, but Josh rejected the offer and joined the Progressive Movement. He played an active role in the achievement of his goal with the help of his like-minded friends such as Sibte Hasan, Majaz, Ali Sardar Jafri and Mohammad Raza Ansari. His most famous poem was "*East India Company Ke Farzandon Se*", which was published in September, 1939 in the progressive newspapers "*Naya Adab*" and "*Kalim*" from Lucknow.[213]

Another Marxist leader of Aligarh was Prof. Mohammad Habib, an eminent historian of India. He associated himself with the Non-Cooperation Movement in Aligarh. He joined the AMU in 1922 as a Reader and in 1923 at the age of barely 28 years he became the youngest Professor of Histroy in any Indian university.[214]

The other radical nationalist of the Socialist group was Mushir Hasan Kidwai. He was the President of the Socialist group of the Legislative Assembly members formed in 1924. He also joined the judicial service and became a senior judge on the Lucknow bench. In 1930s, his activities became more radical and became President of the non-communal All India Independent League. He wrote two books "*Swaraj and How to Obtain it*" (Lucknow 1924) and "*Pan Islamism and Bolshevism*" (London 1937).[215]

Two Kashmiri leaders who played important role in national movement of Kashmir were Shaikh Mohammad Abdullah and Mirza Mohammad Afzal Beg. Both of them after taking educational degrees from AMU joined the Kashmiri National Movement. Shaikh Abdullah became president of the J&K Muslim Conference, and Afzal Beg became its General Secretary. In 1939, the name of Muslim Conference was changed to National Conference. National Conference launched the "Quit Kashmir Movement" in 1946 under the leadership of Shaikh Abdullah against the autocratic rule of the Maharaja. Both leaders were arrested in 1946 and released in

September 1947. When Pakistan organised a raid to annex Kashmir, Shaikh Abdullah along with his followers, including Afzal Beg mobilized popular resistance against the raiders and supported the accession of the state to India.[216]

Raja Mahendra Pratap was an Alig of whose achievements the AMU is proud even to this day. He was a son of a jagirdar Raja Ghanshyam Singh of Hathras. He was admitted to MAO College in 1898 for school education and completed Intermediate from there. However, he could not complete his BA and left the education forever. He was a nationalist leader who created a brilliant history by forming the first Indian Independent Government with its headquarters in Afghanistan. He was very actively supported by Obaidullah Sindhi.[217]

On 1st December, 1915, Raja Mahendra Pratap formed an Independent Government of India in Kabul with the cooperation of King Habibullah of Afghanistan on the occasion of his birthday. Raja Sahib as its President, Maulana Barkatullah as its Prime Minister and Obaidullah Sindhi as its Home Minister took the oath of loyalty. The newly formed Indian Government forged an agreement with King Habibullah. He also tried to have good friendly relations with neighbouring countries, sent ambassadors to the court of Indian Raja's. Maharaja Nabha extended his cooperation to Raja Mahendra Pratap. This government lost its existence when the new king of Afghanistan King Amanullah made a friendly agreement with the British Government.[218]

Loyalists

Besides the nationalists, the other most prominent group of Indian (Alig) Muslims, there was another group of loyalists. This group had the primary aim to get government support for the Muslim community. They were the staunch followers of Sir Syed Ahmad Khan. They thought that time was not ripe for the Muslims to struggle against the British Government. In fact, at that time, the Muslims were not so advanced and forward like their Hindu counterparts. They opined that the Muslims were socially, economically, politically and educationally backward, and that they should first get educated to emerge as strong community to face any situation in India. This could only be achieved, they thought, by the loyalty to the British Government.

The AMU was the only institution which ensured the advancement and prosperity of the Indian Muslims by educating their children. As this institution was running with the help of the British Government, these Muslim patriots followed the path of loyalism to the British Government for the sake of their community. If we see the detail about the loyalist leaders, we find that they were having internal sympathy either to the Congress or Muslim League, and it is well-known that the objective of both the parties was to achieve Constitutional rights for Indians (Hindus, Muslims and others) or to achieve Swaraj or Independence.

The loyalists who determined to ameliorate the position of the Indian Muslims were Dr. Ziauddin Ahmad, Sahibzada Aftab Ahmad Khan, Shaikh Mohammad Abdullah (Alig), Agha Khan, etc. All these leaders were always loyal to the British Government only to improve the position of the Muslims, though they were having national feelings. They were also associated with the national political parties. Shahibzada Aftab Ahmad Khan was of the Congress mentality intellectual. Dr. Ziauddin Ahmad and Agah Khan were associated with the Muslim League and Shaikh Mohammad Abdullah (Alig) had the leanings towards Congress as well as the Muslim League. Their role in the educational development of Muslims had already been mentioned in the preceding chapters of this book.

The other loyalists were Syed Bashir Ahmad, Mohammad Yaqub, Nawab of Chhatari, Sir Mohammad Shafi, Syed Reza Ali, Mir Vilayat Husain, etc. Syed Bashir Ahmad was a member of the AMU Court for twenty five years and member of Executive Council of AMU from 1957-65. He fought for the rights of educationally backward communities without any religious or communal bias.[219]

The other loyalist Mohammad Yaqub took all his education from MAO College. He was also appointed as trustee of the college. He became President of All India Muslim League in 1927 and later on became its Secretary. He was a member of Age of Consent Committee in 1928 and Indian Franchise Committee in 1932. He also played an active part during his membership of AMU Court and Muslim Educational Conference. He also held the honour of Knighthood from the British Government.[220]

Another top rank loyalist was Ahmad Said Khan, the Nawab of Chhatari. He was educated in MAO School Aligarh. He was elected unopposed to the newly constituted UP Legislative Assembly from Zamindar Party in 1920, when the legislatures had been boycotted by the Muslim League and Khilafat Committee. He was appointed the minister in 1923. When Raja of Mahmudabad completed his term as the Home member of the Governor's Executive Council, Nawab Chhatari succeeded him and continued until 1933. He took over charge of Governorship of UP in 1928. In 1932, he became member of the Viceroys Executive Council. In 1941, he became President of Executive Council of Nizam of Hyderabad and continued until 1946.[221]

The other top level loyalist was Sir Mohammad Shafi, a trustee of the MAO College. He was made Vice-President of the Viceroy's Executive Council, and he retained that office until 1925. He also became a member of Education and Health and subsequently the Law member in the Government of India. He was against joint electorate and felt shocked when M.A. Jinnah accepted it on certain conditions in 1927. Presiding over the Lahore session of the Muslim League, he said that it would be in the highest degree injurious to the cause of Indian nationalism.[222]

The most prominent loyalist Syed Reza Ali was educated in MAO College and obtained his Law degree. He was also elected Vice-President of Students Union in 1902. In 1924, he was President of the All India Muslim League. He was a member of the Indian Government deputation of South Africa in 1925-26 and an agent of the Government of India in South Africa in 1935. He was conferred Knighthood and CBE. He considered swarajists to be obstructionist because of their demand for swaraj without adequate safeguards for minorities. He opposed the idea of Constituent Assembly for India and pointed out that the Indians were being maltreated outside India (in South Africa), and British Government should protect them.[223]

Another loyalist Mir Vilayat Husain completed his education from MAO College Aligarh and also appointed as a teacher afterwards. In the early years of his career, he was a khilafatist and opposed the British Government but in 1921, he turned into a loyalist and worked for the betterment of the Muslim community.[224]

All the above titanic loyalist figures always invited the Viceroy, Governor and other high officials of the British Government to visit the Aligarh Muslim University, who patronised and gave generous donations to that esteemed institution. These loyalists, determined for the amelioration of their community, left no stone unturned in securing moral support, demanding safeguards of Muslim interests and Constitutional rights from the British Government.[225]

NOTES

1. Muhammad, Shan, *Successors of Sir Syed Ahmad Khan*, Delhi, 1981, p. 60.
2. *Aligarh Institute Gazette*, 3rd October, 1906; see also Muhammad, Shan, *The Growth of Muslim Politics in India,* New Delhi, 1991, pp. 64-65.
3. *Ibid.*
4. *Aligarh Institute Gazette*, 24th October, 1906.
5. *Ibid.*
6. *Ibid.*
7. *The Englishman*, 31st December, 1906.
8. *Ibid.*
9. *Ibid.*
10. *Ibid.*
11. *The Growth of Muslim Politics in India,* p. 77.
12. *Aligarh Institute Gazette*, 11th October, 1911.
13. *Ibid.,* 1st November, 1911.
14. *Al-Hilal*, 9th October, 1912, No. 13, p. 11.
15. *Aligarh Institute Gazette*, 15th November, 1911.
16. *Ibid.,* 19th October, 1912.
17. *Ibid.,* 30th October, 1912.
18. *Ibid.*
19. *Ibid.*
20. *Ibid.,* 8th January, 1913.
21. *Ibid.*
22. *Naqoosh*, Lahore, January, 1955, p. 4.
23. *Hayat-i-Aftab*, pp. 92-93.
24. *Ibid.*
25. *Aligarh Institute Gazette*, 26th June, 1912.
26. Harding's letter to Chirol of 7th August, 1912, cited in Muhammad, Shan, *The Indian Muslims* (*A Documentary Record*), 1900-1947, Meerut, 1980, p. 121 (Hereafter cited as *The Indian Muslims*).

27. Harding's letter to Butler dated 29th October, 1912, cited in *The Indian Muslims,* p. 12.
28. Muhammad, Shan, *Successors of Sir Syed Ahmad Khan*, Delhi, 1981, p. 109.
29. Sarkar, Sumit, *Modern India 1885-1947*, Madras, 1983, p. 144.
30. *Modern Asian Studies,* Vol. IX, 1975, pp. 227-29; see also Sumit Sarkar, p. 143; and *Successors of Sir Syed Ahmad Khan,* p. 83.
31. Neimeijer, *Khilafat Movement in India, 1919-1924*, Nejheff, 1972, p. 89.
32. *Ibid.*
33. Shakir, Moin, *Khilafat to Partition, 1919-47*, New Delhi, 1970, p. 66 (Hereafter cited as Moin Shakir).
34. *File No. 6*, p. 1, Uttar Pradesh State Archive Lucknow (UPSAL).
35. *Ibid.*
36. *Ibid.*
37. *Young India*, 10th December, 1919; see also Gopal, Ram, *Indian Muslims*, Bombay, 1959, p. 137 (Hereafter cited as Ram Gopal).
38. *File No. 6*, p. 1, Uttar Pradesh State Archive Lucknow (UPSAL).
39. Robinson, Francis, *Separatism among Indian Muslims*, Cambridge, 1974, p. 311.
40. Shaw Stanford, J., and Ezel Kural Shaw, *History of the Ottoman Empire and Modern Turkey*, Cambridge, 1977, p. 332 (Hereafter quoted as Shaw).
41. Manglori, Syed Tufail Ahmad, *Musalmanon Ka Roshan Mustaqbil*, Delhi, 1945, p. 481 (Hereafter cited as *Roshan Mustaqbil*).
42. *File No. 6*, p. 6, Uttar Pradesh State Archive Lucknow (UPSAL).
43. He was elected Aligarh Trustee in 1915, led the Muslim delegation to Viceroy over Turkey in 1922 and 1923. He was granted Knighthood and CBE. Raza, Ali was described by Meston in 1914, "rather unfairly plausible but very third rate member of the young Muhammadans." He was the strongest advocate of Muslim interest in the UP Legislative Council and major protagonist of UP Muslim interest in the UP Municipalities Bill compromise and Lucknow Pact. (A Biography cited in Robinson's *Separatism among Indian Muslims*).
44. *File No. 6*, p. 7, Uttar Pradesh State Archive Lucknow (UPSAL)
45. Hasan, Mushirul, *Mohammad Ali: Ideology and Politics*, New Delhi, 1981, p. 44.
46. *Hayat-i-Aftab*, p. 206.
47. *Mushahidat-o-Taassurat*, pp. 286-290.
48. Quadiri, Khalid Hasan, *Hasrat Mohani*, Delhi, 1985, p. 114 (Hereafter quoted as *Hasrat Mohani*).
49. Hadi, Syed Mohammad, *Ali Biradran Aur Unka Zamana*, New Delhi, 1978, p. 91 (Hereafter cited as *Ali Biradran*).
50. Hasan, Mushirul, *Nationalism and Communal Politics in India 1916-1928,* New Delhi, 1979, p. 173.
51. *Ibid.,* see also *File No. 6*, p. 8, Uttar Pradesh State Archive Lucknow (UPSAL).

52. Ali, Shaikh Shahid, *Majmua Risala-i-Hijrat wa Risala-i-Qurbani Gao*, Farangi Mahal, Lucknow, 1920, p. 150; cited in *Modern Asian Studies*, Vol. 13, Part I, February 1979, pp. 41-57.
53. *Hijrat* was not liked by many Khilafat leaders like Dr. M.A. Ansari, Hasrat Mohani, Hakim Ajmal Khan, Asaf Ali, Mohammad Shafi, Fazl-i-Husain and Dr. Mohammad Iqbal etc. *Modern Asian Studies*, Vol. 13, Part I, February 1979, pp. 41-57.
54. *Ibid.*
55. Hasan, Mushirul, *Nationalism and Communal Politics in India 1916-1928,* New Delhi, 1979, p. 176; see also *Ali Biradran,* p. 91.
56. Interestingly by the same tactics the British Government kept Pandit Madan Mohan Malviya to its support as government had already granted Hindu University at Banaras. Sen, S.P., *Dictionary of National Biography*, Calcutta, 1974 (Hereafter quoted as Sen).
57. Hasrat Mohani, *op. cit.*, p. 219.
58. Azad, Abul Kalam, *India Wins Freedom*, Madras, 1998, p. 11.
59. *Bombay Chronicle,* 16th October, 1920.
60. Shaikh Abdullah incorrectly says that Mahatma Gandhi came directly from Calcutta. Gandhiji had been in Moradabad on 11th October from where he came to Aligarh. (Government of India, Ministry of Information & Broadcasting, *The Collected Works of Mahatma Gandhi*, Vol. 18, New Delhi, 1965, pp. 344-345; see also *Hayat-i-Abdullah*, pp. 106-107).
61. *Mushahidat-o-Taassurat*, pp. 294-95.
62. *Ibid.*
63. *Zia-i-Hayat*, pp. 68-69.
64. *Ibid.*
65. *The Bombay Chronicle*, 16th October, 1920.
66. *Department of Police, Serial No. 16/3*, Uttar Pradesh State Archive Lucknow (UPSAL).
67. *Ibid.,* Mahatma Gandhi's speech reproduced in his *Collected Works*, Vol. 18, p. 345, refers that Mahatma Gandhi on the criticism on the Non-Cooperation being a destructive step, admitted, "This work is certainly destructive, but the seeds which have grown need to be rooted out so that a good crop may be sown." Mahatma Gandhi further questioned the extent of loyalty to the Raj, its bureaucracy and the Union Jack. And finally he allays the apprehension of the students that participation in the Non-Cooperation would lead to the stoppage of government aid. *Collected Works*, Vol. 18, p. 345. Interestingly in his autobiography Mahatma Gandhi refers to his Aligarh visit in few sentences, "A little while after this I was taken by the friends to the Muslim College Aligarh. There I invited the young men to be *Fakirs* for the service of the motherland." M.K. Gandhi, *An Autobiography or the Story of My Experiments with Truth*, Ahmedabad, 1945, p. 540.
68. *Department of Police, Serial No. 16/3*, Uttar Pradesh State Archive Lucknow (UPSAL).

69. *The Bombay Chronicle* gives a contradictory report; it admits that it was a massive meeting in the Union Club of which Mr. Gandhi was already a member, but it also says that Gandhi's meeting got a poor response. The *Aligarh Magazine* reciprocates the same, giving the reference of Mohammad Ali. However, it gives the details of students' response that on 12th October the students did not attend the classes; and that in the meeting which was being held, Zakir Husain declared to for go his scholarship. For details see *The Bombay Chronicle*, 16th October, 1920; *Aligarh Magazine, Special Number 1953-54, 1954-55*, pp. 271-72.
70. *Department of Home-Political, Coll. 210-216 & KW-Dec-A-1920* (National Archives, New Delhi). Shaikh Abdullah says that on 13th October, 1920, a meeting was held in which Ali brothers appealed students for Non-Cooperation. Mr. Mohammad Ali started weeping and decided to move with a verse:
"Nikalna Khuld Se Adam Ka Sunte Aaye The Lekin
Bare Be Aabroo Hokar Tere Kooche Se Hum Nikle."
(We have heard about the dismissal of Adam from Heaven,
With a more humiliation, I am leaving the street on which you live.)
On hearing this heart touching poetry, the students became very much grieved and easily became ready to leave the college. However, keeping in mind of their future, they demanded another college for their study on the condition of leaving the college. See for details in *Mushahidat-o-Taassurat*, pp. 295-96; and *Hayat-i-Abdullah*, pp. 107-109.
71. Mudholi, Abdul Ghaffar, *Jamia Ki Kahani*, Part-I, Delhi, 1964, pp. 21-22; see also, *Aligarh Magazine, 1953-54, 1954-55*, p. 72.
72. *Department of Home-Political, Coll. 59-Dec-Deposit-1920* (National Archives, New Delhi), See also *The Bombay Chronicle*, 10th October, 1920.
73. *Mushahidat-o-Taassurat*, p. 296; and *Hayat-i-Abdullah*, pp. 107-109.
74. *The Leader*, 15th October 1920; see also, *Hayat-i-Abdullah*, pp. 104-105; Ghaffar, Qazi Abdul, *Hayat-i-Ajmal*, Aligarh, 1950, pp. 234-35; and *Zia-i-Hayat*, pp. 69-70.
75. *The Leader*, 18th October, 1920; see also, *The Pioneer*, 18th October, 1920, *The Bombay Chronicle*, 26th October 1920; and *Aligarh Institute Gazette*, 23rd October, 1920, pp. 3-4; and *Aligarh Magazine, September-October 1920*, Vol. XVII, p. 13.
76. *Department of Home-Political, Coll. 210-216 & KW-Dec-A-1920* (National Archives, New Delhi).
77. *The Leader*, 20th October, 1920; see also, *The Bombay Chronicle*, 26th October, 1920; and Gail Minault, *Khilafat Movement*, Delhi, 1982, p. 117.
78. *Ibid.*, 22nd October, 1920, and *Aligarh Institute Gazette*, 20th October, 1920.
79. *The Leader*, 22nd October, 1920.
80. *The Pioneer*, 24th October, 1920.
81. *Ibid.*, Amin Zuberi says that one thousand letters addressed to the Principal in support of his policy and only three were received in support of the Non-Cooperation, *Zia-i-Hayat*, pp. 70-72.

82. *Ibid.*
83. *Ibid.*, 25th October, 1920.
84. *The Pioneer*, 25th October, 1920. The *Aligarh Institute Gazette*, contrary to *The Pioneer*, *The Leader* and *The Bombay Chronicle* says that Mohammad Ali in his speech criticized Sir Syed Ahmad's educational policy. According to the *Gazette*, Dr. M.A. Ansari said that most of the staff of National Muslim University would be Hindus. It had been also published in *The Bombay Chronicle*, 25th October, 1920, *Aligarh Institute Gazette*, 24th October, 1920. Undoubtedly, these were the false points, which had been released to encourage the students in their favour.
85. *The Pioneer*, 25th October, 1920.
86. Hasan, Mushirul, *Nationalism and Communal Politics in India 1885-1923,* New Delhi, 1991, pp. 141-42.
87. Rizvi, Khurshid Mustafa, *Hayat-i-Zakir Husain*, Delhi, 1949, p. 61; see also *Hayat-ul-Bashir*, p. 197.
88. Hasan, Mushirul, *Mohammad Ali: Ideology and Politics*, New Delhi, 1981, pp. 55-56.
89. *Nationalism and Communal Politics in India, 1916-1928*, p. 183.
90. *The Tribune*, 30th October, 1920, writes that a father donated a sum of Rs. 100 to the Khilafat Committee as his contribution.
91. *Department of Home-Political, Coll. 59-Dec-Deposit-1920* (National Archives, New Delhi).
92. *Department of Home-Political, Coll. 210-216 & KW-Dec-A-1920* (National Archives, New Delhi).
93. *Ibid.*
94. *The Pioneer*, 30th October, 1920.
95. *Ibid.*
96. *Ibid.*, see also in *The Leader*, 30th October, 1920. It is also cited in *Bayan* of Dr. Ziauddin Ahmad, Aligarh, (ND), p. 36; *Nationalism and Communal Politics in India. 1916-1928*, of Mushirul Hasan, p. 182; and *Modern Asian Studies*, Vol. 8, Part II, 1974, p. 186.
97. A government dispatch dated 27th October, 1920, thus report the situation in the campus, ".... the college had been closed until the 30th November. There is a great gathering of Musalmans. The situation in unwinding itself. I hope that the invaders will be repelled with loss, but the temper of the Musalmans is queer...." (Letter of Sir Harcourt Butler to Sir William Vincent, cited in File of *Department of Home-Political, Coll. 210-216 & KW-Dec-A-1920* (National Archives, New Delhi).
98. *Ibid.*
99. *Ibid.*
100. *The Leader*, 30th October, 1920.
101. *Ibid.*
102. Correspondent of daily *The Leader* puts a sentence of caution. Mr. Gandhi should note that his supporters were violating the non-violent character of the movement and he should be responsible for all the consequences. *The Leader*, 31st October, 1920.

103. *Ibid.*
104. *Ibid.*
105. *Young India*, 3rd November, 1920. It has been cited in Intelligence Report, *Department of Home-Political, Coll. 210-216 & KW-Dec-A-1920* (National Archives, New Delhi).
106. *Department of Police, Serial No. 16/3*, Uttar Pradesh State Archive Lucknow (UPSAL).
107. *Ibid.*
108. Luke, Sir Harry, *The Old Turkey and New*, London, 1955, pp. 162-63.
109. Beg, Mirza Abdul Ghaffar, *Karachi Ka Tarikhi Muqadma*, Lucknow, 1985, p. 207.
110. *File No. 4/2(1), 1924*, (AMU Archive) (cutting of the newspaper *Englishmen*, 17th July, 1924).
111. The mind of Raja of Mahmudabad diverted in 1903, when the improvement trust of Kanpur decided to demolish a part of Machhli Bazaar Mosque in order to straighten the road. Raja Mahmudabad met the Lt. Governor of UP James Meston in this regard but he rejected his application and instead, accepted the decision of the improvement trust. Raja Mahmudabad also met the Viceroy Lord Curzon to save the mosque and received the sympathy of his Executive Council. He was finally able to save the mosque, but it invited the enmity of James Meston. From that time, he turned into a nationalist fold and assured himself that the aim of the Englishmen was only to divide the Hindus and Muslims of India. (*Fikr-o-Nazar*, Vol. II, pp. 303-304).
112. *Ibid.*, p. 304.
113. *Ibid.*, p. 81.
114. *Fikr-o-Nazar*, Vol. III, pp. 215-17.
115. Syed Mohammad Tonki was a nationalist minded student. He was admitted in the AMU with the effort of Prof. Mohammad Habib and K.M. Ashraf. At that time, Sahibzada Aftab Ahmad Khan was the Vice-Chancellor. When Tonki was completing B.T. (Modern B.Ed.) one of its teachers used to talk of Non-Cooperation leaders in a derogatory manner. One day Tonki stood up in the class and while opposing the teacher, said, "Non-Cooperation made a sacrifice to serve the nation." When the teacher asked, who says that? Tonki replied, "I say today and history will say tomorrow."(*Fikr-o-Nazar*, Vol. III, pp. 215-17).
116. *File No. 51, 1923-24* (AMU Archive).
117. *Annual Report of the Union. 1922-37* (AMU Union Hall).
118. *File No. 51, 1928-29* (AMU Archive).
119. *Annual Report of the Union 1922-37* (AMU Union Hall).
120. *File No. IV/2, 1931-32* (AMU Archive).
121. *File No. 51, 1933-35* and *File No. 51, 1934-35* (AMU Archive).
122. *Hindustan Times*, 25th January, 1937.
123. *Ibid.*

124. Hayatullah Ansari went to Delhi with a letter for Prof. Mohammad Habib. He met Pt. Jawahar Lal Nehru at the house of Prof. Habib and convinced him to visit Aligarh and address the students. (*Fikr-o-Nazar*, Vol. II, p. 298).
125. *Ibid.*, p. 299.
126. *Gazetteer of India*, UP (Aligarh) Lucknow, 1987, p. 41.
127. *Ibid.*
128. *File No. 51, 1924-25* (AMU Archive).
129. *Indian Muslims*, Vol. 8, pp. 114-115.
130. *India in 1925-26*, pp. 78-79; see also *Indian Muslims*, Vol. 8, pp. 114-15.
131. *File No. IV/1*, 1926-27 (AMU Archive).
132. *Annual Report of the Union 1922-37* (AMU Union Hall).
133. Pirzada, Syed Sharifuddin, *Foundation of Pakistan*, Vol. II, New Delhi, 1982, p. 206.
134. *Indian Muslims*, Vol. 8, pp.137-38.
135. *Fikr-o-Nazar*, Vol. II, pp. 194-196.
136. *File No. 82, 1936-37* (AMU Archive).
137. *Ibid.*
138. *Ibid.*
139. *Ibid.*
140. *Indian Muslims*, Vol. 8, pp.137-38.
141. *Foundation of Pakistan*, Vol. II, pp. 36-38.
142. Moin Shakir, p. 84; see also Desai, Mahadeo, *Maulana Azad*, Delhi, 1946, pp. 61-62; and Muhammad, Shan, *Unpublished Letters of Ali Brothers*, Delhi, 1979, p. 234.
143. Desai, Mahadeo, *Maulana Azad*, Delhi, 1946, pp. 60-61.
144. *Ibid.*
145. *Unpublished Letters of Ali Brothers*, pp. 240-41.
146. *Foundation of Pakistan*, Vol. II, p. 169.
147. *India in 1925-26*, p. 66.
148. *Aligarh Mail,* October 1926.
149. *Fikr-o-Nazar*, Vol. III, p. 217.
150. *Roshan Mustaqbil*, p. 439.
151. Chandra, Bipan, *India's Struggle for Independence*, Calcutta, 1992, p. 261.
152. *Indian Muslims*, Vol. 9, p. 3.
153. Munawwar, Mohammad, *Dimensions of the Pakistan Movement*, Lahore, 1987, p. 313.
154. Sumit Sarkar, *op. cit.*, p. 266.
155. *Fikr-o-Nazar*, Vol. II, p. 305.
156. *Gazetteer of India*, UP (Aligarh) Lucknow, 1987, p. 40.
157. *Department of Police, File No. 151/1930,* p. 25, Uttar Pradesh State Archive Lucknow (UPSAL).
158. *Indian Muslims*, Vol. 9, p. 3, and *Roshan Mustaqbil*, p. 439.
159. Panday, B.N., *The Indian National Movement 1885-1947*, Hong Kong, 1979, p. 79 (Hereafter cited as B.N. Panday).

160. Ram Gopal, *op. cit.*, p. 201.
161. *Ibid.*, p. 205.
162. *Ibid.*, p. 206.
163. *Muslim India*, p. 296.
164. Bipan Chandra, *op. cit.*, p. 264.
165. *Roshan Mustaqbil*, pp. 435-36.
166. *Ibid.*, p. 437.
167. Mahadeo Desai, *op. cit.*, pp. 92-93.
168. *Department of Police, File No. 151/1930,* Uttar Pradesh State Archive Lucknow (UPSAL).
169. *Ibid.*
170. *Department of Police, File No. 241/1930,* Uttar Pradesh State Archive Lucknow (UPSAL).
171. *Gazetteer of India*, UP (Aligarh) Lucknow, 1987, p. 41; see also *Department of Police, File No. 151/1930,* Uttar Pradesh State Archive Lucknow (UPSAL).
172. *Ibid.*
173. *Department of Police, File No. 151/1930,* Uttar Pradesh State Archive Lucknow (UPSAL).
174. *Ibid.*
175. *Department of Police, File No. RR-26,* pp. 12-13, Uttar Pradesh State Archive Lucknow (UPSAL).
176. *Gazetteer of India*, UP (Aligarh) Lucknow, 1987, p. 42.
177. Anderson, Sir George, *Progress of Education in India 1927-32*, Delhi, (ND), p. 89.
178. *Addresses and Speeches*, p. 36.
179. *Ibid.*, p. 67
180. *The Hindustan Times*, 20th January 1937; see also *Addresses and Speeches*, p.72.
181. Bipan Chandra, *op. cit.*, pp. 322 and 431.
182. *Department of Police, File No. RR-26,* p. 13, Uttar Pradesh State Archive Lucknow (UPSAL).
183. *Department of GAD, File No. 555/1936*, Uttar Pradesh State Archive Lucknow (UPSAL).
184. *Fikr-o-Nazar*, Vol. III, p. 221.
185. Sumit Sarkar, *op. cit.*, p. 349.
186. In November 1948, Dr. Zakir Hussain became the Vice Chancellor of AMU. He was nominated a member of the Indian University Commission. He was also nominated to the Rajya Sabha and made the Indian representative on the Executive Board of UNESCO from 1956-58. He remained the Chairman, Central Board of Secondary Education until 1957, a member of the UGC until 1957, a member of the University Education Commission in 1948-49, and of the Educational Reorganization Committee of Bihar, UP and MP. In 1957, he was appointed Governor

of Bihar and in 1962, he was elected as Vice-President of India. In May 1967, he was declared elected as Head of State, and was formally sworn in as the third President of Indian Republic until his sudden death on 3rd May, 1969 (Sen, S.P., *op. cit.*, Vol. IV, pp. 463-64).

187. *Fikr-o-Nazar*, Vol. II, p. 113.
188. Jain, Naresh Kumar, *Muslims in India: A Biographical Dictionary*, Vol. II. New Delhi, 1983, pp. 180-181, (Hereafter quoted as *Biographical Dictionary*). While imprisoned with other Congress leaders during Quit India programme, Dr. Mahmood felt convinced after seeking an Omen from *Quran*, that the "British would allow freedom to India" and wrote a letter to Viceroy expressing his dissociation from the programme and urging the latter to renew a negotiation with Gandhi. This release, which followed soon afterwards, caused misunderstanding at the time. (Sen, S.P., *op. cit.*, Vol. III, pp. 294-296).
189. Sen, S.P., *op. cit.*,Vol. II, pp. 355-56; see also *Biographical Dictionary,* Vol. II, pp. 23-25.
190. *Ibid.,* Vol. I, pp. 52-53.
191. *Ibid.,* Vol. I, p. 5.
192. *Ibid.,* Vol. I, p. 6.
193. *Biographical Dictionary*, Vol. II, pp. 157-58.
194. Sen, S.P., *op. cit.*, Vol. II, pp. 351-52.
195. Robinson, *op. cit.*, 377; see also *Biographical Dictionary*, Vol. I, pp. 66-67.
196. *Young India*, 1st January, 1928.
197. Sen, S.P., *op. cit.*, Vol. II, p. 187; see also Robinson, *op. cit.*, p. 378, and *Fikr-o-Nazar*, Vol. II, pp. 310-11.
198. *Ibid.,* see also Robinson, *op. cit.*, p. 378, and *Fikr-o-Nazar*, Vol. II, pp. 310-11.
199. *Ibid.,* pp. 322-23; see also Robinson, *op. cit.*, p. 376.
200. *Ibid.,* see also Robinson, *op. cit.*, p. 376.
201. Sen, S.P. *op. cit.*, Vol. I, p. 153; see also Robinson, *op. cit.*, p. 371; and *Biographical Dictionary*, Vol. II, pp. 206-207.
202. *Fikr-o-Nazar*, Vol. II, pp. 304-305.
203. Sen, S.P., *op. cit.*, Vol. II, p.179.
204. Sen, S.P., *op. cit.*, Vol. IV, pp. 201-202.
205. *Proceedings of the Indian History Congress* (55th Session Aligarh, 1994), Delhi, 1995, pp. 622-627.
206. Sen, S.P., *op. cit.*, Vol. II, p. 350; see also Robinson, *op. cit.*, p. 301.
207. *Ibid.,* p. 151; see also *Biographical Dictionary*, Vol. II, pp. 10-11.
208. *Indian Annual Register*, 1921-22, pp. 64-67.
209. Sen, S.P., *op. cit.*, Vol. II, p. 155; see also Robinson, *op. cit.*, pp. 382-83.
210. Sen, S.P., *op. cit.*, Vol. I, pp. 62-64.
211. Ray, N.R., *Dictionary of National Biography*, Calcutta, 1986, pp. 1-2, (Hereafter cited as 'Ray').
212. *Fikr-o-Nazar*, Vol. III, p. 243.
213. *Ibid.,* pp. 303-304.

214. Nizami, K.A., *Politics and Society during Early Medieval Period*, Vol. I, New Delhi, 1974 (Hereafter cited as 'Nizami').
215. Robinson, *op. cit.*, pp. 379-80.
216. *Ibid.,* pp. 8, 9 & 134.
217. *Fikr-o-Nazar*, Vol. II, p. 344.
218. *Ibid.*
219. Sen, S.P., *op. cit.*, Vol. IV, p. 99.
220. Robinson, *op. cit.*, p. 417.
221. Sen, S.P., *op. cit.*, Vol. II, pp. 308-309; see also *Biographical Dictionary*, Vol. I, p. 62.
222. Sen, S.P., *op. cit.*, Vol. IV, p. 139; see also *Foundation of Pakistan*, Vol. II, New Delhi, 1982, p. 129; taken from *Indian Quarterly Register*, 1927, Vol. II, pp. 369-376.
223. Robinson, *op. cit.*, p. 363; See also *Fikr-o-Nazar*, Vol. II, pp. 357-362.
224. *Aap Biti*, pp. 50-51 and 71; see also Robinson, *op. cit.*, p. 421.
225. *Minutes of the AMU Court,* 1926, pp. 2-6.

6
Political Activities in Aligarh from 1937 to 1947

The decade of 1937 to 1947 was most decisive in the history of Indian freedom movement. The elections of 1937, Pakistan Movement, Quit India Movement, formation of the ministry in 1946 and above all the Partition and Independence of India were happened in this crucial decade of the twentieth century. Generally speaking, it was the most important phase in the modern Indian history and Aligarh that the Aligarh Muslim University was in full form during these periods and participated actively in the every moment of history.

Reaction of AMU over Congress Ministry in 1937

Following the Act of 1935, the election of 1937 was held in almost all provinces of British India. In this election, the Congress won with absolute majority in Madras, Bihar, Orissa, Central Provinces, United Provinces and a near majority in Bombay and formed the government accordingly. Later on, the Congress ministries were also formed in North-West Frontier Province and Assam. Even in Sindh, Congress backed ministry under Allah Bakhsh was installed. Only in Punjab and Bengal ministries were formed under Sikandar Hayat Khan of the Unionist Party and Fazlul Haq of Krishak Praja Party respectively. Fazlul Haq earlier tried to form the government with the support of the Congress as it did not enjoy an absolute majority but having failed to do so he took the support of the Muslim League. He also gave due share to the Muslim League in the Bengal ministry. From this election results, it was clear that the Muslim League had its stronghold nowhere, not even in the Muslim majority provinces.[1]

It must be reminded that till that time Muslim League had no separatist and communal programme. The policies of Muslim League and Mr. Jinnah were national in character and secular in outlook. Mr. Jinnah at Lahore in March 1936 cleared his point by saying, "Whatever I have done, let me assure you there has been no change in me, not the slightest, since the day when I joined the Indian National Congress. It may be I have been wrong on some occasions, but it is never been done in a partisan spirit. My sole and only object has been the welfare of my country. I assure you that India's interest will be sacred to me and nothing will make me budge an inch from that position."[2]

However, the poor election results of 1937 confused Mr. Jinnah and he had to renew his strategy to get the sympathy, at least, of the Muslims. The election results decided that he had no firm footing even among the Muslim masses and the Muslim political parties. Almost all Muslim parties like Jamiatul Ulema-i-Hind formed in 1920 by Deoband Ulema, and Aharar Party founded by ex-Khilafatist in Punjab, supported the Congress and denounced Jinnah as an "out of date politician .... making fetish of constitutionalism and the League as a 'coterie of a few Knigths', Khan Bahadurs and Nawabs."[3]

In UP, Congress and Muslim League leaders like Nawab Mohammad Ismail Khan and Chaudhary Khaliquzzaman were having the gentlemen's agreement in the election of 1937 as the League had no firm footing in UP. They were assured by the Congress that both will be given the ministry if Congress assumed the power provided that they would support the Congress candidate where the Muslim League candidate was not in better position.

According to the pre-poll agreement, the Muslim League leaders like Nawab Mohammad Ismail Khan and Chaudhary Khaliquzzaman worked hard for both Muslim League and the Congress in the election campaign. However, when the Congress came into power with absolute majority, they rejected the coalition appeal of the Muslim League. Nehru and Congress leftists like Narendra Dev and K.M. Ashraf feared that the coalition with

Muslim League would render impossible any radical socio-economic reforms as the League was dominated by upper class and *zamindars*.[4]

Maulana Abul Kalam Azad, on the other hand, was in favour of the coalition government in UP and persuaded other Congress leaders to accept two top rank Muslim League leaders Chaudhary Khaliquzzaman and Nawab Mohammad Ismail Khan. Unfortunately, his advice was not accepted by the Congress High Command. Maulana called it a blunder on the part of the Congress. If Congress had accepted the offer, it might have far-reaching results on the political condition of India.[5]

This political U turn of the Congress against the Muslim League provided strength to the Muslim League in diverting its policy into the communal fold. The Muslim League found it a fair chance to mobilize the Muslim community by quoting the selfish and opportunistic policies of the Congress. Undoubtedly, the Congress had firm footing in Muslim community but being denied from the coalition, the Muslim League gained a momentum in the Muslim majority areas. The Aligarh or AMU intelligentsia was very serious about that sentimental issue and the Muslim League, naturally, influenced the AMU a great deal. Subsequently, the Muslim League leaders got a fair chance to convert the mentality of Aligarh intelligentsia in favour of the Muslim League.

Until 1937, AMU was supported by the Congress whole heartedly and had many expectations from this party. However, the post-poll policy of the Congress gave the Aligarh intelligentsia on Muslim League turn. The Aligarh University Students Union became very aggressive as the proposal of their beloved leaders like Nawab Mohammad Ismail Khan and Chaudhary Khaliquzzaman were spurned by the Congress.[6]

Maulana Zafar Ali delivered a speech in AMU regarding the role of the Congress in ministry formation in UP. His speech greatly influenced many of the students. The students later on due to frustration and dissatisfaction made ugly remarks over the Congress leaders. For the first time in the history of Aligarh, Congress made a question mark on the behaviour of Aligarh students. Since the days of Sir Syed Ahmad Khan, they were marvellous examples of *Tahzib* and *Tamaddun* (civilization and culture) all-over the world.

Pandit Jawahar Lal Nehru wrote a letter to Nawab Mohammad Ismail Khan over the issue of ugly remarks made by AMU students on the Congress and its leaders.[7]

Mr. Mohammad Ali Jinnah found it a golden opportunity to encash the policies of the Congress and used the AMU as his platform to mobilize the Muslim masses. In order to get support of the AMU students and other Aligarh Muslim intelligentsia, Mr. Mohammad Ali Jinnah and other Muslim League leaders annually visited AMU. Their annual visit proved fruitful as most of the students began to consider Mr. Mohammad Ali Jinnah as their only leader. Aligarh students had full faith in the Muslim League and in the leadership of Mr. Mohammad Ali Jinnah. In the meeting of the Muslim University Students Union held on 8th September, 1939, the following resolution was passed:[8]

> "This meeting of the MU Union unanimously resolves that the members of the union have full faith in the leadership of Mr. M.A. Jinnah, the accredited leader of the entire Muslim India. The members of the union further declare most solemnly that students of the Muslim University Aligarh will follow the commands of Mr. M.A. Jinnah whatever they be in this hour of international crisis..."

Muslim League was successful in making more popular image in UP and particularly in Aligarh. It also began to gain strength all-over India, but it was from UP that the League was reorganized. The Punjab Premier and Unionist leader Sir Sikander Hayat Khan and Bengal Premier the Krishak Praja Party leader Fazlul Haq with their followers also became the members of the Muslim League.[9]

The Muslim League, by posing the sole representative of the Muslim community all-over India, enquired about the Muslim's suffering and full details about communal riots, murder, loot and plunder of Muslims and their property, Hindi promoting scheme and ban on cow-slaughter, etc. in the Congress ruled provinces, particularly in Bihar and UP. The League appointed a committee under the Presidentship of Raja Mohammad Mehandi of Pirpur for such purposes. The committee submitted its report and published in late 1938 and became known as the "Pirpur Report". Another committee was also appointed, and its report was published in 1939 known as the "Sherif Report". These were full of atrocities perpetrated by the Hindus in various parts of the provinces.[10]

The data of atrocities committed on the Muslims seemed to be clearly exaggerated. The doubt about the truth of the report was proved by the fact that the Muslim League had rejected the Congress offer of an enquiry by Chief Justice Maurice Gwyer over the charges of the Muslim League.[11] The Muslim League declared that the government in Punjab and Bengal were quite peaceful. The Bengal Premier Fazlul Haq described, "In the Congress provinces riots had laid the country wide waste. Muslim life, limb and property have been lost and blood had freely flowed but here in Bengal not one head had been broken and not one drop of blood had been shed. Here I defy anyone to site a single instance where a Hindu officer had been unfairly treated by us."[12]

In Punjab, Sir Sikandar Hayat, being an Aligarian, had great respect for the secular traditions of Aligarh. His ministry not only included his Unionist colleagues but also Sir Sunder Singh Majithia of Khalsa Nationalist Party and Sir Manohar Lal of National Progressive Party. His reign was very beautifully described by Maulana Zafar Ali as follows:[13]

> "*Kio (Kai) Din Me Yahan Phir Daur-i-Akhar Ane Wala Hai,*
> *Sikandar Hai Abul Fazal Aur Manohar Lal Todarmal.*"

(After a lot of days, the reign of Akbar is about to come here, Sikander is Abul Fazal and Manohar Lal is as Todarmal.)

The Congress ministry barring some unfortunate communal events was very much blamed for its controversial policy of Hindi and Urdu. In the beginning, the Congress adopted the policy of promoting Hindustani, but slowly and gradually it adopted Hindi promoting policy by neglecting Urdu. This was proved by the fact that in UP, in the budget of 1938, a handsome money was given to the colleges of Benaras, where Sanskrit and Hindi languages were being taught. The government did not give any heed to the institution where Urdu, Arabic and Persian were being taught. This pro-Hindi policy of the Congress Government had goaded the

Muslims in the path of darkness, and ultimately they decided to join the Muslim League.[14]

The Aligarh students took the Congress policy of Hindi and Urdu very seriously, and the students union of the Muslim University called a meeting on 26th February, 1939, to discuss the future of 'Urdu' and measures to protect it. It was resolved in the meeting that 'Urdu' should be declared as an official language of the Muslim University Union. To achieve this purpose it is necessary that:[15]

(a) All the narratives of the proceedings would be read and written in Urdu but the discussions, the speeches and narratives would be in English.
(b) In the welcome meetings, condolence meeting and other extraordinary meetings, the proceedings would be generally in Urdu.
(c) All the works of office related to intimation and advertisements would be in Urdu, although English would be included if necessary.
(d) In the regulation of Union some rupees would be sanctioned every year for the publication of Urdu.
(e) Generally, speeches would be in Urdu but those who cannot speak Urdu, would be authorised to make speeches in English with the permission of the President.
(f) Similarly, if any post holder of the Union cannot speak Urdu, would be allowed to deliver his speech in English.
(g) The rules and regulations of the Union with necessary modifications must be compiled in Urdu.

The resolution was unanimously passed by Select Committee of the Union. It was the initial measures adopted by Aligarh University for the promotion of Urdu.[16]

In the provinces of Congress ministry, particularly in UP, there were many anti-social elements that not only tried to subjugate the Muslims but divided the Muslims in such a way that they kept fighting with each other. In Lucknow, the Shia-Sunni controversy was the example. Muslim League claimed that it was the Congress Government which was really responsible for all that controversy.

Khaksar Movement tried its level best to console the two sects of the Muslim community Shia and Sunni but its efforts were frustrated by the government by imposing ban on the movement and by imprisoning the workers of the movement.[17]

The Aligarh students were furious over the ban on Khaksar Movement in UP and arrest of its volunteers. Over this issue, the Union called a meeting to show their resentment. The meeting passed the following resolutions:[18]

> "This meeting of the MU Union views with deep resentment to the fascist policy of repression pursued by the Congress Government, of UP towards the Khaksars who are working to bring about an understanding between the two leading sects of Musalmans at Lucknow. While protesting against the drastic measures and inhuman treatment meted out by the government to the Khaksars, it urges upon the All India Muslim League and Congress High Command to realize the need of forming in this hour of national emergency, a united front to check the menace of repression and exert their influence on the UP Cabinet to bring about an immediate and unconditional release of the Khaksar prisoners and to lift ban imposed upon the said movement."

They also persuaded university authorities and prominent Muslim leaders to go to Lucknow and console both the sects of the Muslims. Prominent Muslim leaders from all-over India rushed to Lucknow and appealed the Shias and Sunnis of Lucknow to stop this useless and absurd controversy. Sir Reza Ali, Dr. Sir Ziauddin, Sir Mohammad Yaqub, Sir Sikandar Hayat Khan and A.K. Fazlul Haq tried their level best to bring compromise between the two but failed to change their mob mentality. Even Congress leader Maulana Abul Kalam Azad could not evolve a compromising formula.[19]

In the Congress ministry in UP, the most undesirable event took place in Aligarh on 26th January, 1939. In the evening of 26th January, 1939, most of the university students had gone to the exhibition. The students of university school known as Minto Circle had also gone with their Headmaster Mr. G.C. Woods. In the exhibition, a policeman chided an innocent student. This event provoked the rest of the students present in the exhibition ground. It was also said that some volunteers of the Hindu Sewa Samiti had attacked the students. A responsible police officer and constable took side of the samiti volunteers and ordered '*lathi* charge' on the Muslim students. Even revolver shots were used by the police officers. This rendered the situation from bad to worse, and many camps were set fire in that very rumpus.[20]

This incident of Aligarh exhibition left a reactionary effect on the Muslims all-over India, especially the Aligs. About this incident, the Muslim Association of Allahabad held an emergent meeting on 3rd February, 1939, under the Secretaryship of Shah Hafeez Alam Jung and passed the following resolution:[21]

> "The Muslim Association of Allahabad is alarmed at the news emanating from Lucknow that the Congress Government is taking serious view of Aligarh incident. The association warns the government that any mishandling in this matter will set the whole province ablaze for which the Congress Government will be responsible. The association demands the immediate transfer of district officials."

Another meeting of Old Boys Association of Hyderabad held on 3rd February, 1939 was presided over by Muhiuddin Yar Jung. A copy of the resolution was sent to Vice-Chancellor and University Union. The general meeting of Hyderabad Old Boys resolved, "This meeting greatly admires and appreciates the sense of discipline shown by the students against grave provocation and requests the Vice-Chancellor to convey to boys this expression of sincere administration from their elder brothers of Hyderabad."[22]

The Muslim University Union on its part also held a meeting on 27th January, 1939, a day after the event had taken place. They passed a resolution which reads as follows:[23]

(1) That the members of the MU Union strongly condemn the irresponsible and callus treatment of the Aligarh district

police towards the students of the Muslim University in district exhibition. They demand from the district authorities to take necessary action against those police constables and officers who took aggressive part in the quarrel, assaulted the students and made *lathi* charge upon them.

(2) That the members of the MU Union sincerely sympathise with those fellow students who have been seriously injured.

(3) That the Aligarh district exhibition must be completely boycotted and no student of the university or any of its allied institutions should visit the exhibition.

(4) To give expression to our self-respect, the members of the Union should not go to the exhibition until and unless the district authorities, being persuaded by the *dukandars*, ask the police to apologize for their misbehaviour.

(5) That the members of the Union strongly condemn and challenge the inaccurate and misleading statement issued by the District Magistrate and published in '*The Hindustan Times*' of the 27th January, 1939.

In the Central Provinces in the Congress ministry, another incident happened. The Congress leaders in the league with the Arya Samaj created disturbances in Hyderabad State. In Hyderabad, the Hindus, particularly Arya Samajists made an agitation against Nizam. To cite one Mr. Baldev and Arya Samajist preacher, "There should be no trace of Muslims in India, there should be Hindu Raj, we have to secure the throne of Nizam within six months."[24] A popular song sung by them meant that they will kick out the Muslims from the state. A Congress leader and speaker of the Central Provinces Assembly was very much active in this movement.[25]

As the Nizam of Hyderabad was closely associated with Aligarh, the Aligarh students always cherished him. At this hour of crisis, the Aligarh students tried their level best to pacify the problem and also threatened the CP Government and communal ogranizations to stop the said movement in the Nizam's territory. They called a meeting of the Union and expressed their resentment against the activities of Hindu Mahasabha and the Indian National Congress because these parties were not only holding tumultuous agitations against the Government of Nizam Hyderabad but also instigating his subjects. They declared emotionally that if conditions would not get normal and the activities of Hindu Mahasabha and Indian National Congress would continue against the Government of Nizam, the Muslim university students who belonged to different parts of India would involve wholeheartedly with all their power and would not hesitate in sending their service in favour of Nizam.[26]

League Propaganda

Throughout the twenty seven months rule of the Congress in the provinces, Muslim League kept up an intense propaganda. It made countrywide tour against Congress ministry and mobilized the Muslim masses and particularly the Muslim intelligentsia. For that very purpose, the Muslim League blamed the Congress for its anti-Muslim policies. In 1938, Mr. Mohammad Ali Jinnah in his Presidential address of the Muslim League said, "The High Command of the Congress is absolutely determined to crush all other communities and cultures in this country and establish Hindu Raj in this country."[27]

In addition to the countrywide tour, Mr. Mohammad Ali Jinnah made the almost annual visit to the Muslim University and made the position of the Muslim League stronger. The AMU students also cherished him and regularly invited to attend the seminars and debates and preside over the functions of the University Union. The speeches of Mr. Mohammad Ali Jinnah left a deep impression on his listeners.[28]

In 1938, when Mr. Mohammad Ali Jinnah was invited as a chief guest in a function of Muslim University, he delivered a very long and impressive speech. The excerpt of the same is being quoted here. He addressed the students saying, "....To a very great extent Muslim League has freed the Musalmans from the clutches of the British Government. But now there is another power which claims to be the successor of the British Government, call it by whatever name but it is Hindu and Hindu Government..."

Mr. Jinnah continued, "My appeal is to you come to the platform of the League. If Muslims are united, the settlement will come sooner than you think. You will have established your claim to achieve freedom. After a few months' work the League's name is known to every corner of India, lakhs of people are joining it. Even those who are against us will realize that they are under a serious delusion and their only course is to join the League and make Musalman with one voice."

Mr. Jinnah further said, "I am convinced that you will agree with me that Congress policy is to divide the Muslims among themselves. It is the same old tactics of the British Government. They follow the policy of their masters. Do not fall into their tarp…"

While inviting the youths to join the Muslim League, Mr. Jinnah said, "…. I find in front of me the finest recruiting ground. Lacs are ready to serve the platform and flag of the All India Muslim League…. The British Government is always thinking of what the Congress is doing, to be repercussions of the British policy in the Congress camp. But will the British Government think of you? No, because you are not an organized power and established your solidarity. The Muslim League is determined to win freedom but it will be a freedom not only for the strong and the dominant but also for the weak and suppressed."[29]

Besides the above mentioned visit of Mr. Jinnah, he visited Aligarh three times, in January and September 1939 and in March 1940, and addressed Aligarh youths for the cause of nation and Muslim League.[30] He made Aligarh students a strong supporter of Muslim League. Mr. Jinnah also claimed from the Congress to recognise the League a sole representative body of the Indian Muslims. However, Congress rejected the claim. Chaudhary Khaliquzzaman admits with frankness, "Congress rejection of Jinnah's position was a piece of good luck for us, for if Congress had accepted the position at the time when the demand was made by the League, I wonder what positive demands we could then have made."[31]

It must be reminded that at that time there was no issue before the Muslim League to strengthen its position and continue its separatist movement. However, the policies of the Congress definitely provided a new platform to the Muslim League to launch a fatal movement of partition of India.

On 3rd September, 1939, when Second World War started, British Government without consultation of Indian leaders thrown up India into the war. Congress felt humiliation and ultimately all the Congress ministries in the provinces resigned from the office in the protest in early November of 1939 and in pursuance of Section 93 of the Government of India Act, 1935, Governors assumed control of the legislative and administrative powers within the provinces. Muslim League observed that day a 'Day of Deliverance' as a sign of relief on the resignation of the Congress ministries in the provinces.[32]

As its Lahore session held in March 1940, the Muslim League enunciated the theory that the Muslims were not "a minority" but a "nation" and they must have their homeland, their territory and their state (Pakistan). "That is the area in which the Muslims are numerically in a majority, as in north-western and eastern zones of India, should be grouped to constitute independent states in which the constituent units shall be autonomous and sovereign."[33]

The observance of 'Day of Deliverance' and launching of a movement for separate homeland by Muslim League was highly condemnable. If we go through the words of Jinnah that the Congress ministries were actuated by a decidedly anti-Muslim policy and suppose that Jinnah was correct yet the circumstances did not allow him to do so. This was the question of humiliation of the Congress party by a foreign power or British Government in India. The Muslim League must have shown its sympathy with the Congress.

If the Congress was the anti-Muslim during its tenure of government, then what action Mr. Jinnah had taken for 80 million Muslims of India in such circumstances? Why there was no movement against such atrocities committed by Congress ministry? Why had they waited for 30 long months for its resignation? Mr. Jinnah and his followers observed the 'Day of Deliverance' only when the Congress ministry resigned by their own choice and free will. The League crossed the limits of excessive communalism when in 1940 it passed the 'Pakistan' resolution. This famous resolution created a permanent rift between the Hindus and the Muslims and finally divided the country between two nations, viz. India and Pakistan.

AMU's Response over Congress and British Policies

Although the cherished leaders of AMU Chaudhary Khaliquzzaman and Nawab Mohammad Ismail Khan were deprived from the Congress ministry in UP, the Congress could not lose its base in AMU.[34] The Congress leaders were being welcomed whenever they visited Aligarh Muslim University. Dr. Syed Mahmood, Minister of Education in Bihar; Pandit Govind Ballabh Pant, Premier of UP and Rafi Ahmad Kidwai, Revenue Minister of UP visited AMU. Their aim was to check the hold of Muslims League in the university, and they became quite successful in their aim. However, due to the annual visit of Mr. Mohammad Ali Jinnah and his provocative speeches affected the students very much. It resulted in the creation of another section of students who was a staunch supporter of the Muslim League.[35]

The visit of the Congress and League leaders resulted the division of AMU students into two groups, one supporting the Congress and the other follower of Muslim League, that too, due to the UP policies of the Congress. No doubt Muslim League tried its level best to create a Muslim League atmosphere among the Indian Muslims but the independent, secular and national traditions of Aligarh always encouraged them for the cause of India. Most of the Aligarh Muslim leaders also could not control their nerves to support the national policies of the Congress in spite of being members of the Muslim League. Nawab Mohammad Ismail Khan, the President of the UP Muslim League, in spite of being deprived from the ministry in UP, had the friendship with almost all the top-most Congress leaders. In the AMU Court, the majority was of the Congress men. Even on the key posts of the AMU many Congress minded men were appointed.[36]

A letter of the Muslim League leader of Aligarh Mr. Sattar Khairi to Mr. Mohammad Ali Jinnah on October 12, 1941 throws much light on the political conditions of AMU. It needs to be quoted as follows:[37]

> ".... Mr. Jinnah you remember, three years ago both Dr. Ziauddin and Nawab Ismail Khan on your advice withdrew their names from being the candidate for the

> Vice-Chancellorship.... Pandit Govind Ballabh Pant was angry with Nawab Ismail Khan on account of withdrawing his name. Mr. Pant had made all arrangements for leave, etc. for such members of the University Court, who were to vote for Nawab Sahib. Nawab Ismail Khan has been the greatest supporter of Dr. Zakir Husain of Jamia Millia who had been doing his best to introduce Congress minded members in the staff and the Court. Another great friend of Nawab Sahib has been Khan Bahadur Deputy Habibullah, the bitter enemy of the League workers in the university. About this Dr. Abid Husain, Mr. Jamiluddin Ahmad and myself protested once to Nawab Sahib. So far, once he stayed at Dr. Abid's house when he came on League business and we three and few others spoke to Nawab Sahib about Dr. Zakir. Upon this Nawab lost all self-control and was full of rage. Now, the thing has been exposed. They have been intriguing to bring in Congresswalas in the key position in the university. It were these three persons who had been in Executive Council of the university—Tasadduq Ahmad Sherwani, Abdul Majid Khwaja, Abdul Hameed. ... I pray that God shall give you strength in this great hour of trial and true insight into the needs of the Indian Muslims."[38]

The way of the Congress in AMU remained unaffected until the selection of Dr. Ziauddin Ahmad as Vice-Chancellor of AMU in 1941. Members of the Muslim League in the university regarded the selection of Dr. Ziauddin as the greatest victory of the Muslim League.[38] Dr. Ziauddin was a loyalist, a true Musalman and a member of the Muslim League also. In 1941, when anti-Congress propaganda by Muslim League was at its height, he became the Vice-Chancellor of AMU. At the beginning of the new session in August 1941, he addressed the students, "This university is a Muslim institution which has preserved an Islamic atmosphere and respect for Islamic tenets. For those who oppose and underline Islamic belief and practices in addressing the students of the Muslim University are over."[39]

During the Second World War, Pandit Jawahar Lal Nehru and many other Congress leaders visited Aligarh several times. Pandit

Nehru explained the Congress attitude towards the Second World War and paid particular attention to the need for the enrolment of the Congress volunteers. Subhas Chandra Bose also addressed the Aligarh people in January 1940. He described India's poverty to the British rule and made an impassioned appeal advocating immediate mass struggle for the country's independence.[40]

The Aligarh Political Conference was held on April 30th and May 1st, 1940 in Aligarh. It was presided over by Acharya Narendra Deo. The other speakers were Kailash Nath Katju, Krishan Datta Paliwal and Malkhan Singh. They explained that how British were using Indian men and money to carry on the war despite opposition of the Congress. They said that the exploitation would never end until the British imperialism was destroyed. In this conference, the resolutions condemning the Second World War were passed. In 1940, Individual *Satyagraha* was launched particularly against the war funds, and a number of people courted arrest.[41]

Actually, the beginning of the Second World War changed the entire political scenario all-over India. While Congress had anti-war policy and protesting against exploitation of Indian resources for imperialistic ends and demanded that "India must be declared an Independent nation." The All India Muslim League started its Pakistan Movement during this World War crisis. Thus, non-Congress ministries in Punjab, Sindh and Bengal extended their full support to the British Government. The Indian states as usual also offered their full support to the British Government with men and money. The Hindu Mahasabha and National Liberal Federation also offered unconditional support to the British Government.[42]

The conflicting ideology of the politicians all-over India affected the political activities of Aligarh very much. They also divided themselves into 'pro' and 'anti' of the British Government by following their policy-makers. The loyalist elements which had developed from very beginning got strength and started supporting the British Government fully in order to get its sympathy. During the war time, the local landlords and other loyalists helped the government in recruiting programme and other war efforts. Their cooperation was to get support of the wealthy and powerful hands of the government for their own sake or for the sake of their community.

In Aligarh, Dr. Ziauddin Ahmad, who was also a member of the Muslim League, followed the ideology of Muslim League, but much against the wishes of the League leaders, he adopted loyalist attitude with government. He thought that the Muslim community could not be powerful without the support of the government. For that cause, Dr. Ziauddin Ahmad sometimes did loyalist activities for the happiness of the British Government. On the occasion of the celebration of the coronation of Their Majesties King George VI, Emperor of India, and Queen Elizabeth, on 12th May, 1937, Dr. Ziauddin along with his loyalist friends illuminated the university clock tower and organised a university dinner followed by a cinema show.[43]

On that occasion almost all the Raises of Aligarh district also celebrated the coronation at Darbar Pandal near Lal Diggi, Aligarh. The hosts of this function were Nawab Bahadur of Bhikampur, Nawab Sadar Yar Jang of Habibganj, Rai Bahadur Sultan Singh M.B.E. of Lucknow, Khan Bahadur Haji Ghulam Mohammad Khan Dadon, Rai Bahadur Pratap Bhan Singh of Kapasia, Kunwar Raj Kumar Singh of Baraulu, Rai Bahadur Seth Chiranji Lal Bagla of Hathras, Mohammad Abul Muqit Khan of Bhikampur, Kunwar Ram Singh of Lucknow, S. Ali Asghar of Jalali, Shah Udai Ram of Vajidpur, Rai Bahadur Dwarka Prasad Bhargawa of Sasni, Raja Bahadur of Murson, Khan Bahadur Obaidur Rahman of Bhikampur, Rai Bahadur Sheodhan Singh of Piswa, Kunwar Deo Raj Singh of Gabhana, Rao Madho Singh of Suhawali, Mr. Abid Khan of Bhikampur, S. Mahmud Hasan of Asgharbad, Seth Mahabir Prasad of Beswan, Kunwar Gulzar Singh of Piswa, Netrapal Singh of Jiroli, L. Harish Chandra of Sikandra Rao, Rai Bahadur Mathra Prasad of Man, Rai Bahadur Laxmi Raj Singh of Gabhana, Nawab Bahadur of Talibnagar, Khan Bahadur Mohammad Jan Khan of Dadon, Rai Bahadur Raghubir Singh of Surajpur, Khan Bahadur Munis Khan of Jatauli, Kunwar Rohini Ramandhwaj Prasad Singh of Beswan, Cap. Swaleh Khan of Bhikampur, Kunwar Jaipal Singh of Jalaipur, S. Masudul Hasan of Asgharabad, Rai Bahadur Mathra Prasad Bhargawa of Sasni, Kunwar Virendra Singh of Birpura, S. Ali Azhar of Jalali, M. Hadi Ali Khan of Sikandra Rao and Chhattar Singh of Bhartau.[44]

Pro- and Anti-League Atmosphere in AMU

Aligarh had always been the arena of different political parties and the personalities of different ideologies. However, with the defeat of Muslim League in the election of 1937, the academic atmosphere of the university suffered greatly. It further worsened due to the political activities at the AMU campus. The leader of the Muslim League Mr. M.A. Jinnah visited the Aligarh several times and tried his level best to mobilise the Muslims in favour of Muslim League both in the Aligarh city and in AMU campus.[45] His visit was always eagerly looked forward by everyone connected with the university and his thought-provoking speeches and discussions became a source of inspiration for the students.[46]

Besides Mr. M.A. Jinnah, other leaders like Nawabzada Liaqat Ali Khan, Hon'ble Sir Firoz Khan Noon and Hon'ble Dr. B.R. Ambedkar visited the AMU and delivered thought-provoking speeches under the auspices of the AMU Students Union.[47] Congress also had its strong hold in the university staff and students which caused a tussle among the intelligentsia of different political ideologies.[48] Because of the political rivalry between the Congress and Muslim League in the university campus, the administrative problems arose and caused a set-back to the educational development of the university.

Dr. Ziauddin Ahmad, a devout Muslim and an active member of the Muslim League, became Vice-Chancellor of the AMU three times in the duration of 1935 to 1947. His Vice-Chancellorship gave a further boosting to the Muslim wave in the university. In Aligarh, Jinnah was always given a very warm reception every time and a band of students was prepared for the service of the Muslim League and Mr. Jinnah.[49] In 1943, Dr. Ziauddin offered Jinnah the honourary degree of Doctor of Laws[50], but in hesitation he replied, "I am thankful to the Court of the Muslim University Aligarh, I have most reluctantly to say that I have lived as plain Mr. Jinnah and I hope to die as plain Mr. Jinnah, I am very much averse to any title or honour and I will be much happy if there was no prefix to my name."[51]

Muslim League had many good followers in the Aligarh district and Aligarh Muslim University, and they opposed the Congress programmes whenever were launched by the party. In October 1940, the Congress inaugurated an Individual Civil Disobedience campaign. The majority of the Aligarh Muslims actively opposed the Congress policy as already in March 1940 in the Lahore session of the Muslim League Mr. Jinnah declared that the Muslim nation must have a separate state.

Regarding the Individual Civil Disobedience, the Students's Union of AMU passed a resolution on 17th Februrary, 1941:[52]

> "This meeting of the MU Union places on record its considered view that the real object of the *satyagraha* movement launched by the Congress is to force the hands of the British Government to let down the Muslims and coerce them into submission to the demands of the Congress which are calculated to bring about complete Hindu domination over the entire country. The claim that the struggle is being waged to vindicate liberty of speech is falsified by the fact that the civil and religious liberties of the Muslims were severely suppressed under Congress ministries."
>
> "The union sounds a note of warning that if any settlement is made over the heads of the Musalmans without their approval and consent it will lead to disastrous consequences and trusts that the government will not allow itself to be stampeded into taking any action, which would adversely affect the interests of Muslims."
>
> "The Musalmans, being fully alive to the gravity of the world situation, are always prepared to cooperate with other parties on an equal footing to ensure the safety of India as a whole. But so far the settlement of the final constitutional issues is concerned, the union reiterates its firm faith that whole future, fate and salvation of the Musalmans be bound up with the scheme of independent states in regions of Muslim majority."
>
> "The Union reaffirms its fullest confidence in Mr. Jinnah and assures him that the Muslim youth are prepared to obey his commands and make every sacrifice to achieve the national goal of Musalmans."

A Muslim organization 'Khaksar'[53] which was in the form of a movement engaged actively with the Muslim problems and sufferings. Government imposed ban on its movement and its popular leader Allama Inayatullah Khan Mashriqi was put behind the bars. It greatly initiated not only the Aligarh people but also the Muslims all-over India. In a meeting of the MU Union held on 26th November, 1941, it was resolved, "this meeting of the MU Union issues with great concern and anxiety the report that Allama Mashriqi has been fasting since the Ramdhan in the Vellore jail as a protest against the treatment meted out to him by the jail authorities and that his health has been declining. It expresses its profound sympathy with the Allama and urges on the government to show the difference to the sentiment of the Muslim public all-over India by releasing him immediately."[54]

On 1st April, 1942, Muslim University Union again met and urged the government the necessity to remove immediately the restrictions imposed on Allama and of lifting ban on the Khaksar movement. It also said that at a time of national crisis when political prisoners of all shades of opinion had been released it was very unfair to restrict movement of Allama Mashriqi.[55]

Most of the Aligarh students influenced by Muslim League always welcomed any idea or call given by Mr. Jinnah, who was generally called as '*Qaid-i-Azam*'.[56] In 1942, Mr. Jinnah made an appeal to the Muslims for a fund of the Muslim League, the Muslim University Union quickly responded and charged Re. 1/- per head from every member of the Union. The money was sent to Mr. Jinnah with the assurance that the members of the union would faithfully carryout his command.[57]

Besides the Muslim League supporters, there were a lot of people, including both the students and staff in AMU who were bitterly against the Muslim League and Mr. Mohammad Ali Jinnah. Most of them were the Congress sympathizers and true patriot of their motherland. Not only the Congress but the other like-minded secular political parties also had their firm footing in the AMU.

Dr. Ziauddin Ahmad for his pro-Muslim League policy faced much opposition in the Aligarh Muslim University. In 1935, when he was elected Vice-Chancellor for the first time, he was criticised by Khan Bahadur Maulvi Habibullah Khan, Maulvi Tufail Ahmad,

Quazi Azizuddin and Mr. Zafar Umar regarding university administration. They also made personal attacks on him.[58]

When Dr. Ziauddin Ahmad was elected Vice-Chancellor for the second time, the Old Boys Association also firmly opposed him. As a mark of protest, Nawab Mohammad Ismail Khan, Dr. Zakir Husain and Khan Bahadur Maulvi Habibullah Khan resigned from the Executive Council on 7th May, 1941. Again in 1943, seven members of the Court published a large pamphlet in which Dr. Ziauddin Ahmad was not only criticized for his policies in the university affairs but there were also attacks on his personal life. The pamphlet was signed by Khan Bahadur Habibullah Khan and hid friends. Dr. Ziauddin Ahmad in return requested the Executive and Academic Councils for an enquiry about it. The report was sent to the Court, and it showed its disfavour over the publication of the pamphlet. However, Khan Bahadur did not keep quiet and a mark of protest he resigned from the Court on January 31, 1944 through a letter. In that letter he criticized Dr. Ziauddin Ahmad saying that the work of Dr. Ziauddin about the development of the university and the movement for the Medical College was mere a propaganda.[59]

Dr. Ziauddin Ahmad always faced a bitter opposition and criticism from many members of the Court and local personalities, but they had to yield before his success. In the later years of his life, he could not succeed to quell the opposition and it led to tragic end of his Vice-Chancellorship. According to Amin Zuberi during the year of 1946, the Communist wave was on its peak and there was a special lobby of Communists in the university. This lobby included both staff members and the students.[60]

By the end of December 1946, the anti-Ziauddin and anti-League staff of the AMU hatched a conspiracy against the Vice-Chancellor Dr. Ziauddin Ahmad. In this conspiracy, students were utilised by the lobby. In this conspiracy, a student of Aftab Hall, Abdul Qadir Rizvi, who was also the editor of the university magazine, published a note without showing the censor of the university. The note included the role of Congress Government and Hindus about the happenings in Bihar. When its news reached to the District Magistrate of Aligarh, he intimated it to Dr. Ziauddin and Dr. Sahib seized all the copies of the magazine with immediate effect. Abdul Qadir and his friends along with the lobby made a propaganda that Dr. Ziauddin is about to hand over the editor of the university magazine to the police. This news spread like a wild fire and students demanded the resignation of the Vice-Chancellor immediately.[61]

Following this rumour, a large gathering of the students' proceeded towards the office of the Vice-Chancellor and forced him to resign. Dr. Ziauddin Ahmad realized the situation and by writing the word 'resign' on a piece of paper he handed it over to the students. On this untoward episode, the other faction of the students or pro-League condemned this event and requested the Vice-Chancellor to take back his resignation. However, Dr. Ziauddin Ahmad did not accept their request.[62]

On 1st January, 1947, a special meeting of the Executive Council was held to discuss the resignation of Dr. Ziuaddin Ahmad. The Council concluded their discussion with words, "As Dr. Ziauddin Ahmad has requested for his resignation but Council opines that this is not a resignation and this meeting is not ready to accept it. So his resignation should be placed before the Court of the university. During this period the work of Vice-Chancellor should be carried on by the Treasurer Maulvi Obaidur Rahman Khan Sherwani."[63]

During rejection and consideration of his resignation, Dr. Ziauddin Ahmad was persuaded to take back his resignation, but he didn't become ready to take back his step. Eventually, Dr. Ziauddin Ahmad accepted the request of the Council to supervise the matters related to Medical College, Polytechnic School and Dairy Farm. On 2nd March, 1947, a special meeting of the AMU Court was held and the Court, like the Executive Council, requested him to continue as Vice-Chancellor but Dr. Ziauddin Ahmad deliberately refuted the request. The Court ultimately accepted his resignation. Mr. Mohammad Ali Jinnah and Nawabzada Liaqat Ali Khan proposed the name of Mr. Zahid Husain for the Vice-Chancellorship. By the request of Liaqat Ali Khan, Dr. Ziauddin became ready to work until April 1947.[64]

The Budget Session of the AMU Court was held on 20th April, 1947, and requested Lord Rector to appoint Dr. Ziauddin Ahmad as Rector of the university. Consequently, Dr. Ziauddin Ahmad became Rector of the university.[65]

By concluding all the events it can rightly be said that the AMU was full of the persons of all ideologies and parties. They played active part whenever they got opportunity. However, by Mr. Jinnah's efforts, the AMU Students Union was completely dominated by Muslim League activists. They spoke from the platform of the union regarding all national and regional events mainly concerning Muslim population.

From the activities and resolutions of the union, it should not be presumed that the whole of AMU students were pro-Muslim League. However, it must be kept in mind that the influence of Muslim League and its separatist policy was always challenged by the secular leaders of the Muslim community in AMU. It was long cherished tradition of the AMU that whenever any large meeting or gathering was convened, the lesson of secularism was always taught to the students. In the convocational address of 1st January, 1941, Sultan Ahmad addressed, "there is no gainsaying the fact that racially and politically we (Hindus and Muslims) are all-Indian, we breathe in the same atmosphere and till the same land. We are inheritors of the same proud civilization and whatever we may privately think and aspire after, our destinies are linked together. Our political and social salvation can only lie in both Hindu and Muslim pooling their energies together for the reconstruction of a better India. However, much you try there is no other road of salvation. Any other road will lead India to chaos, anarchy, bloodshed and perpetual subjection .... And I conjure you earnestly, all young men both Hindus and Muslims, to remember this hard sane and incontrovertible fact when you enter a larger sphere of life."[66]

These lessons of unity and secularism very much affected the youths and it bound them to work for India and for their own community. They carried their national work sometimes themselves or by joining with Aligarh city nationalists who were both Hindus and Muslims.[67]

Revolutionary Activities in Aligarh

The Aligarh was also known for its revolutionary activities. In the freedom movement of India, the revolutionary type people of Aligarh also did a lot. In the Aligarh city the nationalistic activities were mostly revolutionary and the city worked as a workshop for making arms for revolutionary elements generally known as '*Krantikari*'. It was quite interesting that in spite of having the revolutionary ideology, they made Mahatma Gandhi as their ideal.

Aligarh was the source of supplying bombs to the All India Revolutionary Organization at its headquarter in Delhi. Generally, bomb action was avoided in Aligarh itself for the fear of defection of the supply.[68] It all became possible due to the lock industry of Aligarh and Government Metal Working School Aligarh. Some of the revolutionaries also used the Engineering College workshop of Muslim University in the bomb making process for the revolutionaries.[69]

The group of revolutionaries of Aligarh mostly included a high-class technician and electrician. They were of the good heart and brain and having zeal to do a lot for their country. Most famous among them were Krishna Lal Verma, Deo Datta, Panna Lal, Bhagwat Deo Mishra, Satya Murti, Mahendra Pal Singh, Durga Prasad, Rajendra Kumar, Kailash Ram Singh of Harduaganj, etc.[70]

They all belonged to the Aligarh city. Only Kishan Lal was the student of the Muslim University in the War Technician's Course. He used to bring some cast iron from the university workshop and also had a few friends in AMU who were engaged in his work, but their active role was not very clear.[71]

For the smooth workings of their activities, the revolutionaries formed themselves into three committees: (1) Finance Committee, (2) Secret Committee or Bomb Party, and (3) Propaganda Committee. The first committee was to get money for the party by fair or foul means such as robbery, dacoity, cheating or securing voluntary financial help from the public. The chief function of the second committee was to arrange all possible anti-government and anti-British actions, influence bank officials for private servants of government officers so that they might prove useful in party actions. The third one the Propaganda Committee was to enlist as many youth for the party as possible who should all be ready to sacrifice not only their lives but also that they possess for the party work.[72]

Most of the revolutionaries styled themselves with the name of revolutionaries and politicians of all-India level, e.g. Deo Datta was styled as Allama Mashriqi and Krishan Lal as Jinnah and other revolutionaries also styled like that.[73] These revolutionaries enlisted new members in their group only after being fully satisfied with their courage and patriotic feelings. One of the methods was cutting a portion of the body and saying, *"Jaisa Main Ab Khun Baha Raha Hun, Bharat Mata Ke Liye Waise Hi Bahata Rahunga."*[74]

When the Cripps Mission arrived in India, the revolutionaries of Aligarh were very much frustrated. They expressed their frustration by singing a Hindi poetry copied from the Daily Hindi *Milap,* Lahore, of 25th September, 1942. The poem was entitled as "Cripps Ke Chane" and was something as follows:[75]

> *"Chana Zor Garam, Ghana Zor Garam,*
> *Gandhi Main Laya Mazedar,*
> ....
> *Charh Na Saka Gandhi Pe Rang."*

There was another Urdu poem by Josh Malihabadi, which was being sung by the revolutionaries of Aligarh:[76]

> *"Kis Zuban Se Kah Rahe Ho Ai Saudagaron,*
> *Dahar Men Insaniat Ke Naam Ko Uncha Karo,*
> *Ek Kahani Waqt Likhega Naye Mazmun Ki,*
> *Jiski Surkhi Ko Zarurat Hai Tumhare Khun Ki."*

When the Quit India Movement was launched by Mahatma Gandhi, the Aligarh revolutionaries actively participated in this movement.[77] They took the responsibility for providing bombs to the militants of other cities also. Qayyum Lohar of the Muslim University was also active in moulding the shells to prepare the bombs. In this connection, Aruna Asaf Ali came to Aligarh in the middle of September 1942. She met the revolutionary elements of Aligarh and told that bomb should be made in plenty. She was pleased to note that the Aligarh revolutionaries were working with zeal for the country and was quite satisfied by the work done by them.[78]

For the purpose of bomb making, readymade iron and tin containers were purchased from Sufi Kabari, Abdul Majeed or Abdul Hameed motor mechanic. Motor brake drums were also purchased for that purpose. Out of these materials, the bombs were prepared with the help of Amir Bakhsh Lohar and Mullah Naimullah. All the bombs prepared in Aligarh were distributed to Delhi, Kanpur and Muzaffarpur.[79]

Somehow, the activities of the revolutionaries were leaked to the police, and the police started repression against the revolutionaries. Subsequently, the revolutionaries decided for a bomb action in Aligarh. Kishan Lal took a shell to the University Engineering College workshop and did the needful with the permission of Mr. Aziz turner instructor on the pretence that it was the work of Allanur an A.R.P. Mistri, who was known to him. Deo Datta and Satya Murti filled the shell with explosive and watch was also fitted to serve as a time bomb.[80] At the railway station, near the post box, the bomb was planted, and it exploded when the Bareilly Passenger had gone. Krishan Lal, Bhura Singh, Sheo Das and Ghanshyam went on to the university, a safest place for the shelter.[81]

During that period, the AMUSU was busy with the programme of the Muslim League and did not participate in the Quit India Movement launched by the Congress. About this movement, the Chancellor of the AMU Nizam III and the Viceroy felt satisfaction over the aloofness of the students. On 30th November, 1942, Nizam wrote to the Vice-Chancellor Dr. Sir Ziauddin Ahmad:[82]

> "As a Chancellor of the university, I feel, I must express my satisfaction of the good conduct and behaviour which the students of the said university have shown during the subversive movement caused by the 'Congress' throughout the country. Not only this, but have come to know that His Excellency the Viceroy as Lord Rector of the said university has appreciated this very much. Under the circumstances, I ask you to let the student know that I have written to you in this connection and say that I have every hope that they will continue to show good conduct in future as well, especially at a time when India is passing through troublous time and that preservance and many character are the chief necessary factors to combat the evil forces that are unfortunately rampant in the country. So, it is all the

more necessary that we should overcome them by our sagacity and prudence at all costs. I trust, the students will listen to my advice given in their own interest."

However, it must not be forgotten that the aloofness of the university union and majority of the students of AMU regarding Quit India Movement was due to their involvement in the movements launched by Muslim League and Mr. Mohammad Ali Jinnah, not by any other reason or due to their loyalty to the British Government.

AMU and Demand for Pakistan

Since the very beginning, Mr. Jinnah had special attachment with the students. When he entered the politics, he realized that there is immense strength in the students who could properly be used at the time of political crisis. From the time of his political setback, during the elections of 1937, he began to visit AMU and other educational institutions. However, his love and attachment with the students was even before the elections of 1937. Its proof was that he had founded All India Muslim Students Federation in 1937, before the election, at Lucknow on the pattern of All India Students Federation. Its provincial branches were opened in most of the provinces of India.[83]

Mr. Jinnah had tremendous faith in Muslim youth, and he succeeded in winning them to his side. In response the student community regarded Jinnah as equal to none. Mr. Jinnah sent messages to student moots and publications, he addressed their gatherings especially at Aligarh which he visited almost every year, and he also inaugurated and presided over student's conferences. At Aligarh Mr. Jinnah was their "Beau-ideal" during the decisive decade of 1937-47.

Most of the Aligarians joined the UP Muslim Students Federation, and they actively propagated the Muslim League ideology through this federation. In 1944-45, Prof. A.B.A. Haleem, President of the UP Muslim Students Federation sent deputations to different districts in the province in order to popularize the federation. It was aimed that by doing so, they would form and reorganize the district units of the federation. The most important persons who carried the deputation were M/s Nazrul Hasan, Abdul Khair, Malik Hamid, Mohammad Farooq, etc. who visited Moradabad, Bareilly, Saharanpur, Muzaffar Nagar, etc.[84]

The Muslim students helped to generate enthusiasm, galvanise the masses behind the League and its demand for Pakistan, for which the resolution was passed in the Lahore session of All India Muslim League on March 22-24, 1940.[85] In order to fulfil his goal, Mr. Jinnah tried his level best to mobilize the Muslim students in his favour. He targeted the AMU students who were already considering him as their cherished leader. To make his programme successful, Mr. Jinnah planned to visit the Muslim University annually. In this process of mobilizing the Muslim students, Mr. Jinnah provoked them through his speeches in Aligarh. On 10th March, 1941, Jinnah addressed the Aligarh students as follows:[86]

> "...In England instead of democracy a few influential sections are ruling. When this system (Democracy) is not successful to a country where only one community is living and there is no doubt of being one community for them, then in India not more but at least very different two communities are living, how this system can be successful. On the contrary promulgation of this system would mean rule of majority over minority community and would enslave the later one. You have accepted this fact that the position of the Muslim is of minority and declared that Muslims are a separate nation and their national position should be accepted. You have told that the Pakistan is only solution of communal problems of India. That means only that where Muslims or Hindus are in majority, they should rule there independently....You have said that Pakistan is not a new thing but it existed earlier and still exists and it will remain till resurrection. Of course, it was being seized from us and now we are trying to get it. To get it back is not so easy but we should have to continue our fight with full strength for it...."

The Muslim League Working Committee opened its branch in AMU for canvassing, promotion and propagation of Muslim League programmes into the students. For this purpose, the Muslim University branch of the Muslim League Working Committee drafted a comprehensive programme. The most important items were (1) enrolment of the 1,000 members, (2) literary centres, (3) distribution and circulating libraries in different hostels, (4) series of lecture on political problems, and (5) group discussions and talks. The university branch of Muslim League was very much influential as most of the students actively and staff members formally took much interest in it. Almost all post holders of students union were active members of it and were ready for any sacrifice.They were true followers of Jinnah.[87]

Mr. Nusrat Hasan on the occasion of his installation as Vice-President of the Muslim University Students Union in October 1941 opined about the Pakistan, "Paksistan is our creed and our politics is based upon it. The dream of united nationalism cannot be realized in this country because the majority does not permit us to live a life of peace and comfort. Pakistan and Pakistan alone is the best solution of the problem." Referring to the Muslim League he said, "I am in a complete agreement with the programme of Muslim League. This is the platform which has given real political insight. This is the organization which has taught us to speak with one voice and which has given us strength and solidarity. My victory is the victory of the Muslim League. My success represents the success of the Muslim League. Muslim League is the source of my strength and encouragement."[88]

Mr. Nusrat Hasan also cleared, "The Muslim University Students Union is not working a debating society, it is a mirror reflecting the thought and sentiments of the Musalmans of India." He also declared, "Musalmans are a living nation and will never allow the sinister design of their antagonists to be realized."[89]

Mr. Jinnah arrived in Aligarh again on 1st November, 1941. The students gave an enthusiastic reception at the railway station and hailed him with slogans, "*Quaid-Azam Zindabad*", "*Muslim League Zindabad*", "*Pakistan Zindabad*". This time he came here in order to attend the Aligarh Muslim League Conference. He gave a stirring address to the University Union on 2nd November, 1941. Other important Muslim League leaders who were present were Nawabzada Liaqat Ali Khan, Mr. H.S. Suhrawardy, Qazi Isa Khan and Maulana Hasrat Mohani.[90] In the honour of Mr. Jinnah a poem was presented to him, on 2nd November, 1941, by a student Ahmad Mohiuddin.[91]

Giving a survey to the present political situation Mr. Jinnah said that India's politics could be divided into two parts—the present and the future. As for future, he said that the Viceroy on behalf on His Majesty's Government, made a declaration of 8th August, 1940, which was simplified by Mr. Amery on the 15th August, 1940, to effect that no future Constitution of India would be framed without the consent and approval of the major elements in India and that it could only be adopted when there was an agreement between the principal parties in India.[92]

Regarding the present, Mr. Jinnah said that the Muslim League was willing as far back as November 1939 to help the British Government, in the successful prosecution of the war. Some of the excerpts of the speeches of Mr. Jinnah are as follows:[93]

> "We had realised that there was a great danger to India", Mr. Jinnah continued, "It was in our own interest that we should have a share and power to defend our homes and hearths, and therefore, within the framework of the present Constitution we must be ready and willing to cooperate with the British Government with authority and power both at the centre and the provinces. The August declaration of the Viceroy recognised that principle, but when that principle came to be translated into action, it was completely frustrated. The terms of the offer were such that no self-respecting party could agree to it. The Muslim League therefore rejected the offer also."

Referring to the independent and sovereign Muslim State, Mr. Jinnah said, "if the British Government, do not make it clear as to what their intentions are, regarding Muslim States and also that they have no design on their sovereignty and independence, it would be very difficult to control Muslim India any more. Some of the Hindu leaders have been suggesting that Pakistan is more a danger to the British Government than to the Hindus and therefore, the only way to fight this danger is to disrupt existing independent

Muslim States. So, that the Hindus could rule over the whole of India easily, I say that it is foolish."

Referring to Mahatma Gandhi's statement hinting at civil war, Mr. Jinnah said that if it comes it would come as a result of Congress policy of repression and domination over Muslim India. Mr. Jinnah declared, "Muslim India is demanding only one fourth of India leaving the rest to the Hindus, while the Congress wants to have whole of this vast sub-continent for the Hindus. If, therefore, India is plunged into civil war it would only be on account of the Congress and nobody else."

Mr. Jinnah refuted the allegations of Mr. Munshi in his speech at Lahore that non-Muslims in Pakistan would be treated as untouchables, Mr. Jinnah said, "let me tell Mr. Munshi that untouchability is only known to his philosophy. Pakistan scheme is based on what Islam has taught us. Islam stands for equality of manhood. It stands for justice and fair play, pay generosity to non-Muslims who are like brothers to us and would be the citizens of the state."

The thought-provoking speeches of Mr. Jinnah further strengthened the base of Muslim League in the Aligarh Muslim University. Muslim University Union also expressed its deep sense of loyalty to the cause and the aim of the AIML and its full faith in Mr. Jinnah.[94]

On 3rd November, Mr. Jinnah also addressed the Muslim University's Day Scholars Union and said that he did not appreciate a separate union for day scholars in one and the same university. They should learn to live and work on one platform unitedly and for that purpose it would be better that they should merge themselves into one university union.[95]

Mr. Jinnah established himself on such a position that no one could reach up to that point. He was not only cherished by the Aligarh students but also by the staff and higher authorities of the university. On 25th December, 1943, the birthday of Mr. Jinnah was celebrated in the university with great enthusiasm and zeal by both the students and the staff members. The Pro-Vice Chancellor of the university Prof. Haleem and Vice-Chancellor Sir Ziauddin Ahmad paid special tribute to Mr. Jinnah's capacity to keep himself above all temptations which was a rare quality found even in the foremost Indian leaders. Sir Ziauddin Ahmad fervently prayed and wished long life and prosperity for Mr. Jinnah.[96]

In 1944 on 25th of December, the birthday of Mr. Jinnah was again celebrated in AMU with great pomp and show. Vice-Chancellor Sir Ziauddin Ahmad paid glowing tributes to Mr. Jinnah's character, integrity and achievements as a leader. On a query by a British officer why Mr. Jinnah was so popular among the Muslims, Dr. Ziauddin Ahmad replied, "at a time when British Government had handed over all the Muslims of India to the Hindu Congress to treat them the way they liked, it was Mr. Jinnah who had the courage to stand up in defence of the Muslims and to save them from destruction."[97]

On that occasion of Mr. Jinnah's birthday, Mr. Mohammad Ali Khan, Secretary of the AMU Union, has sent the following telegram to Mr. Jinnah, "Students of the Muslim University rejoice and express their heartiest greetings on your 68th birthday and pray Allah for your long and happy life. May Muslim India achieve its cherished ideal of Pakistan under your inspiring leadership."[98]

The height of the popularity of Muslim League and Mr. Jinnah could be observed that even the children of Aligarh formed a 'Bachcha Muslim League'. According to its Secretary, a meeting of the 'Bachcha (Child) Muslim League' was also held under the Presidentship of Fashiuddin Ahmad. He said, "*Qaid-i-Azam* has made us a nation and has given us a definite goal and platform and it is up to us to carry this teaching successfully for the attainment of Pakistan."[99]

Unfortunately, Mr. Jinnah was attacked by some anti-social elements, but he was escaped with a little injury. Over this mishappening, Aligarh expressed its sense of indignation and abhorrence to the attackers and felt profound relief at his providential escape. The students and the staff held a meeting and passed a resolution about it and prayed for his speedy recovery from the injuries sustained and complete restorations to health, strength and vigour. The same resolutions were passed by Muslim University Union, MU Muslim League, MU Executive Council and Teacher's Training College.[100]

Along with their strong faith in Mr. Jinnah, most of the Aligarh students were being taught the only pet lesson of Pakistan. They did not spare even the Viceroy for his reference to the geographical unity of India, addressed to the Central Legislature. The Muslim University Union held a meeting and passed a resolution of strong protest regarding this. The meeting resolved as follows:[101]

> "It is a subcontinent in which there is found a great diversity of relief climate, nature, vegetation, economic production and the people. It consists of four clearly marked regions: (1) Indus Basin, (2) Upper Gangetic Basin, (3) Lower Gangetic Basin, and (4) Deccan Plateau. These regions are separate entities not only from the point of geography but also from the point of view of religion, ethnography, culture, historical traditions and economic conditions. It will not be mere geography, which will determine the formation of Pakistan but also the will of the hundred millions of Musalmans of India. This speech of the Viceroy is a challenge to a Muslim youth and all the lovers of India's independence."

While suggesting the students, the MU Union said, "The Muslim students must play an important part not only for a new awakening to the Muslim masses but also in organising and consolidating their strength for securing their just rights...."

The year of 1944 was the year of progress in the history of University Muslim League. In order to popularise Muslim League, the moving libraries were set-up in all boarding houses to enable students to understand about Pakistan and its contortions. This work became possible due to the free donation of 400 books by Nawabzada Liaqat Ali Khan and by means of UP Muslim League. Different pamphlets were also published on the topic of present situations. A debating contest was also convened about Pakistan and other related topics. Due to these efforts, about 45 National Guards from AMU went to attend the Karachi session of the All India Muslim League.[102]

The Aligarh Muslim University Union not only did its level best for the demand of Pakistan but also mobilized the newcomer students in favour of it. For that purpose, a general conference was convened in reception of fresher students on 4th August, 1945 by Vice-President of the Union Kunwar Ishrat Ali Khan. He told them that Muslim League was the only representative party of Indian Muslims and the Union was following its policy. He also said that in the Congress, besides some misguided senseless Muslims, no other Muslims were there.[103]

In Aligarh Muslim University, whenever there was a Union meeting, fullest confidence, faith and loyalty were expressed in Mr. Jinnah and appreciated him for his sagacity, statesmanship and sincerity for the cause of Musalmans and Muslim India. Whatever policy Mr. Jinnah adopted, the University Union approved it by passing a resolution in its favour.

On 6th August, 1945, Kunwar Ishrat Ali Khan, the Vice-President of the Union convened a meeting in which he endorsed the refusal of the All India Muslim League to accept the Wavell Plan. He argued that it did not guarantee the establishment of Pakistan as envisaged in the Lahore resolution of All India Muslim League and failed to recognise the first claim of the AIML to represent all the hundred million Muslims of India. He further said that it failed to give the right to nominate all the Muslim members of the proposed Executive Council of the Viceroy. This meeting also resolved that each member of the Union should contribute Re. 1/- in the "Muslim League Election Fund" in response to the appeal made by Mr. Jinnah.[104]

On 11th August, 1945, Mr. Aebey, Secretary of the American Commissioner in India visited Aligarh. On his arrival, the AMU Union convened a welcome meeting for him. Kunwar Ishrat Ali Khan said in the meeting that in India two communities Hindu and Muslim are residing, and both are different from each other in all respects. He cleared the point, "we, as being a separate community demand a separate country. We consider *Qaid-i-Azam*, Mohammad Ali Jinnah as our leader and in his guidance we shall have Pakistan."[105]

On 22nd September, 1945, Mr. Liaqat Ali came to Aligarh in order to prepare the students for the campaigning of elections of Central Legislator. He told the students, "there comes time in the life of a nation when every other activity has to be subordinated to that big issue of life and death to the Muslims. I want the Muslim students.... to play their part boldly and honourably in the issue which would mean either emancipation or perpetual domination

....what use would be of a degree if the future is dark and disappointing. Hence, the students should come out of their classrooms and support the Muslim League even at the cost of the one academic year."[106]

Aligarh students quickly responded to the call for canvassing in favour of Muslim League. They spread all-over the country, especially Northern India, to compaign for the forthcoming elections. Fearing by the respond of Aligarh students, Congress issued some false propaganda against AMU. Regarding that propaganda University Union appealed to the government and public in general and Muslims, in particular, not to be misled by this propaganda. The Union said that the real aim of the propaganda was hampering the Aligarh students from taking free and active part in the general election campaign. They warned the press that such misguided policy would only result in exacerbating bitterness between the two nations.[107]

In the Second World War, England became victorious and in India, the British Government also celebrated its victory. Some peoples of India, mostly Muslims, organized demonstrations against these victory celebrations. Over these demonstrations, the British Government used brutal force in Delhi. These repressions followed by firings in Calcutta, Meerut, Bombay, Madras, etc. The Aligarh Muslim University students abhorred over these firings and started criticizing the government. They convened a meeting and passed a resolution as follows:[108]

> "This meeting congratulates the brave sons and daughters of the Indian people in general and those of the Muslims, in particular, who faced the imperialist bullets heroically. They with their blood have written a new chapter in the Muslim politics of the country. In the name of those martyrs, this meeting pledges to follow in the footsteps of those heroes in the battle for Pakistan and freedom."

On 12th May, Mr. Jinnah sent to the Cabinet Mission a memorandum containing Muslim League's minimum demands in which he termed the group of six provinces, i.e. Punjab, NWFP, Baluchistan, Sindh, Bengal, and Assam as Pakistan group, which was to be autonomous in all matters except Foreign Affairs, Defence and Communication. Responding to the Jinnah's demands, the Cabinet Mission grouped the provinces into three categories ABC of which B&C were claimed as Pakistan.[109]

Regarding the Cabinet Plan, Aligarh students went a step further than that of Mr. Jinnah. They didn't accept the proposal of the Cabinet Mission. Regarding that the AMU Students Union passed a resolution on 27th May, 1946 in which they rejected the British Cabinet proposal which had denounced Pakistan in a language that betrayed total disregard of the sentiments of the Musalmans. According to them, these proposals were not sincere attempts to solve the Indian communal problems as they left the question of parity between Pakistan and Hindustan Federations to the Centre, which was the fundamental precondition to the Muslim acceptance of an All India Centre to the Constituent Assembly in which the Muslims would be in helpless minority.[110]

The AMU Students Union further resolved that the checks provided for safeguarding the interests of the Musalmans and the depressed classes were ineffective and could only result in confronting the Confederation Government and even the Constituent Assembly with absolute deadlocks. They declared that these proposals, therefore, were merely a clever attempt to prolong the British imperialist hold in India. While reiterating the full confidence in the statesmanship and leadership of *Qaid-i-Azam* Mr. Mohammad Ali Jinnah, it attempted the Muslim League High Command and the All India Council, to declare once for all that there could never be the slightest compromise on Muslim nation's right of self-determination and assured them to the complete readiness of the Muslim University students for any struggle that would be launched to defeat this Anglo-Brahmin 'Big Business' conspiracy and to achieve Muslims long cherished goal of Pakistan.[111]

The AMU Students Union further demanded from the British Government that separate sovereign assemblies of Hindustan and Pakistan be immediately set-up, and that they should transfer the power to these Constituent Assemblies, and they also should quit India with bag and baggage, leaving them to come to any agreement about the formation of any All India Centre. The Union warned the representatives of the alien rule that any attempt to impose a Constitution which was not duly approved by the Muslim League, would be resisted by all means.[112]

When the discussion of partition plan was going on between the Viceroy Lord Mountbatten and Indian leaders, the Aligarh students could not keep themselves quiet and sent a telegram to the Viceroy and expressed their feelings regarding the division of the Punjab and Bengal. They told the Viceroy, "we students of Aligarh Muslim University want to impress upon your most Exalted Excellency by urgent need of realizing that the division of the Punjab and Bengal is calculated to prove utterly detrimental to the cause not only of Muslim League but is bound to have repercussions on Indian politics too. We are totally against it and we are confident that you shall graciously listen to the voice of the student community which is, in fact, the voice of the Muslim community."[113]

No doubt the students of Aligarh and rather Aligarh intelligentsia as a whole vehemently supported the cause of Pakistan by all means. However, they also knew the fact that whenever the division would be materialized, they would remain in India and in India alone because of the geographical position of Aligarh. Then the question arose why they had supported Jinnah with so much curiosity? As a matter fact, it was clear from the Muslim League demands to the Cabinet Mission Plan for grouping of the provinces, and they did not have in their mind the complete separation of Pakistan from India. The speeches of Mr. Jinnah and his dialogues with the other political leaders and the Viceroy during 1946-1947 also proved the fact. It was also a hard sane fact that the Aligarh students were never in favour of partition or complete separation of Pakistan from India.

Aligarh students also thought that there would be an independent Pakistan within India with the common centre of India and Pakistan. Undoubtedly, the Muslim League and Mr. Jinnah used the Muslim University as a platform for gaining their goal but Mr. Jinnah himself was not sure to get the separate Pakistan in his lifetime. Being the power-hungry politician, Mr. Jinnah wanted power share in the Government of India, and he used the term Pakistan as mere a tool. However, the Congress leaders considered Mr. Jinnah as a thorn in the peaceful governance of Independent

India. It was really shocking when the Congress leaders accepted not only the Pakistan but the partition proposal in the last moment.

Formation of Interim Government

The British Prime Minister Clement Attlee sent a Cabinet Mission to India on March 24, 1946. The Mission was consisting three members of the British Cabinet-Secretary of State Pathic Lawrence, Stafford Cripps and A.V. Alexander. The objective of this mission was to devise a machinery to draw up the Constitution of Independent India and make arrangements for Interim Government. Thus, the mission was like a declaration of India's Independence.

The Muslim University Union, which was the over-sensitive regarding the affairs of the Indian Muslims and Muslim League, expressed its concern over the Cabinet Mission. The Muslim University Union held a meeting on March 23, 1946 and warned the Cabinet Mission that any attempt at jilting the Musalmans and by-passing the Muslim League would be resisted with force and that any attempt at persuading the Muslims to compromise was pre-deemed.[114]

After the full conversation of the Indian leaders and representatives of the different communities, the Cabinet Mission announced its own recommendations on May 16, 1946. The Cabinet Mission said that there shall be a Union of India which was to be empowered to deal with the defense, foreign affairs and communications. The Cabinet Mission recommended an undivided India but assured that the minority's autonomy must somehow be safeguarded within the framework of a united India. It also provided for formation of the constituent assembly on the democratic principle of population. The Constituent assembly had to comprise 389 members out of which 292 members were elected by the Provincial Legislature, 4 members represent Chief Commissioner's Provinces from the British Provinces and 93 members from the Princely States. The representation of the Provincial legislatures was to be break up into 3 sections. Section A—Madras, UP, Central provinces, Bombay, Bihar and Orissa; Section B—Punjab, Sindh, NWFP, Baluchistan; and Section C—Assam and Bengal, which meet separately to decide on group Constitutions. The Cabinet Mission also decided that there would be a common centre controlling defence, foreign affairs and communications.[115]

Mr. Jinnah wanted that any agreement either for the formation of Interim Government or partition in the Constituent Assembly should be based on Hindu and Muslim parity. However, his proposal of parity was rejected by the Congress. The rejection of the Hindu-Muslim parity in political agreements by the Congress frustrated the Muslim League and finally it strengthened its demand for Pakistan. Even many Muslim organizations which were considered sister organization of the Congress also felt malign by the Congress policy. It was this time when Muslim League demanded separate and independent homeland for the Muslims, having no connection with India.

Maulana Mazhar Ali Azhar, Secretary All India Ahrar Committee, said, "Congress has rejected the Congress-Muslim League parity or parity between Hindus and Muslims and has thus torpedoed the hopes of framing on Interim Government or placing the country on the road of freedom. Before the nationalist Muslim groups met the Cabinet Mission, the nationalist formulae containing the Hindu-Muslim parity in the Interim Government as well as in the future Central Government was known to and approved by responsible Congress leaders. But after getting Pakistan rejected by the Cabinet Mission they have now decided to oppose Hindu-Muslim parity tooth and nail. They thus compelled the all nationalist Muslims to revise their stand in respect of the future Constitution of India and thus marred the chances of success of any negotiations."[116]

Aligarh Muslims also advocated the idea of parity in the formation of Interim Government and other political agreements. Sir Ziauddin Ahmad, the Vice-Chancellor of AMU suggested that the portfolios for the Interim Government should be grouped together, and one from each group should go to the Muslim League and the other to the Congress and other minorities. He suggested the following panel groups:[117]

Finance and Planning,
Food and Defence,
Commerce and Supply,
Home and Communications,

Food and Agriculture,
Labour and Education,
Miscellaneous and Health, and
Industry and PWD.

About the matter of parity in the formation of the Interim Government Mr. Arthur Moore, former editor of the *Statesman*, expressed his feelings over Congress and said, "The Congress has been thinking too much about its own prestige and too little about India, over and over again it has said it would accept any Indian Government for the sake of freedom. Now, it has the chance of not only of freedom but of unity, because the Muslim League, realising that in the atomic age the sovereign state is a dead conception, has wisely dropped its claim for sovereign state and wants a Pakistan within a Federal India."[118]

Mr. Arthur Moore further said, "the natural ultimate gaurantee for a race or a religion, namely to have somewhere a cultural homeland of its own. The Congress should rejoice in this acceptance of federation and offer to serve. They have brilliant men whom the country needs... Let Mr. Jinnah be asked to form a purely Indian Government and to choose his own colleagues. His first thought will be to get as many Congress men as he can to cooperate with him. Indian rancour is sometimes fierce but rarely deep. Jinnah and Jawaharlal teamed together would soon recognise each other's qualities and bless each other's work. Youth of India are today disappointed. The hungry sheep look and it is high time that they were led."[119]

Mr. Mohammad Ali Jinnah wanted to hold the political power and was ready to cooperate the Congress on his own terms. He was a self-styled arrogant who considered him equal to none. He never considered the Congress leaders as good politicians. He denoted Jawahar Lal Nehru as a "literary figure" who should have been an English Professor, not a politician. To Mr. Gandhi, Jinnah said "a cunning fox", "a Hindu revivalist."[120]

It was due to his superiority complex Mr. Jinnah was not ready to cooperate on forming the Interim Government under Nehru or any other Congressman. Undoubtedly, he should have been agreed to drop the idea of Pakistan if he had been given the offer of forming the Interim Government. However, the Congressmen were not prepared for that. They were not even ready to get cooperation of Muslim League on equal terms.

The Cabinet Mission had rejected the Pakistan move, but Mr. Jinnah thought it a green signal for grouping of Indian states on the communal basis by the Mission. Following the Cabinet Mission proposal, the elections of Constituent Assembly were held in July 1946, and the following result appeared:[121]

- **Section A:** Madras, Bombay, Orissa, U.P., Bihar, Coorg, Delhi, Ajmer, and Marwar
  — Congress: 164 seats
  — Muslim League: 19 seats
  — Independent: 7 seats
- **Section B:** Punjab, NWFP, Sindh, Baluchistan
  — Congress: 9 seats
  — Muslim League: 19 seats
  — Unionist: 3 seats
  — Independent: 1 seat
  — Sikh: 4 seats (vacant)
  — (Sikh seats were vacant due to their anti-Cabinet Mission Movement)
- **Section C:** Bengal, Assam
  — Congress: 32 seats
  — Muslim League: 35 seats
  — Communist: 1 seat
  — Scheduled Caste Federation: 1 seat
  — Krishak Praja Party: 1 seat

However, after the election results Mr. Jinnah and Muslim League changed their stand and rejected the plan due to the intransigence of the Congress, on the one hand, and the breach of faith with the Muslims by the British Government on the other.[122] The Council of the Muslim League by rejecting the Cabinet Mission proposal called the Muslim community to join for Direct Action from 16th August to achieve Pakistan.[123]

Whatever Muslim League had given the pretext, but its changed stand was only due to poor results of Muslim League in the elections and no hope in forming the Interim Government. The Congress under Pandit Jawahar Lal Nehru decided to form the Interim Government. The Congress could not understand the grave consequences of the Direct Action Plan of the Muslim League. The Congress tried its level best to include Muslim League members in their cabinet. However, they were not ready surrender the power. Surely, it was not the matter of Pakistan or division of India but the matter of power, which the Congress was not ready to surrender for Mr. Jinnah even at the cost of partition of India.

The day of Direct Action on 16th August, 1946 may be marked as the 'Black Day' in the history of united India. It followed a series of communal riots on an unprecedented scale, starting with Calcutta, touching Bombay, spreading Noakhali in east Bengal, Bihar, Garhmukteshwar in UP and Punjab. Murder was the primary objective in the riots, not as often earlier communal outbreaks, demolition of temples or mosques, rape, or attacks on the property of relatively privileged groups belonging to the opposite community. In these communal riots, the loss of the Muslims was much more than the Hindus. This fact was not only hinted by Mr. Wavell but also Sardar Patel.[124]

Amid of series of communal riots and hatred between the two major communities, the Congress tried its best to reach an agreement with the Muslim League in the formation of the cabinet. After failing to reach on any agreement, the Congress formed the cabinet of its own on 2nd September, 1946. The following members were included in the cabinet: Jawahar Lal Nehru, Sardar Ballabh Bhai Patel, Rajendra Prasad, M. Asaf Ali, C. Rajgopalachari, Sarat Chandra Bose, John Mathai, Baldeo Singh, Shafaat Ahmad Khan, Jagjivan Ram, Ali Zaheer and C.H. Bhabha.[125]

The Muslim League declared 2nd September, 1946 as the day of mourning and Mr. Jinnah advised to display black flags. However, with the mediation of prominent leaders and the Viceroy, Jinnah agreed to nominate five persons to the Interim Government. These were Liaqat Ali Khan, I.I. Chundrigar, Abdur Rab Nishtar, Ghazanfar Ali Khan and Jogindra Nath Mandal. By this agreement, the Muslim League entered the Interim Government, but it was without commitment to join the Constituent Assembly.[126]

After joining the Muslim League, the portfolio of the Interim Government were as followes:[127]

Jawahr Lal Nehru: PM and External Affairs
Sardar Ballabh Bhai Patel: Home, Information & Broadcasting
Baldeo Singh: Defence
John Mathai: Industries and Supplies
C. Rajgopalachari: Education
C.H. Bhabha: Works, Mines and Power
Rajendra Prasad: Food and Agriculture
M. Asaf Ali: Railway
Jagjivan Ram: Labour
Liaqat Ali: Finance
I.I. Chundrigar: Commerce
Abdur Rab Nishtar: Communications
Ghazanfar Ali Khan: Health
Jogindra Nath Mandal: Law

On joining the Interim Government by Muslim League, Aligarh felt pleased and the Muslim University Union convened a meeting on 1st November, 1946, in which the Union congratulated the working committee of the All India Muslim League on their decision. According to the Union, Muslim League worked all the vain and monstrous design of the Congress to perpetuate the Hindu supremacy over this entire subcontinent.[128]

The happiness of the Union over joining the government by Muslim League shows the fact that Aligarh or Aligarh Muslim University was never in favour of partition of India and creation of Pakistan totally separate from India. Whatever the students of AMU favoured Muslim League and its agenda was only to advocate for proving proper share to Muslim community within India. They were fully aware that after the partition of India, the AMU will remain with India due to its geographical position. They perhaps thought that Pakistan was only a tool to get share in the government by Indian Muslims. Even Mr. Mohammad Ali Jinnah was not sure of getting Pakistan in his lifetime.

Although the Muslim League joined the government under pressure but his dream of heading the government was never fulfilled. So, except Liaqat Ali Khan, Mr. Jinnah nominated all the League nominees the second-rate politician. It shows that the responsibility was the main objective of the Muslim League. League members frequently questioned the actions taken by the Congress members and generally refused to attend the informal meetings. After joining the Interim Government, the Muslim League further boosted their demand of Pakistan.

Muslim League had entered the cabinet with the prime object of preventing the Congress from consolidating its position to the detriment of League's interest. According to Mr. Jinnah, the Interim Government was a continuation of civil war by other means.[129] Mr. Jinnah further said that Muslim League could not take orders either from Jinnah or from the Congress as long as the policy of the Congress was to torpedo the demand of Pakistan.[130] Liaqat Ali said that he was in the Interim Government to get a foot hold to fight for his long-cherished goal of Pakistan.[131]

Communal Riots and Repression

From the beginning of the 1946, a communal atmosphere was developed all-over India. In these communal atmospheres, the elections were held and the Congress became victorious on many seats. After defeat of the Muslim League, a new disastrous programme, the Direct Action was started by Muslim League, which followed the communal riots all-over India. Even before the Direct Action programme the communal riots were common in many parts of India. Both Hindus and Muslims were embittered with poisonous intentions of political leaders. Thousands of people were killed, and their property was looted and burnt. Aligarh was also set ablaze on communal frenzy.

Chaudhary Khaliquzzaman complained about the dubious and suspicious behaviour of the government machinery. He said that in Aligarh, there was some trouble and two ministers were sent by the government to prepare a report. Nevertheless, while Muslim shops and houses were burnt in Kasgunj and the mosque was set on fire, not even one minister was sent there. Chaudhary Khaliquzzaman attacked the Congress by saying that this time the Congress minister came into power with more murderous intentions than in 1937.[132]

In the series of communal riots which started in Aligarh on 29th March, 1946, a lot property looted and burnt. In these communal riots, in Aligarh the total loss estimated was Rs. 50 lakh. For the first time, the AMU was alleged in these riots. Mr. L.N. Mathur, a local lawyer and senior Vice-Chairman of Aligarh Municipal Board alleged that posters inciting students for violence against Hindus had been discovered inside AMU compound. He also rumoured that one of these posters came into possession of District Magistrate.[133]

However, it was merely an allegation of Mr. L.N. Mathur, whose record was suspicious during the riots. He not only charged the AMU students but also attacked local officials, particularly the District Magistrate, Mr. Abdul Hamid Khan, the city Deputy Superintendent of Police, and Mr. Abdul Jabbar, the City Kotwal, before the enquiry conducted by the Commissioner and the Deputy Inspector General. Nawabzada Mushtaq Hasan Khan, member of the AMU Court stated that the enquiry committee was not properly represented by the Musalmans but the Hindus took active part in it under the leadership of Mr. Mathur. He also claimed that another minister who did not even come to Aligarh gave objectionable statement. He further said that as expected all of them threw the whole blame on the students of AMU.[134]

The matter of Aligarh riots was also raised in the U.P. Assembly in the discussions. The Muslim leaders like Chaudhary Khaliquzzaman and Professor A.B.A. Haleem asked a number of supplementaries on the conduct of investigation at Aligarh after the riots.[135]

Over the situations of the Aligarh riots, AMU expressed its cordial sympathy with the innocent Muslim victims who had suffered a lot. According to the Union they suffered at the hands of cruel Hindu aggressors in defending their religion, life, honour and property. Referring to the communal riots in Bihar, the Muslim University Union stated that Bihar was controlled by the caste Hindu Congress, the provincial Congress Government and the dummy Governor of Bihar. They were solely responsible for the terrible massacre because it was done according to a pre-planned scheme with the deliberate negligence and connivance of the provincial authorities. The Union strongly urged upon the Central

Government, which had terribly failed so far to take strong measures immediately to prevent this lawlessness which might spread to other provinces as well and for which they alone would be entirely responsible.[136]

Aligarh also condemned the Unionist-Congress coalition Government of Punjab, where the Muslim National Guard Organization was declared unlawful for which Muslim League leaders courted arrest. In the meeting of the Muslim University Union, held on 25th January, 1947, they condemned the Burhanpur officials and of the Congress ministry in Central Provinces. The Union called their attitude as communal and also charged that it was directly responsible for creating communal tension in that town on 29th December, 1946. The Central Provinces Government allowed the Sikhs to take out a procession with naked swords in their hands on a disputed route which created panic. The union also alleged the government for imposition of a punitive force and the imposition of the Goonda Act. It demanded to withdraw the Act. The Union also demanded the immediate transfer of the D.S.P. and S.D.O. from Burhanpur.[137]

The Muslim University Union had much sympathy not only with the Muslims of UP and Aligarh but the entire Muslim population of all-over India. On 2nd March, 1947, University Union paid great tribute and homage to the martyrs of the Khaksar Party, describing them as brave and selfless Mujahids of the Punjab. The martyrs of the Khaksar Party sacrificed themselves not only for the Muslims but for the peace-loving members of all the communities.[138]

The Aligarh students never appreciated the Congress policies and suspected the Congress Government for engaging it with anti-Muslim activities. Earlier on 3rd May, 1946, the Aligarh Union charged the Congress Government in Assam for starting the Muslim victimization campaign.[139]

The Union meeting further charged the Congress Government in Assam for, "the ruthless and inhuman eviction of the settlers simply because they happen to be Muslim and the brutal annihilation of their houses and standing crops when the serious food shortage is in the country…." The Union meeting demanded that all orders of eviction passed by the present Congress

Government be immediately cancelled and those cultivators be allowed settlements of the lands under their cultivation. The Union further called Government of India and the Government of Assam to take immediate steps to withdraw the invidious and illegal line system prevailing in Assam. The AMU Students Union also decided to raise a fund in response to the appeal made by the Assam Muslim League to help the poor emigrants who were being evicted by the Congress regime. The Union fixed that each member of the Union would contribute Re. 1/- towards this fund and this contribution would be collected through the Provost Office.[140]

The Aligarh students never criticised the Muslim League for its shirking of responsibilities and creating administrative problems to run the Congress Government peacefully. Even when the Muslim League was in power in the Central Government it did not show any responsibility. It was more devoted to its only aim of achieving Pakistan and creating disturbances. Congress also, being frustrated with the activities of the League, never tried to win over the hearts of the Muslim community. Definitely, the bone of contention was the separatist activities of the Muslim League and its demand for Pakistan which they had strengthened after formation of the Interim Government under the Congress leader Pandit Jawahar Lal Nehru.

Partition and Independence of India

After failing to emerge as a popular and powerful party, the Muslim League played at last the religious game to polarize the Muslims in its favour. The frustration and failure goaded the Muslim League on the path of separatism. The Congress also provided the Muslim League full opportunity by rejecting its petty demands. The failure of the Muslim League and non-cooperation by the Congress from the elections of 1937 to 1946 further strengthened the separatist demand of the Muslim League.

In 1940, Muslim League launched a separatist movement popularly known as Pakistan Movement. However, the proposed Pakistan was not totally separate from Indian subcontinent. Muslim League demanded a region (Pakistan) within India with some administrative autonomy. Later on, the Muslim League started repeated its demand for Pakistan with more regions. In these intolerable situations, both Congress and Muslim League felt it impossible to live together with such different ideologies.

On the one hand, Mr. Jinnah wanted more power, which was not in proportion of the seats he won in the election of 1946. On the other hand, the majority party Congress was not ready to work under a minority party like the Muslim League. Both were power hungry and none of them was ready to sacrifice for the cause of the unity of India. Actually, the situations and political developments further widened the gap between Hindus and Muslims and this rift became one of the major causes of division of the country into two nations—India and Pakistan. Congress also accepted that the survival of both the parties with such different ideologies was impossible.

Congress was almost agreed that there was no solution except partition, but it had not given clear indication of partition of India or division of Punjab and Bengal. Many intellectuals of Congress and Muslim League started to search the agreeable solution. The big question was that how partition would be made. Many schemes were formulated for partition of India. Many political intellectuals of India suggested the scheme of partition. Even the Aligarh intellectuals Professor Syed Zafrul Hasan and Professor Mohammad Afzal Husain Qadri also proposed a plan. They proposed the area and population-wise plan to divide India into three wholly independent and sovereign states along with independent state of Hyderabad as follows:[141]

(i) Pakistan-Comprising of Punjab, NWFP, Sindh, Baluchistan and the State of Kashmir & Jammu, Mandi, Chamba, Sakit, Sumin, Kapurthala, Maler Kotla, Chitra, Dir, Kalat, Loharu, Bilaspur, Simla-Hill States, Bahawalpur, etc.
Total Populaton—3,92,74,244
Muslims—2,36,97,538 (60%)

(ii) Bengal (Excluding Howrah and Midnapur District), Purnia District (Bihar), Sylhet Division (Assam)
Total Populaton—5,25,79,232
Muslims—3,11,18,184 (57%)

(iii) Hindustan: Comprising the rest of India and Indian States (excluding Hyderabad, Pakistan, Bengal and the states included therein)

(iv) Hyderabad: Comprising Hyderabad, Berar and Karnataka (Madras and Orissa)
Total Population—2,90,65,098
Muslims—21,44,010 (7.5%)

(v) Delhi Province: Including Delhi, Meerut Division, Rohilkhand Division and the District of Aligarh (Agra Division)
Total Population—1,26,60,000
Muslims—35,20,000 (28%)

(vi) Malabar Province: Consisting of Malabar and adjoining area, i.e. Malabar and South Kanara.
Total Population—49,00,000
Muslims—14,40,000 (27%)

Aforesaid three states of Pakistan, Bengal and Hindustan should enter an offensive and defensive alliance on the following basis:

(i) Mutual recognition and reciprocity;

(ii) Pakistan and Bengal be recognized as the homeland of Muslims and Hindustan as the homeland of Hindus, to which they can migrate respectively, if and when they want to do so;

(iii) In Hindustan the Muslims are to be recognized as a nation in minority and part of a larger nation inhabiting Pakistan and Bengal;

(iv) The Muslims in minority in Hindustan and non-Muslim minority in Pakistan and Bengal will have: (a) representation according to population, and (b) separate electorate and representation at every stage, together with effective safeguards by all the three states. Separate representation in proportion to population may be granted to all considerable minorities in the three states, e.g. Sikh non-caste Hindu, etc.

(v) An accredited Muslim political organization will be the sole official representative body of the Muslims in Hindustan.

The Aligarh intellectuals Professor Syed Zafrul Hasan and Professor Mohammad Afzal Husain Qadri also proposed that each of the three independent states of Pakistan, Hindustan and Bengal will have separate treaties of alliance with Great Britain and each with the separate crown representatives if any. They will have a joint court of arbitration to settle any dispute that may arise between themselves or between them and the crown. Hyderabad commanded an exclusive position. It was recognized as an ally by the British Government. In truth, it was a sovereign state by treaties. Berar and Karnataka were taken from it by the British for administrative reasons, and so they must be restored. Hyderabad with its restored territories should be recognized expressly as a sovereign state, at least as sovereign as Nepal. With Karnataka restored it will have sea coast and will naturally become southern wing of Muslim India.[142]

Many similar schemes were also proposed by other intellectuals of different political parties. However, the movement for separation of India and creation of Pakistan made the situation from bad to worse. Under this worsened situation, the Congress had to accept the division of Punjab and also Bengal, if necessary.[143]

In these alarming situations, Lord Mountbatten assumed the office of Governor General on 24th March, 1947. He was deeply moved by the rapid deterioration in communal relations as he was eager to solve the communal problems without any delay. He held talks with important leaders of all political parties. He knew the Mahatma Gandhi's opinion about the partition of India. Mahatma Gandhi said to him that India would be divided over his dead body. So long as he was alive, he would never agree to the partition of India. Then Mountbatten assured Mahatma Gandhi that dividing India would be last solution for him. Mahatma Gandhi placed an alternative before Mountbatten to avoid partition, which was to give Mr. Jinnah the whole of India instead of just the part he wanted. He proposed that to let Mr. Jinnah form the government. On asking by Mountbatten that whether his own Congress party would accept his plan, Mahatma Gandhi replied that the Congress wanted above all to avoid partition, they would do anything to prevent it.[144]

However, the pupils of Mahatma Gandhi who once blindly obeyed him could hardly agree this point. They kept silent about this matter. Mahatma Gandhi unsuccessfully urged his colleagues to accept his plan to hold India together. The meeting of Congress

High Command held in the evening of 1st May, 1947, in which Mahatma Gandhi's plan was outrightly rejected. Mahatma Gandhi said to a friend later "they (Congressmen) call me Mahatma but tell you I am not even treated by them as a sweeper."[145]

Pandit Jawahar Lal Nehru, Sardar Patel and all the other Congressmen felt that the partition was the only way to save the country. Sardar Patel was prepared to accept partition even before Mountbatten's arrival. He argued that Jinnah should be given his state, but it would not survive anyway, within five years the Muslim League would be knocking at the door begging for India's reunification. Pandit Jawahar Lal Nehru too stood out against the man he had followed so far.[146]

For the solution of partition, Lord Mountbatten also held talks with Muslim League leader Mr. Jinnah. During the first fortnight of April 1947, he held many talks with him.[147] Mr. Jinnah also said that India had never been a true nation, it only looks that way on the map. He declared that, "The cows, I want to eat, the Hindus stops me from killing. Every time a Hindu shakes hands with me, he has to go wash his hands. The only thing the Muslims has in common with the Hindus is slavery to the British."[148]

After having failed, in compromising between Congress and Muslim League, Mountbatten also felt that partition of India was the only solution of the present political crisis. On 18th May, Mountbatten proceeded to London to seek the advice of the British cabinet and after his return prepared a plan which came to be known as Mountbatten Plan of 3rd June, 1947. He announced that the British Government had accepted the principle of partition, which would be effective from 15th August, 1947.[149]

Both the Congress and Muslim League accepted the plan of partition, but Sikhs were dissatisfied with this plan. Khan Abdul Ghaffar Khan also showed his disagreement by putting forward the demand for independent Pakhtoonistan.[150]

After agreement of partition by both the major parties, a Boundary Commission under the Chairmanship of Sir Cyril Radcliff was appointed. The Commission decided that West Bengal and East Punjab would go to India and West Punjab, Sindh and Baluchistan would be part of Pakistan. The district of Sylhet also joined Pakistan.[151]

On 15th August, 1947, India became Independent with a blot of partition over it. Since that very time it has been a long controversy that why the India was divided? Why the Congress accepted the plan of partition and who was responsible for the partition, Mr. Jinnah or Pandit Jawahar Lal Nehru?

No doubt Mr. Jinnah and his Muslim League worked hard for a separate homeland Pakistan for the Muslims, but as the historical events witness, he used the Pakistan movement as a tool to get more power beyond the proportion of his seats. He also claimed that Muslim League would be considered sole representative body of the entire Muslim India which was mere an imaginary approach and away from ground reality. The Congress also could not save itself from responsibility of partition because it was the Congress who changed its policy of national aim to political gain. It was the Congress which facilitated the way for the separatist movement of Muslim League since 1937.

Pandit Jawahar Lal Nehru, Sardar Patel and Mahatma Gandhi in 1947 accepted the long term failure of the Congress to draw in the Muslim masses to the national movements launched by the Congress and stem the surging wave of Muslim communalism.[152]

It must be cleared that until 1946, the Congress leaders were bitterly against the partition. In 1946 when Pandit Jawahar Lal Nehru and Dr. Syed Mahmood were in Ahmedabad jail, Syed Mahmood told Jawahar Lal that if they were compelled to accept partition, they would not agree to the partition of Punjab and Bengal. Then Jawahar Lal Nehru got enraged and said, "how this idea came to your mind? I am bitterly against partition. The partition can exist only on our bones."[153]

Here the question arises that when Pandit Jawahar Lal Nehru was not ready even to listen the word 'partition' then what forces compelled him to accept it? No doubt Jinnah used all possible tools of the Muslim society for the propaganda of Pakistan, but he was quite sure that it was not an easy job. If we see the historical background, we can conclude that Mr. Jinnah created such a situation in order to get heavy share in the power game or wanted to hold the supreme leadership of Indian Union over and above Mahatma Gandhi and Pandit Jawahar Lal Nehru. Mr. Jinnah frequently addressed Mahatma Gandhi as Mr. Gandhi not with

Mahatma or any other title, while Mahatma Gandhi after 1944-45, always addressed Mr. Jinnah as '*Qaid-i-Azam*.'

To a great extent Pandit Nehru and Sardar Patel easily accepted the partition plan to avoid Mr. Jinnah and his associates. These Congressmen were sure that in the presence of Mr. Jinnah and his associates, it would be not easy to rule peacefully over India after Independence. The Congressmen had also the threat of 'Direct Action' of Muslim League and many communal riots spreading all-over India. Above all the partition was the situational mishappening which provided Mr. Jinnah a separate homeland rather than a heavy share of power within India. Mr. Jinnah, who was bent upon to get Pakistan undergone in the shocking situation when Congress accepted the Pakistan proposal. No doubt Mr. Jinnah had love for this country and wanted the leadership.

When India was partitioned and Mr. Jinnah was about to leave India, he murmured to his A.D.C. Syed Ahsan Ali, "I suppose this is the last time I shall be looking at Delhi."[154] Mr. Jinnah spent the entire flight silently and absent mindedly lost in the newspapers. Not even the slightest trace of emotion appeared on his face as he read those laudatory accounts of his achievements. Not once during his entire trip did he speak or reveal even the slightest hint of his feeling, the meagrest indication of what this flight to a realized dream meant to him.[155] When Mr. Jinnah reached Karachi he whispered harshly to Syed Ahsan, "Do you know, I never expected to see Pakistan in my lifetime."[156]

These words and feelings of Mr. Jinnah show that he had great love for India and wanted only power share and popularity by threatening the Congress through the weapon of Pakistan. His feelings were clearly understood by Mahatma Gandhi and he persuaded the other Congressmen to let Jinnah form the government, but his efforts were unsuccessful.

When the partition was accepted by the Congress leaders, Mahatma Gandhi commented that the leaders of the Congress were yearning for power. Even Pandit Jawahar Lal Nehru confessed, "Well, I suppose it was a compulsion of events. A large India would have constant troubles, constant disintegrating pulls... And so we accepted." He further said, "Let us built-up strong India... The truth is that we were tired men.... We saw the fire burning in Punjab and heard every day of the killings. The plan for partition offered a way out, and we took it."[157]

There was clear intolerable bitterness between Congress and Muslim League from the 1946 elections. Over the formation of the Interim Government, Pandit Jawahar Lal Nehru wrote to Wavell on 22nd August, 1946, "We are not going to shake hands with murderer or allow it to determine the country's policy."[158]

Over the acceptance of the partition plan Mahatma Gandhi was unhappy with Pandit Nehru, Sardar Patel, etc., but this poor fellow was helpless to do anything. His inaction has been explained in terms of his forced isolation from the Congress decision making council. His pupils, who had followed him faithfully for many years at a great personal sacrifice, were succumbed to the lust for power.[159]

Larry Collins and Dominique Lapierre in their book *Freedom at Midnight* have stressed upon Mr. Jinnah's illness of Tuberculosis. They opined that if the secret of illness of Mr. Jinnah were known to Mountbatten, Nehru and Gandhiji, the division of India might have been avoided. Tuberculosis had gravely invaded the lungs of Mr. Jinnah. The damage of lungs was so extensive that he had barely one or two years to live. His treatment was going on under a Bombay physician Dr. J.A.L. Patel. According to him, Mr. Jinnah had been living for the past decade on "will power, whiskey and cigarette." The secret of illness was only known to his doctor and his sister Fatima. Liaqat Ali Khan was aware of his illness in the last six months of his life. Even his daughter Wadia could come to know of her father's illness only after his death.[160]

Mr. Jinnah was aware that if the Congressmen came to know that he was dying, their whole political outlook would change. They might try to wait, for the moment, of his going into the grave. Mr. Jinnah never wanted to abandon his move of ameliorating the position of the Indian Muslims. He wanted to provide the due power to the Indian Muslims even at the cost of partition.

Dr. Patel suggested Mr. Jinnah for bed rest. However, he told Dr. Patel that there was no question of abandoning his life's crusade for a sanatorium bed. Nothing except the grave was going to turn him from the task he had given himself, that of leading India's Muslims at the critical juncture in their history.[161]

In the last days of united India, Mr. Jinnah realized that he was the only thorn in eyes of the Congress. He maintained the secrecy of his illness in order to give the moral boost to the Muslim League leaders and Indian Muslims for their goal. Mr. Jinnah perhaps thought that if the Congress leaders had known about his illness, they would not have even talked about Pakistan and also not got agreed to give the proper share to Muslims within India.

The Aligarh students, who were since long being used by their so called '*Qaid-i-Azam*', were after partition became helpless and full of fear and shy for their attachment with Muslim League. They said, as quoted in the *Aligarh Magazine*, "we have got the freedom, who can doubt the freedom being the biggest boon. But no one told us that the biggest luxury demands biggest sacrifice.... Aligarh needs us and we needed Aligarh and our nation needs us both. We should pledge that our Aligarh and our nation shall be the basis of power and fame of each other."[162]

After the Independence of India, the ruling party Indian National Congress tried its level best to mobilize the Muslim population in its favour. Congress also sent its leaders to Aligarh. The ever beloved leader of Aligarh students Sarojini Naidu, the Governor of UP visited Aligarh on 12th November, 1947. She was given a very warm welcome. She delivered speeches in Girls College, University School, Stretchy Hall and Students Union. She intelligently mobilized the students for the love of the nation and the Congress. Her arrival brought a joyful and hopeful change in the atmosphere of Aligarh. She also might have carried a very good impression along with her.[163]

After Independence, both the Congress and Aligarh came closer to each other. The Government fully satisfied the Indian Muslims to safeguard their honour and interests and provide them the power and facilities. The Aligarh and AMU changed their attitude and were bent upon the loyalty to the nation and faith in the Congress Government under the leadership of Pandit Jawahar Lal Nehru.

NOTES

1. Sumit Sarkar, *Modern India 1885-1947*, Madras, 1983, pp. 353-355.
2. Gopal, S., *Jawahar Lal Nehru—A Biography*, Vol. I, Delhi, 1947, p. 223, f. n. 5, (hereafter cited as *Nehru—A Biography*).

3. Sumit Sarkar, *op. cit.,* p. 354.
4. *Ibid.*
5. Azad, Abul Kalam, *India Wins Freedom*, Madras, 1988, pp. 160-161.
6. *Aligarh Magazine, March 1939*, p. 4.
7. Aziz, K.K., *Muslims under Congress Rule, 1937-39*, Vol. I, Delhi, 1978, p. 208, (hereafter cited as Aziz).
8. *Private Business Meeting Register, MU Union 1937-44*, 8th September, 1939, (AMU Union Hall).
9. Ram Gopal, *Indian Muslims*, Bombay, 1959, p. 273.
10. *Ibid.,* pp. 258-259.
11. Sumit Sarkar, *op. cit.,* p. 355.
12. Ram Gopal, *op. cit.,* p. 258.
13. Gilmartin, David, *Empire and Islam*, California, 1988, pp. 146-247.
14. *Aligarh Magazine*, March 1939, pp. 4-7.
15. *Select Committee Proceedings Book, 1935-44*, 26th February, 1939, (AMU Union Hall).
16. *Ibid.*
17. *Private Business Meeting Register, 1937-44*, 6th October, 1939, (AMU Union Hall).
18. *Ibid.*
19. *Muslim India*, pp. 382-383.
20. *Hindustan Times*, 27th January, 1939; see also Aziz, *op. cit.,* p. 414; also cited in A.K. Fazul Haque's *Muslims Sufferings under Congress Rule*, Calcutta, December 1939; and *Fikr-o-Nazar*, Vol. XI, p. 255.
21. *File No. 79*, 1938-39 (AMU Archive).
22. *Ibid.*
23. *Private Business Meeting Register, 1937-44*, 27th January, 1939, (AMU Union Hall).
24. *Muslim India*, pp. 383-384.
25. *Ibid.*
26. *Private Business Meeting Register, 1937-44*, 2nd February, 1939 (AMU Union Hall).
27. Bipan Chandra, *India's Struggle for Independence,* Calcutta, 1992, p. 434, taken from *M.A. Jinnah, Speeches and Writings*, edited by Jamiluddin, Vol. I, Lahore 1960, pp. 69-70 and 72-73.
28. *File No. 51, 1939-40* (AMU Archive); see also *Annual Report of AMU 1939* (AMU Archive) and Mujahid, Al Sharif, *Qaid-i-Azam Jinnah*, Delhi, 1993, pp. 581, 585, 588 and 592 (Hereafter quoted as *Qaid-i-Azam*).
29. *Muslim India*, pp. 334-340.
30. *Qaid-i-Azam*, pp. 585, 588 and 592.
31. Sumit Sarkar, *op. cit.,* p. 355; quoted from Chaudhary Khaliquzzama's *Pathway to Pakistan*, p. 192.
32. *Ibid.*
33. Dutta, Kali Kinkar, *Rajendra Prasad*, New Delhi, 1974, p. 208.

34. *File No. 51, 19 /-38* (AMU Archive); see also Pirzada, Syed Sharifuddin, *Qaid-i-Azam Jinnah's Correspondence*, New Delhi, 1981, p. 184, (Hereafter cited as *Jinnah's Correspondence*).
35. *File No. 51, 1937-38* (AMU Archive), see also *Muslim India*, pp. 334-340.
36. *Jinnah's Correspondence,* p. 184.
37. *Ibid.,* pp. 184-185.
38. *Ibid.,* p. 185.
39. *Ibid.*
40. *Aligarh Gazetteer*, p. 42.
41. *Ibid.*
42. Bakshi, S.R., *Abdul Kalam Azad—A Secular Leader*, Delhi, 1991, p. 117.
43. *File No. IV/1, 1936-37* (AMU Archive).
44. *Ibid.*
45. *File No. 51, 1942-43, 1943-44 & 1945-46* (AMU Archive); see also *Annual Report 1943 & 1944* (AMU Archive).
46. *Ibid.*
47. *File No. 51, 1942-43* (AMU Archive).
48. *Zia-i-Hayat*, p. 172.
49. According to Amin Zuberi in *Zia-i-Hayat*, when Mr. Jinnah arrived in Aligarh in 1938, a great preparation was made for his welcome on the part of the university. The railway station was full of students and staff. When Mr. Jinnah sat in the car then university scout showed its performance. Dr. Ziauddin in honour of Mr. Jinnah gave a dinner in *Zaka Manzil* on the large scale. He made a stay for the three days and these three days he was very busy. He met the students of the different ideologies and gave a long impressive speech in the Union Hall (*Zia-i-Hayat*, p. 172).
50. *File No. 4, 1942-43* (AMU Archive).
51. *Ibid.*
52. *Private Business Meeting Register MU Union, 1937-1944*, 17th February, 1941 (AMU Union Hall).
53. Khaksars had been in existence since 1931, but it was in 1939-40 that its activities became felt. It was a semi-military organization whose membership was estimated about four lakh until 1940. Armed with the spade, the Khaksars were brought under iron discipline and implicit obedience to order from the higher command involving in some cases of breach and public flagging. In the early summer of 1940, they came into violent conflict with Government of Punjab leading to police firing and number of casualties (Low, Francis, *The Indian Year Book and Who's Who 1940*, Vol. XXVII, p. 885).
54. *Private Business Meeting Register MU Union, 1937-1944*, 26th November, 1942 (AMU Union Hall).
55. *Ibid.,* 1st April, 1942.

56. It was very funny that Qaid-i-Azam of the Muslim community Mr. Jinnah had no more Muslim qualities. According to *Freedom at Midnight,* he drank frequently, ate pork, rarely entered a mosque and ignored the *Quran.* (Collins, Larry, & Lappiere, Dominique, *Freedom at Midnight*, 1975, New York, p. 152).
57. *Private Business Meeting Register MU Union, 1937-1944*, 1st April, 1942 (AMU Union Hall).
58. *Zia-i-Hayat*, p. 173.
59. *Ibid.*
60. *Muslim University Union Ministry Report, 1945-52 and 1946-47*. 20th November, 1946 (AMU Union Hall); see also *Zia-i-Hayat*, p. 191.
61. The students were very much infuriated with Dr. Ziauddin because the matter of Bihar was sentimentally attached with the students. They were actively participated in the collection of Bihar relief fund and also worked in the elections (*Zia-i-Hayat*, p. 191).
62. Students Union held a meeting and resolved "this meeting of the MU Union highly condemns the attitude of certain undesirable students who behaved with the VC so indecently on 26th December, 1946." (*Muslim University Union Ministry Report, 1945-52*, 31st December, 1946).
63. *Zia-i-Hayat*, p. 191.
64. *Ibid.*, p. 192.
65. *Ibid.*, p. 193.
66. *Aligarh Institute Gazette*, 1st January, 1941.
67. In 1946, more than 32,000 primary members were enrolled by the Aligarh District Congress Committee. About 1000 Muslims also got themselves enrolled as members of the Congress. (*The Hindustan Times*, January 11, 1946).
68. *Department of Police, File No. RR 26*, p. 50, Uttar Pradesh State Archive Lucknow (UPSAL).
69. *Ibid.*, p. 52.
70. *Ibid.*, pp. 41-42.
71. *Ibid.*, p. 43.
72. *Ibid.*, pp. 33-34.
73. *Ibid.*, p. 131.
74. *Ibid.*, p. 126.
75. *Ibid.*, p. 142.
76. *Ibid.*, pp. 143-44.
77. *Aligarh Gazetteer*, pp. 42-43.
78. *Department of Police, File No. RR 26*, pp. 46-47, Uttar Pradesh State Archive Lucknow (UPSAL).
79. *Ibid.*, pp. 47-48.
80. *Ibid.*, pp. 50-52.
81. *Ibid.*, p. 54.
82. *Aligarh Institute Gazette*, 1st January, 1943.

83. *Qaid-i-Azam*, p. 442.
84. *The Dawn*, 23rd December, 1944.
85. *Foundations of Pakistan*, p. 347.
86. *Aligarh Institute Gazette*, 1st April, 1941.
87. *Ibid.*, 15th October, 1941.
88. *Ibid.*
89. *Ibid.*
90. *Ibid.*, 15th November, 1941.
91. *Welcome Welcome, Oh! Paragon of the East,*
    Hero of the day, freshly crowned with never dying fame,
    Fighting for freedom, victory-Pakistan,
    Struggling for thy nation? an illustrious warrior of thy land.

    Shower your paramount golden beams,
    Thus make us from our deep slumber,
    Infuse us again and again with life and light,
    Create in us unity, duty, discipline and sacrifice.

    Stabilize our fickle minds and bless us with faith and action,
    Give us planes, tanks, destroyers, and all,
    Well, the strength of the arm is not looked,
    The sharpness of the sword is not counted.

    But the skill and valour that is amounted,
    So shall we march, onward, onward, still,
    Advance forward with skill,
    Beyond time beyond space near the horizon.
    (*Aligarh Institute Gazette*, 15th November, 1941).
92. *Aligarh Institute Gazette*, 15th November, 1941.
93. *Ibid.*
94. *Ibid.*
95. *Ibid.*
96. *Ibid.*, 1st January, 1944.
97. *The Dawn*, 29th December, 1944.
98. *Ibid.*
99. *Ibid.*, 27th December, 1944.
100. *Aligarh Institute Gazette*, 1st August, 1943.
101. *Private Business Meeting Register 1937-44*, 3rd March, 1944 (AMU Union Hall).
102. *Aligarh Magazine*, March, 1944, p. 9. A few sentimental students of AMU styled themselves as 'National Guards' in order to support and propagate the programmes of the Muslim League.
103. *Muslim University Union Ministry Report, 1945-52, 1945-46*, 4th August, 1945 (AMU Union Hall).

104. *Ibid.,* 6th August, 1945.
105. *Ibid.,* 11th August, 1945.
106. *Qaid-i-Azam*, pp. 446-447, quoted from the newspaper "*The Star of India*", 24th September, 1945 (Calcutta).
107. *Muslim University Union Ministry Report, 1945-52, 1945-46*, 1st October, 1945 (AMU Union Hall).
108. *Ibid., 1945-46*, 12th March, 1946.
109. *Qaid-i-Azam*, p. 629.
110. *Muslim University Union Ministry Report, 1946-47*, 27th May, 1946 (AMU Union Hall).
111. *Ibid.*
112. *Ibid.*
113. *Ibid.,* 1947-48, 30th May, 1947.
114. *Ibid., 1945-46*, 23rd March, 1946 (AMU Union Hall).
115. Bipan Chandra, *op. cit.,* pp. 492-93.
116. *The Dawn*, 17th June, 1946.
117. *Ibid.,* 24th June, 1946.
118. *Ibid.,* 28th June, 1946.
119. *Ibid.*
120. *Freedom at Midnight*, p. 117.
121. Das, M.N., *A Contemporary History of the Indian National Congress*, Vol. 3, New Delhi, 1985, p. 707 (Hereafter cited as 'Das').
122. *Qaid-i-Azam*, p. 506.
123. *Qaid-i-Azam*, p. 507.
124. Sumit Sarkar, *op. cit.,* p. 432.
125. Bakshi, *op. cit.,* p. 149.
126. *Ibid.,* pp. 149-150.
127. Das, *op. cit.,* p. 704.
128. *Muslim University Union Ministry Report, 1946-47*, 1st November, 1946 (AMU Union Hall).
129. Bipan Chandra, *op. cit.,* p. 494.
130. Das, *op. cit.,* p. 706.
131. *Ibid.*
132. *Foundations of Pakistan*, Vol. II, p. 517, taken from *A Pledge for Pakistan, full Proceeding of League Legislators Convention*, Delhi, 1946 (New Era Publication, Lahore).
133. *The Hindustan Times*, 2nd April, 1946.
134. *The Dawn*, 15th June, 1946.
135. *The Hindustan Times*, 24th July, 1946.
136. *Muslim University Union Ministry Report, 1946-47*, 9th November, 1946 (AMU Union Hall).
137. *Ibid.,* 25th January, 1947.
138. *Ibid., 1947-48*, 2nd March, 1947.
139. *The Dawn*, 15th June, 1946.

140. *Muslim University Union Ministry Report, 1946-47*, 3rd March, 1946 (AMU Union Hall).
141. *India Divided*, pp. 181-183; see also Kumar, Kamlesh, *Role of Muslim in Indian Politics (1857-1947)*, New Delhi, 1985, p. 236.
142. *Ibid.,* see also Kumar, Kamlesh, *Role of Muslim in Indian Politics (1857-1947)*, New Delhi, 1985, p. 236.
143. Bakshi, *op. cit.,* p. 150.
144. *Freedom at Midnight*, p. 107.
145. *Ibid.,* pp. 132-133.
146. *Ibid.,* pp. 133-134.
147. Jinnah told the Mountbatten that it was like a court case that he had handled a dispute between two brothers embittered by the shares assigned to them by their father's will. Two years after the court had adjudicated their dispute. Now, they were the greatest friend, and that would be the case in India. (*Ibid.,* p. 118).
148. *Ibid.*
149. Sharma, Brij Kishore, *Introduction to the Constitution of India*, (7th Edition), Delhi, 1915, p. 27.
150. Bakshi, *op. cit.,* pp. 151-152.
151. *Ibid.*
152. Bipan Chandra, *op. cit.,* p. 500.
153. *Fikr-o-Nazar,* Part II, p. 118.
154. *Freedom at Midnight*, p. 262.
155. *Ibid.,* p. 263.
156. *Ibid.,* p. 264.
157. Bakshi, *op. cit.,* p. 153.
158. Nehru, Jawahar Lal, *Selected Works* edited by S. Gopal, Vol. 15, New Delhi, 1984, pp. 3 & 6-7.
159. Bipan Chandra, *op. cit.,* p. 503.
160. *Freedom at Midnight*, pp. 124-25
161. *Ibid.,* p. 125.
162. *Aligarh Magazine, 1947*, pp. r-z.
163. *Ibid.,* p. 2.

7
Conclusion

The present work deals with the history of the Indian Muslims particularly associated to Aligarh Movement and Aligarh Muslim University and their role in the freedom movement right from the rebellion of 1857 to the Independence of India in 1947. In the chapters included in this book, we saw that how Sir Syed Ahmad Khan saved the Muslims who were badly targeted for conspiring and regulating the rebellion against the British in 1857. There is no doubt that Indian Muslims were participating in the rebellion as their positions were badly worsened after the fall of the Mughal Empire and other Muslim principalities. In the repercussion, the heavy hand of the British Government fell upon them. At that crucial time Sir Syed Ahmad Khan, although being a government official, took the cause of the Muslims.

During the rebellion Sir Syed Ahmad Khan was at Bijnor as a subordinate Judge. He mediated between the rebellious leader Nawab Mahmud Khan and Englishmen. He became successful not only saving the life of the Europeans but also congratulated the Nawab on receiving the country of his ancestors. In this furious rebellion Sir Syed Ahmad Khan lost many of his family members, including his mother.

After the suppression of the revolt, he was rewarded for saving the life of the Europeans, but he was painful as the Muslims were branded as the main conspirators of the rebellion. As the Muslims and the *Ulema* class were the worst sufferers after failure of the Uprising, Sir Syed Ahmad Khan, while negotiating the British authorities, deliberately hided the real facts as well as participation of the Muslims in the rebellion. Sir Syed Ahmad Khan firmly stood to defend the Indian masses in general and Muslims in particular. He was the first person who declared that the British policies were the sole cause of the rebellion while defending the people of India.

At the time of crisis, Sir Syed Ahmad Khan, tried his level best to prove the Muslim community loyal to the British Government on the basis of the loyalty of a few people whose name he has mentioned in his book *Asbab-e-Baghawat-e-Hind*. However, the fact also could not be denied that the number of those people was like salt in the cooked food, and it is evident that these were the Muslim *Jihadis* or *Mujahideen,* who fought the war until their last breath.

In order to restore the power and prestige of the Muslim community, he advised them to follow the policy of loyalism towards the British Government. He convinced that like the Hindus the Muslims could improve their position only with the aids and cooperation of the British Government. Sir Syed Ahmad Khan realized that the Indian Muslims were educationally, socially, politically and economically backward and the panacea of all the evils was to persuade them to receive western education. That's why he established many schools wherever he was transferred.

In 1859, he founded a primary school in Moradabad, in 1863 Victoria school in Ghazipur. In April 1864, Sir Syed Ahmad Khan got transferred at Aligarh where he continued his educational work. In 1867, he was transferred to Banaras but he was determined to open a school at Aligarh. He toured for England for this purpose and after his return, he established a school "Madarsatul Uloom Musalmanan" in Aligarh on 24th May, 1875. This school was raised to Mohammadan Anglo Oriental College on 8th January, 1877. Subsequently, after the death of Sir Syed Ahmad Khan, this college was raised to the status of Aligarh Muslim University in 1920.

Sir Syed Ahmad Khan opposed the Muslim entry into the active politics. Sir Syed thought that the Muslim's entry in the active politics would create a hindrance in British help, cooperation and in his mission of Muslim's upliftment. He advised the Muslims not to join the Indian National Congress and devote their full time and energy only in educating themselves. His opposition to the Indian National Congress was based upon his personal experiences keeping in view of the ultimate good of the Muslims as understood by him. It however does not mean that he was totally against the nationalist movement and spirit of nationalism. He was of the view that the participation of the Muslims at this stage in political activities would be premature. They should first acquire education, attain perfection in various worldly affairs and then decide their own political course.

His mission and efforts of Muslim upliftment through western education are known as the Aligarh Movement. He felt that the Muslim community, in order to take its rightful place in the country, must undertake all-embracing reforms, including religious belief and practices, social life and education, manners and customs, etc. Sir Syed Ahmad Khan wanted to make all Muslims realise the significance of the age and take up challenge of the time.

As for the fulfilling the dream of Sir Syed Ahmad Khan and founding the Muslim University in Aligarh, the pupils and associates of Sir Syed Ahmad Khan launched a movement for the same in 1911. They were the true follower of Sir Syed Ahmad Khan and exactly followed the policy of loyalism in order to achieve their cherished aim of establishing the Muslim University and ameliorating the position of the Muslim community.

They wanted that their university should have the affiliating power and more autonomy. Naturally, these objections delayed the granting of the charter to the university while Madan Mohan Malviya became successful in getting the Hindu University in 1916 on liberal terms. The First World War gave a setback to the Muslim University movement. However, after the end of the war, the movement got a fresh impetus and finally in December 1920, the dream of Sir Syed Ahmad Khan was fulfilled by sacrificing the affiliating power out of the Aligarh city.

It is a matter of debate as to why did the British Government pass the AMU Act in 1920? Were they really sympathetic to the Muslim community? As far as the first question is concerned, the government had taken this step due to various reasons. As the Aligarh Muslims were staunch followers of Sir Syed Ahmad Khan and had at his behest followed the policy of loyalism to benefit the Muslim community of India. Nevertheless, the British Government did not care a fig for them, and this frustrated the young generation of the Muslims into becoming nationalists. Their participation in the

Khilafat and Non-Cooperation movements alarmed the government. These situations compelled the government to change its policy and ultimately fulfilled the demand of Muslim University in order to satisfy the Muslims of India. The government became very clear that their delay in this regard would change the mentality of the Indian Muslims.

The British Government was not against the Muslim education, but it was deliberately delaying the Muslim demands in order to maintain its hold over them. The government wanted to use the Muslims against the Hindus by awakening them about their share in power. However, the government was also afraid of educating the Muslims and thought that by complete education, the Muslims would emerge a stronger, efficient and reasonable community like the Hindus and will create disturbances for the government. That's why the government provided the university to the Muslims but did not allow the Muslim University the affiliating power out of the Aligarh district. The government was not ready to take a risk that the loyalists who were always begging for their rights, should start an all-India movement to get their share in the power and politics.

However, it must not be forgotten that before the elevation of the MAO College to a Muslim University, the nationalist movement in Aligarh had already gained momentum, and the Muslims were participating in good strength. Due to the Muslim participation in politics, the tussle between the loyalists and the nationalist Muslims had almost reached its zenith. The loyalists of Aligarh were happy because their dream of establishing a Muslim University was about to fulfil. The nationalists on the other hand, wanted a university free and independent from British control. The nationalist Muslims after failing to reach any compromise, decided to set-up an independent university. For the establishment of the National Muslim University the nationalists invited both Hindus and Muslims to attend its inaugural ceremony on 29th October, 1920 and successfully the National Muslim University was founded at Aligarh.

The National Muslim University had the blessings and financial support of Mahatma Gandhi and Indian National Congress. This institution was later renamed as 'Jamia Millia Islamia.' Maulana

Mohammad Ali prepared a syllabus, and then the teaching got underway at the National Muslim University. Maulana Mohammad Ali himself started teaching English and Modern History. Senior students of AMU were also roped in order to function as teachers. The curriculum prepared by Maulana Mohammad Ali was predominantly on nationalistic pattern.

It was the same time when the Aligarh Muslim University also started its teaching in December 1920. While Aligarh Muslim University started its functioning under the complete control of the loyalists, the nationalists with their independent and national outlook kept themselves engaged in Jamia Millia Islamia which later on shifted to Delhi in 1925.

When the Aligarh Muslim University started its functioning, it established many new departments but its sources for grants were too limited. It became very difficult to carry on full-fledged teaching in some departments. However, when the required money was received from different sources, many appointments were made for that purpose and regular teachings, and full-fledged departments were started. At the beginning, the process of development was quite slow as its first Vice-Chancellor Raja of Mahmudabad, due to his busy schedule, could not give much attention to the university affairs. However, when Sahibzada Aftab Ahmad Khan was elected as Vice-Chancellor, the strength of the students rose greatly and many new departments of study were opened in the university.

The Pro-Vice-Chancellor Dr. Ziauddin Ahmad also made many revolutionary improvements in the university. Dr. Ziauddin Ahmad was a pure academician and was really concerned about the Muslim problems. On many occasions, he introduced some reforms suitable to the students which were objectionable to the Vice-Chancellor. One of his very remarkable reforms was starting the policy of holding private examinations.

Aligarh Muslim University was imparting very valuable education; its courses of study were both general and professional, but the unique thing of this university was its pattern of education, culture and traditions. The discipline, traditions and culture of Aligarh were modelled, to some extent, on the pattern of Oxford and Cambridge. At Oxford and Cambridge, the students' attendance at church service and recitation of a few verses from the Bible in the dining hall everyday before lunch was considered necessary for the formation of the character of the students. Similarly for the development of culture and character, saying of the daily prayers and attending the Friday Sermon was enforced on Muslim students in Aligarh Muslim University. It was the general belief that religious and spiritual life would greatly help in formation of character of the students. Aligarh always insisted on the development of sound judgement, good manners, common sense and self-sacrifice as essential elements for education. Aligarh Muslim University did never betray any kind of bios or prejudices against or in favour of any particular community.

Sir Syed Ahmad Khan was the ideal of Dr. Ziauddin Ahmad, and he had the same dream of educating the illiterate persons, particularly the Muslims all-over India. Both Sahibzada Aftab Ahmad Khan and Dr. Ziauddin Ahmad were determined to popularise the Muslim University and tried to attract the Muslims towards the educational movement of Aligarh. They got an opportunity to materialize their objective in 1925, when the institution was completing its 50 years since its establishment in 1875. They decided to mark the occasion a scheme by celebrating the jubilee of its foundation. To make the jubilee celebration attractive, successful and popular, the meetings of the other bodies were also arranged. These bodies included All India Mohammedan Educational Conference, All India Urdu Conference, The Muslim Rajput Conference, All India Muslim League, Tanzeem and University Convocation. Many debates, games and tournaments were also organised.

The jubilee celebration benefited the university a lot. On the one hand, the Muslim University became popular all-over India and received attention of the Muslim community. On the other hand, it received a large sum of money in donations, i.e. Rs. 1,76,000/- in cash, and assurances were made for more than Rs. 3,00,000/-.

While the Muslim University was gaining momentum, the pupils of Sir Syed Ahmad Khan, like Dr. Ziauddin Ahmad, Sahibzada Aftab Khan, Shaikh Abdullah, etc. were badly affected with the internal bitterness and jealousy. Much attention is required to dig up the reason behind their bitterness. Actually, all the associates of

Sir Syed Ahmad Khan were of high positions and belonged to almost the same pedestal. They equally devoted their energies in founding the AMU. When the university was founded, they took charges of running the institution but their appointments were not of equal grade.

Dr. Ziauddin Ahmad had devoted all his life to Aligarh and always tried to do the best for the institution. During the crisis of 1920, when the Khilafat and Non-Cooperation movements were on its peak, Dr. Ziauddin Ahmad saved this institution from the clutches of politicians. However, after the foundation of the university, he was appointed as Pro-Vice Chancellor of AMU. While Raja of Mahmudabad, a second-rate alumnus, was given the Vice-Chancellorship. After Raja Sahib, Sahibzada Aftab Ahmad Khan became Vice-Chancellor but Dr. Ziauddin Ahmad remained on the same position. All these persons had different ideologies, which came into conflict with one another. The Vice-Chancellor Sahibzada Aftab Ahmad Khan wanted to run the university strictly according to the rules and regulations, but Dr Ziauddin Ahmad was having the interests and benefits of the students uppermost on the rules.

The Pro-Vice Chancellor Dr. Ziauddin Ahmad was a unique personality and always considered himself as the real successor of Sir Syed Ahmad Khan in educating and promoting his community. In the lifetime of Sir Syed Ahmad Khan, he has promised him to serve this institution until death. No doubt he remained true to his promise and acted boldly whenever the MAO College and later on the AMU has to face any problem. He thought that the ultimate aim of the university was to educate the students in general and Muslim students, in particular, and the rules restricting the interests of the students must be avoided. According to him, rules and regulations were mere technical restrictions which he always waived in most of the cases.

However, the position of Dr. Ziauddin Ahmad in the university was secondary as he was the Pro-Vice Chancellor and hence not in a position to do what was good for the cause of the university or students. Subsequently, he was constrained to implement his schemes, but he did so without the consultation of the Vice-Chancellor Sahibzada Aftab Ahmad Khan. His nature of independent thinking and idea of educating the Muslim youth by flouting the regulations in certain cases created a band of opponents in the university led by his own colleagues and friends. These were the reasons which created a serious rift between the Vice-Chancellor and the Pro-Vice Chancellor and were a cause of bitterness between them. A lot of negative propaganda was made against Dr. Ziauddin Ahmad, the main focus of which were that the standard of the university was falling down, and the rules and regulations were being violated openly.

As a result of these differences and allegations over university functioning, the government paid its attention over AMU and an enquiry committee popularly known as "Rahmatullah Enquiry Committee" was appointed to look into the whole affair. The committee after enquiring all the departments of the university and interviewing many related persons submitted its report. According to the recommendations of the report, many reforms were made. The report also requested Dr. Ziauddin Ahmad to resign from his post of Pro-Vice Chancellor while appreciating his services for the institution.

The next personality who developed the university was the grandson of Sir Syed Ahmad Khan and the Vice-Chancellor of the Muslim University Sir Ross Masood. His important works were the inclusion of Intermediate College and schools in the university, improvements in Urdu, Geography, introduction of Hindi, and drainage and electrification of the university, starting of VC fund for the poor students, building of gymnasium and swimming bath, etc. His most important and highly appreciable work was the starting of the Science College and collection of Rs. 25 lakh. He also started research provision and appointed able staff for that purpose.

However, in spite of the remarkable works of Sir Ross Masood, the lobbying in the university could not spare him. Some of the authorities and staff members polarized against him began to criticise his works. It was the endeavour of Sir Ross Masood to give a practical shape to his grandfather's dream. He never expected that anybody will oppose his works. He had not the responsibility by post only but by blood too. The opposition of his own men made him sentimental, he was particularly aggrieved. He tendered his resignation in April 1934 and left for Europe.

Dr. Ziauddin Ahmad, who once resigned from the Pro-Vice-Chancellorship of the university following the Rahmatullah

Committee Report, was also appointed as the Vice-Chancellor. Dr. Ziauddin Ahmad was also an able man and took the challenging responsibility. Until 1947, he made many developments in the university. His first step was to acquire the Aligarh fort to meet the needs of the lands for the development of the university. Many new departments and courses of study were also opened. A few among them were Journalism, Military Drill, Agriculture, Commerce, Geology, etc.

The faculty system which was introduced in 1944 marked further development in the educational system of AMU. Dr. Ziauddin Ahmad played a very important role in establishing many war-related courses. With the help of the government, he established many courses like War Technician, A.R.P. Chemical Industry, Military College, Flying Club, Radio, Naval Training, etc. Sir Agha Khan suggested him to establish a Medical College and also gave a handsome donation for that purpose. Under the guidance of Dr. Ziauddin Ahmad, many deputations toured throughout the length and breadth of the country, and until 1947 about Rs. 50 lakh were collected for the purpose of establishing the Medical College.

As far as Engineering College was concerned, the teaching for diploma courses had started as early as 1924, but its real beginning was possible only in 1935, when the Technical Institute was started. In 1940, the Department of Technology was established. Tibbiya College also made a noticeable progress for the first time since its establishment in 1927, and its diploma holder Hakim began to be recruited by UP Government.

In the field of girls' education, the work of Shaikh Abdullah is well known. By the efforts of Shaikh Abdullah, a girls' school was also started in 1907. He felt that the social problems of the ladies were of a really serious nature, and their emancipation was only possible through the modern education. However, giving it a practical shape was undoubtedly a difficult task in the orthodox Muslim society. The work of Shaikh Abdullah was not only opposed by orthodox section of the Muslim community and general masses but also by some highly educated persons of the community and even by his own friends.

He faced great difficulty in collecting donations for his school, recruitments of the teachers and in the admission of the girl students.

The most difficult work was to mobilise the people to send their daughters to his school. Another problem was that those who had so far opposed his work through speeches and writings only, now came out openly against him and started creating problems in his path. In 1914 when boarding house completed its construction, no parents were ready to lodge their daughters in the boarding house. However, after untiring efforts of Shaikh Abdullah and Begum Abdullah, a few parents became ready to lodge their daughters after a lot of enquiry. From then the lodging process increased day by day.

From 1921, this small girls' school rose to the status of a Girls High School and in 1929, UP Board recognised it as an Intermediate College. In 1930, this college got affiliated to the Muslim University. But the grant from the Muslim University was too meager and Shaikh Abdullah thought it better to convert it into provincial college in order to get a bigger grant from the UP Government. By the joint efforts of Dr. Ziauddin Ahmad and Shaikh Abdullah this college became a provincial college under the UP Government in 1942.

As for the political role of the Aligarh Muslim University students and its alumni, they had both the responsibilities of nation and the community. They were of the opinion that without the sound position of the community, the national service cannot be performed perfectly. However, the people generally misunderstood the service of the community and service of the nation and began branding the service of the community as separatist movement or pro-Pakistani leanings. Actually, Aligarh was not a merely institution but a school of thought, which naturally moulded the destiny of the nation. The educational importance and political awareness in Aligarh were started with the ideology of Sir Syed Ahmad Khan, who continuously worked for the betterment of the Muslim community after the shocks of 1857.

At the beginning, the British Government was very hostile to the Muslim community. The British considered that they have seized the power from the Muslims, and the Muslims could never be friendly with the British Government. They also made the Muslims responsible for the rebellion of 1857. Sir Syed Ahmad Khan tried his level best to save the Muslims from heavy hands of the British Government. He advocated that the Muslims could get prosperity only with the cooperation of the British. He changed the mentality of the British Government. Following the ideology of Sir Syed Ahmad Khan, the Muslims progressed themselves.

After the death of Sir Syed Ahmad Khan, the Muslim leaders of that time decided to meet the Viceroy and put before him certain demands for Muslims' security and interest in India. On 1st October, 1906, a deputation of 35 members reached Shimla to present their address to the Viceroy Lord Minto. This deputation is popularly known as 'Shimla Deputation'. They asked the Viceroy to provide Muslim community the right to select their representatives by electorates confined exclusively to their community. They also demanded that Muslim representation should be proportionate not merely to their numerical strength but should reflect the significance of their community as an important factor. Lord Minto also assured the deputation that their political rights and interests would be safeguarded in administration with which he was concerned. The Viceroy fully encouraged the Shimla deputation, so these prominent Muslim leaders began to think to unite the Muslims in the form of an association.

When the Muhammadan Educational Conference was over on December 30, 1906 at Decca, Nawab Salimullah Khan convened a meeting to discuss the scheme of a Muslim organization. Ultimately, with the general consensus, the All India Muslim League was formed. The work of the Muslim League was to unite to Muslims all-over India, to demand and get share in the power and remain loyal to the British Government. Fortunately, the Muslim League gained much attention and favour from the British Government. The Act of 1909 was the reward of the Muslim League in which they got the historic separate electorate.

Indian Muslims were not only concerned with the position of the Indian Muslims but they were worried about the Muslim problems of the all-over world. When the Tripoli War was started in 1911, it caused great concern among Indian Muslims. The Muslim League passed a resolution appealing the British Government to put a stop to this brutal war. Aligarh students, responding to the call of the Muslim League, contributed to the funds raised for Tripoli victims. They also began to boycott the Italian goods. Aligarh Muslims thought that the British Government would certainly favour the sentiments of the Muslims. However, the British Government's announcement of neutrality in the war embarrassed the Indian Muslim community. The defeat of Turkey frustrated the Indian Muslims, particularly Aligarh Muslims, because they had much expectation from the British Government.

Unfortunately, soon after the Tripoli War, Balkan War began from October 1912. During the progress of this war, anti-British feelings gained ground among educated young Muslims, especially at Aligarh. On 17th October 1912, after the Friday prayer at the MAO College Mosque, the Muslims prayed for Turkish betterment. Maulana Shaukat Ali proposed volunteers to fight against Balkans and asked for government's help. However, in the Balkan War, much against the wishes of the Indian Muslims, the British Government once again pleaded and advised neutrality. The Aligarh Muslims never followed the advice of the British Government.

Most of the Aligarh teachers, students and other Muslims felt that the Balkan War was not merely a political but a religious war for the entire Muslim community. This consideration was based upon the fact that the Austrians and Russians were also supporting and helping the Balkan states. Maulana Shibli, on the commencement of the Balkan War, was very much grieved and wrote a poetry entitled "*Shahr-Ashooh-i-Islam*." In this poem Maulana Shibli described that how Islam is being attacked by combined European forces.

The MAO College students of Aligarh were very much emotional due to the Balkan War and the British diplomacy. In order to raise money for Turkey they demanded to the College management that the total of the fund collected for the establishment of the Muslim University should be given to Turkey. In order to cure the war victims of Turkey, a Medical Mission led by Mukhtar Ahmad Ansari accompanied by Chaudhary Khaliquzzaman, Abdur Rahman Siddiqui, Shoaib Peshawari from MAO School was sent to Turkey in December, 1912.

The Turkish issue had created a chasm among the Aligarh Muslims. Most of them, frustrated with the policies of the British Government, adopted the nationalist stand. These nationalists, by taking the advantage of the situation, held a series of secret meetings of students exposing the role of British Government in India and tanned their sentiments by citing the fate of Islam in Morocco, Persia and Turkey. Political agitation in Aligarh thus reached on its peak, causing great concern to the British high officials.

Most of the Aligarh Muslims openly advocated pursuance of a policy of joint struggle against the British by joining hands with the Indian National Congress. Following the ongoing international situations now there was a clear shift among the youths of Aligarh and sure departure from Sir Syed's policy. The Turkish problems in the First World War further strengthened the anti-British feelings among the MAO College students.

The Khilafat and Non-Cooperation Movement played the most important role in the Aligarh politics. Most of the Aligarh Muslims participated in these movements. These movements disturbed the British Government, and they in repercussions, intensified their policy of divide and rule. The government immediately granted the charter to the Muslim University to bring the Muslim back to its fold. However, still much to the chagrin of the government the AMU and other Muslims actively participated in the Khilafat and Non-Cooperation Movements.

The Indian *Ulema* and the Congress led by Mahatma Gandhi also supported the Khilafatists. Gandhiji invited all Hindus to support the Muslims on the Khilafat issue. The Khilafat along with Non-Cooperation Movement united all the Hindus and Muslims of India on one platform. Actually, by supporting the Khilafat Movement, Mahatma Gandhi had made a great diplomatic effort of bringing the Muslims into the freedom struggle. The Aligarh nationalists like Ali brothers, Hasrat Mohani, Ajmal Khan, etc. played a leading role in his effort. However, a few Aligarh Muslims still had great expectations from the British Government and they decided to remain loyal to it.

In Aligarh, the Muslims were divided over the issue of supporting the British Government and Khilafat Movement. They were denoted by the name of the nationalists and loyalists. These Aligarh Muslims of two different ideologies waged a cold war against each other through pamphlets and ballots. They held a number of secret meetings to woo the students on their respective sides. However, it is noteworthy that the majority of the students had great sympathy and support for the nationalist stand. The Khilafat and Non-Cooperation movements thus brought about a remarkable change in the Aligarh politics.

One thing must be cleared here, whether the Khilafat question was really an issue? Whether really the *Khalifa* was Muslim religious head of all-over world, including India? In fact, the *Khalifa* was a Turkish Sultan and had nothing to do with rest of the world. In order to make their seat safe, they promoted themselves as the successor of the traditional *Khalifa* of rather the real *Khalifa*. Similarly, the Khilafat Movement in India was an expression of hate towards the British, who had enslaved the Indian people since long. The politicians find it a golden opportunity to unite the Muslims against the British, who were considered the traditional British supporter after the Aligarh Movement of Sir Syed Ahmad Khan.

This Khilafat Movement not only polarized the Indian Muslims against the British, but due to the efforts of Mahatma Gandhi and launching of Non-Cooperation Movement, united Hindus and Muslims against the British Government. It was nothing to do with the Islam or rest of the Muslim world. It was a good pretext to propagate the nationalist feelings among the Muslim masses. Mahatma Gandhi appealed to the Hindus to help their Muslim brethren in this hour of Muslim crisis. It soon developed into a movement and resulted in an unprecedented Hindu-Muslim unity and took the form of a tough struggle of nationalist movement against the British Government. The Non-Cooperation further added fuel to the enthusiasm of the nationalists. These movements coupled with the Hindu-Muslim unity broken the backbone of the British Government.

When Aligarh came into limelight due to its political interest and activities, both Muslim League and Congress tried their level best to obtain a foothold in Aligarh. However, as Muslim League was not having much been following even among the Muslims until 1937, the Congress succeeded in making a stronghold for itself in Aligarh. Since the time of Non-Cooperation Movement, Aligarh became a favourite campaign ground for the nationalist leaders. Almost all the top rank Congress leaders had visited MAO College and later on AMU and received a very positive response from the students. Its alumni joined the Congress, Khilafat and Swaraj party in order to serve the nation and played a memorable role in history of freedom movement.

The Aligarh was a centre of Hindu-Muslim unity, quite away from the clutches of the British policies of divide and rule. In the midst of the communal riots and *Shuddhi* and *Sangathan* movements, Aligarh always gave the message of peace and tranquility. In Aligarh Shaikh Abdullah founded the Independent Muslim Party. This party criticised the communal minded leaders and decided to cooperate with any political party whose aim would be to achieve the Hindu-Muslim unity and in the interest of the country. This party attracted many secular Muslims by its campaign of nationalism and communal harmony. The loyalist group also shared the ideology of Shaikh Abdullah. They all tried to promote the Hindu-Muslim unity, and this process continued until 1937.

When the Simon Commission arrived in India, many Muslim leaders like Maulana Abul Kalam Azad, Dr. M.A. Ansari, Mr. T.A.K. Sherwani formed the Muslim Nationalist Party in order to mobilise the Muslim masses in favour of the national movement and to boycott the Simon Commission. Besides this, the Muslim League led by Mr. Jinnah, Jamiatul Ulema, Khilafat Committee, etc. opposed the Commission. Among others who opposed the Commission were Syed Hasan Imam, Maharaja of Mohmudabad, Maulana Mohammad Ali and Shaukat Ali.

In the anti-Simon protest, the active participation of Aligarh students was doubtful. According to the loyalists, the university was an educational institution and participation of the students in political movements could ruin of their carriers. Besides, the university was running with the aid of the British Government and political participation of the students meant disaster for the university also. So, even the members of the university bodies involved in politics never allowed the students into political participation.

It is also noteworthy that the AMU students were full of political awareness. The role of the students union was mainly to hold debates and discussion on the topics of social, economic, educational and particularly political problems. For that purpose, many political leaders were being invited from time to time. Thus, it was just impossible for the AMU students to keep quite regarding political movements when they were so thoroughly coloured with nationalism and secularism. However, as no written records are available about their role in these movements, it may be safely assumed that they showed remarkable maturity on partial aloofness from these political developments.

The Civil Disobedience Movement started in 1930, gave a further momentum to the freedom movement and blazed the national feelings all-over India. Although, the British Government adopted the policy of keeping the Muslims away from the movement but the irresistible Muslim leaders like Maulana Abul Kalam Azad, Dr. Ansari, Dr. Syed Mahmood, T.A.K. Sherwani, Mr. Rafi Ahmad Kidwai, Khan Abdul Ghaffar Khan, etc. could not be contained. Muslim Nationalist Party, Jamiatul-Ulema-i-Hind, Ahrarul Islam, Khudai Khidmatgar, etc. gave great sacrifices for the movement. The followers of Mr. Jinnah kept aloof in the movement due to the inconsistency of the Congress policy towards Muslims regarding Nehru Report.

Muslim League had a very weak position in UP, where it was no more than a small group led by Nawab Mohammad Ismail Khan and Chaudhary Khailquzzaman. These Muslim League leaders were not against the Congress or its policies. They thought that the service of the nation was only possible by the joint efforts of Hindus and Muslims without any sectional difference. They proved their nationalist and secular credentials by supporting the Congress at many places in the election of 1937. The Congress in return assured them at least two cabinet seats in their government. However, after the sound victory of the Congress in the election, the Congress refused to fulfil the pre-poll assurances.

These opportunistic policies of the Congress leaders frustrated the Muslim League leaders. Muslim League not only turned against the Congress to its policies in UP, but started working day and night for strengthening its position. Mr. Jinnah also got an opportunity to mobilise the Muslim youths by citing the example of the Congress attitude in distributing the portfolios of the UP cabinet. Nawab Mohammad Ismail Khan and Chaudhary Khailquzzaman were, undoubtedly, the cherished leaders of Aligarh and the breach of trust also frustrated the Aligarh Muslims and *alumni*. Naturally, most of the Aligarh students turned against the Congress.

In the election of 1937, when the Congress won a mammoth majority of seats, it was fair chance for it to merge most of the smaller political parties with itself. Even the most prominent Muslim League Leader Mr. Jinnah had much hope from the Congress. However, here the Congress played a negative role. In Bengal, when Fazal-i-Husain, a Krishak Praja Party leader, pleaded with the Congress for its support, the Congress declined the request. If Congress had supported the Krishak Praja Party, it would definitely have become a part of the Congress or a Congress supporting party. Similarly in UP, if the Congress had taken the two Congress minded Muslim League leaders Chaudhary Khaiquzzaman and Nawab Ismail Khan, then at least in UP Muslim League would have lost even its roots. The Congress by its policies indirectly supported in strengthening the Muslim League at every step.

Thus the Aligarh, which was once dominated by the Congress mentality people, became a workshop of the Muslim League. Slowly and gradually, in the last few years of the freedom movement Mr. Jinnah could get support of AMU students in favour of its separatist policies. The Muslim League, deceived by the Congress, started poisoning the minds of the Muslims against the Congress and branded it as a Hindu organization. The Muslim League blamed the Congress for its anti-Urdu, anti-Islamic and anti-Muslim policies and alleged that only the Congress was responsible for the communal riots, and for the butchering of the Muslim masses in the Congress ruled provinces.

The anti-Congress propaganda of Muslim League was because of the presence of some leaders in the Congress, who were also having membership of communal organization like Hindu Mahasabha. These leaders always tried to embitter the relations between Muslims and the Congress. Although a good many Muslim leaders were still there in the Congress party but their position was merely of advisors and hardly of any value.

In spite of such an anti-Congress move at Aligarh, there were many students in the university who were still the supporter of the Congress party. Whenever the Congress leaders visited Aligarh and AMU, they were very warmly welcomed, and the students listened to them with great enthusiasm. However, the university authorities never gave any encouragement to the nationalist feelings among the students, following the loyalist ideology. Perhaps they were afraid of the British Government as the AMU was running by its financial aid. Sometimes, they showed their nationalist feelings by secretly supporting parties like Muslim League, Congress and the Communist Party.

At the beginning of the Second World War, a new political crisis developed in which many Congress ministers resigned from their Provincial Government. They complained that the British Government involved the India into the war without the consultation of the Congress. During this crisis, the Muslim League got a fair chance to knock down the Congress, and it not only observed the 'Day of Deliverance' but in the following year it started the Pakistan Movement also. The non-Congress ministries in Punjab, Sindh and Bengal pledged their full support to the Government in the Second World War. Indian States as usual also offered their support with men and money while Congress was still opposing the Government tooth and nail in this war.

In the AMU campus, almost all parties were trying to get sympathy of the students. It created an atmosphere of the diverse thinking process. Sometimes it was the followers of the Congress who seemed to have become powerful, at others it was the turn to the communists, but mostly it was the Muslim League which dominated over the students. The Muslim League was the most favoured party not only of the students but also of the Aligarh authorities. Actually the portfolio distributing episode in UP after the 1937 election, the controversy over Urdu language, atrocities committed upon the Muslims during the Congress rule and suppression of the Khaksars maligned the Muslims as a whole that the Congress could never be a saviour of the Muslims. The stirring speeches of Mr. Jinnah further convinced the Aligarh Muslims whom the only alternative of the Congress was the Muslim League.

However, the nationalists of Aligarh could not be convinced by the speeches of Mr. Jinnah, and they always opposed the separatist policies of Muslims League. In the Aligarh city, the nationalistic activities were carried on in two ways; one in peaceful Gandhian way and the other, in a revolutionary way. The revolutionary movement flourished a great in Aligarh largely due to its Metal Work Industry. These *Krantikaris* were great experts in preparing bombs and supplied them to different revolutionary organizations all-over India.

If we particularly talk about Aligarh Muslims, we bound to accept the hard sane fact that the number of nationalist Muslim began decreasing after 1940 when Pakistan resolution was passed by Muslim League. It must not be forgotten that this Pakistan was not a totally Independent nation but an autonomous nation within India. Whatsoever it was, but it was a fact that during this period, Muslim League began to instigate the Muslim youths of Aligarh by making them believe that Islam and Muslims were in danger, and that the British wanted to impose Hindu rule upon them. By striking this sentimental card, Mr. Jinnah had been succeeding in wooing the Aligarh students in 1937 and now again in 1940, he succeeded in alluring them by the dream of Pakistan, although even Mr. Jinnah was not sure of its future.

Ironically, the Muslims of India forgot that their religious leaders were *Ulema* who were in favour of Congress and unity of India; they did not realize that they were being seduced by a man who wants political gain only. He was no doubt a Muslim by name but far away from Islam and Islamic traditions. Mr. Jinnah founded AIMSF (All India Muslim Students Federation) which became his real weapon to popularise the Muslim League and getting support of the Muslim masses in favour of Pakistan. In the elections also these students helped and campaigned for the League.

The Aligarh students knew the fact well that Pakistan was only an autonomous Muslim majority state within India. They never even dreamt about Independent Pakistan. They supported this movement in order to react to the Muslims sufferings according to the propaganda spread by Mr. Jinnah, who visited Aligarh annually and gave stirring speeches to mobilise the students. As a result of these efforts, the Muslim youths founded a branch of Muslim League in AMU. Its branch was also opened in Aligarh city. More interestingly even children of Aligarh founded 'Bachcha Muslim League' in Aligarh to show their sympathy with Mr. Jinnah and his so-called movement for Pakistan.

In 1942, Mahatma Gandhi launched 'Quit India Movement' in the growing danger of Japan's victory over British. He was sure that Japan would certainly occupy the Indian subcontinent if it remains in the possession of the British. All-over India the Quit India Movement was started and both the Hindus and Muslims participated actively. Even Muslim League did not remain behind, by following the Quit India Movement of the Congress, although a bit differently giving the call for 'Divide and Quit'. The British Government rejected Pakistan proposal by many delegations of England which arrived in India to solve the Constitutional problems. However, the Cabinet Mission gave green signal to the Muslim League by grouping the provinces on the communal basis for the election of Constituent Assembly.

The election of the Constituent Assembly was held, and the Congress won the mammoth majority. A process of formation of the Interim Government was started under Pandit Jawahar Lal Nehru. Mr. Jinnah was also invited to share the cabinet of Pandit Nehru. Mr. Jinnah declined the offer because by nature, he was a dictator and an egomaniac, and he wanted to hold the position of supreme leadership of India. How could Nehru, a leader of the majority party had agreed to the leadership of Mr. Jinnah, a leader of a minority party? Subsequently, Jinnah was left with no alternative but to strengthen the call of Pakistan. For that purpose, the 'Direct Action' programme was started by Muslim League.

Here it must be cleared that in the 'Direct Action' programme of Muslim League, the Aligarh Muslims never cooperated the Muslim League or Mr. Jinnah. No doubt they talked enough about the communal riots and openly criticized the communal forces and leaders. In the last moment when the Pakistan Movement became violent and led to many communal riots, the Aligarh intelligentsia kept aloof with Mr. Jinnah and the League. Perhaps they were aware that the nature of Pakistan was completely changed from autonomous state within India to a separate independent state. The Aligarh Muslims were sure that a separate Pakistan would never benefit the Aligarh due to its geographical position. They were also perhaps aware about the greedy nature of their leader Mr. Jinnah, who wanted to hold power at any cost.

The Direct Action programme of the Muslim League followed a series of communal riots all-over India. Especially in Bengal, thousands of men were killed and the property estimated at many lacks was looted and burnt. The situation became uncontrollable and the leaders began to seriously think about its solution. After the hectic negotiations, Mr. Jinnah condescended to let some of his colleagues join the ministry of the Interim Government but his motive was not to support the Government, but to oppose the Congress policies.

Following the worsened situations, Lord Mountbatten arrived in India as the Viceroy and tried his level best to diffuse the political crisis by having many talks with topmost Indian leaders. He found that except Mahatma Gandhi all the other Congress leaders were prepared to handover the Muslim majority areas to Mr. Jinnah. A few leaders of the Congress thought that Pakistan would not remain for long as it was situating on two corners of India. They were confident that a few years later Muslim League would beg for reunification of India. When the Muslim League leaders sensed a hint of acceptance of their demand by the Congress stood for their demand firmly, and clearly told the Mountbatten that they would achieve the Pakistan otherwise India would perish.

Sardar Ballabh Bhai Patel, already in favour of India's partition in 1946, was prepared to handover the Pakistan to the Muslim League. He was against any conciliation with Muslim League about its demand. Sardar Ballabh Bhai Patel was sure that the Pakistan Movement was a drama of power share and leadership, and he was not ready at any cost to handover India's fate into the hands of Mr. Jinnah. The Congress leaders better thought that in the presence of Mr. Jinnah and Muslim League, they would never rule India peacefully. Both the parties were power hungry and wanted to have the leading position in India. Perhaps it was Sardar Ballabh Bhai Patel, who had also convinced Pandit Jawahar Lal Nehru to agree for partition of India.

Mahatma Gandhi opposed the partition plan tooth and nail, but his pupils had become quite strong by the time India achieved Independence. They refused the plan of the man whom they had since long obeyed. As far as Maulana Azad was concerned, he was in a dilemma as to whether he should follow Mahatma Gandhi or his colleagues Nehru and Patel, who were going to become the rulers of India. Being a Muslim if Maulana Azad had supported Mahatma Gandhi, then the fate of Azad like a true Congressman would have become more precarious along with the rest of Muslims in free India. It was a good diplomacy at a really testing time that Maulana Azad adopted keeping quiet and leaving on Nehru and Patel to decide the fate of India.

When India was partitioned the Aligarh community was shocked as the Pakistan was an impossible dream for them. Definitely, the Pakistan or the partition of India was a situational result and nobody thought of its materialization. Even Mr. Jinnah was not sure to get Pakistan in his lifetime. It was the power and politics which divided the India into two Independent nations. The Aligarh Muslims were, to some extent, ashamed of being the traditional supporter of Muslim League and Pakistan. After the Independence of India, the Congress adopted the Aligarh with fair deal. The Congress leaders visited Aligarh and the students as well as the rest of the intelligentsia of AMU actively cooperated with them and responded positively to their call of nationalism and patriotism.

Bibliography

Primary Sources: Newspapers, Confidential Files, Reports, Proceedings and Journals

Al-Hilal, 9th October, 1912, No. 13.
Aligarh Institute Gazette, 10th December, 1935.
Aligarh Institute Gazette, 11th October, 1911.
Aligarh Institute Gazette, 12th December, 1935.
Aligarh Institute Gazette, 12th June, 1897.
Aligarh Institute Gazette, 14th November, 1935.
Aligarh Institute Gazette, 15th July, 1943.
Aligarh Institute Gazette, 15th November, 1911.
Aligarh Institute Gazette, 15th November, 1941.
Aligarh Institute Gazette, 15th October, 1919.
Aligarh Institute Gazette, 15th October, 1941.
Aligarh Institute Gazette, 15th September, 1920.
Aligarh Institute Gazette, 19th October, 1912.
Aligarh Institute Gazette, 1st April, 1941.
Aligarh Institute Gazette, 1st August, 1943.
Aligarh Institute Gazette, 1st January, 1941.
Aligarh Institute Gazette, 1st January, 1943.
Aligarh Institute Gazette, 1st January, 1944.
Aligarh Institute Gazette, 1st June, 1943.
Aligarh Institute Gazette, 1st March, 1890.
Aligarh Institute Gazette, 1st May, 1886.
Aligarh Institute Gazette, 1st November, 1911.
Aligarh Institute Gazette, 1st September, 1920.
Aligarh Institute Gazette, 20th October, 1920.
Aligarh Institute Gazette, 21st August, 1874.

Aligarh Institute Gazette, 23rd October, 1920.
Aligarh Institute Gazette, 24th October, 1906.
Aligarh Institute Gazette, 24th October, 1920.
Aligarh Institute Gazette, 26th June, 1912.
Aligarh Institute Gazette, 28th April, 1926.
Aligarh Institute Gazette, 30th October, 1912.
Aligarh Institute Gazette, 30th October, 1920
Aligarh Institute Gazette, 31st March, 1926.
Aligarh Institute Gazette, 3rd October, 1906.
Aligarh Institute Gazette, 7th March, 1926.
Aligarh Institute Gazette, 8th January, 1913.
Aligarh Institute Gazette, 8th September, 1920.
Aligarh Institute Gazette, 1st November, 1920.
Aligarh Magazine, 1928.
Aligarh Magazine, 1947.
Aligarh Magazine, 1953-54 & 1954-55.
Aligarh Magazine, 1953-54-1954-55.
Aligarh Magazine, 1953-54-55.
Aligarh Magazine, December, 1932.
Aligarh Magazine, January-February, 1929.
Aligarh Magazine, July-October, 1921.
Aligarh Magazine, March, 1939.
Aligarh Magazine, March, 1944.
Aligarh Magazine, October-December, 1929.
Aligarh Magazine, September-October, 1920.
Aligarh Magazine, Special Number, 1953-54, 1954-55.
Aligarh Mail, October 1926.
AMU Act of 1920 (AMU Archive).
AMU Annual Report 1944 (AMU Archive).
AMU Annual Report, 1931 (AMU Archive).
AMU Annual Report, 1933 (AMU Archive).
AMU Annual Report, 1934 (AMU Archive).
AMU Annual Report, 1935 (AMU Archive).
AMU Annual Report, 1936 (AMU Archive).
AMU Annual Report, 1939 (AMU Archive)
AMU Annual Report, 1940 (AMU Archive).
AMU Annual Report, 1943 (AMU Archive).
AMU Annual Report, 1944 (AMU Archive).
AMU Annual Report, 1947 (AMU Archive).
AMU Calendar, 1921-25 (AMU Archive).
AMU Calendar, 1932 (AMU Archive).

Court Minutes of AMU, 1926 (AMU Archive).
Department of GAD, File No. 555/1936, Uttar Pradesh State Archive Lucknow (UPSAL).
Department of Home-Political, Coll. 210-216 & KW-Dec-A-1920 (National Archives, New Delhi).
Department of Home-Political, Coll. 59-Dec-Deposit-1920 (National Archives, New Delhi).
Department of Police, File No. 151/1930, Uttar Pradesh State Archive Lucknow (UPSAL).
Department of Police, File No. 241/1930, Uttar Pradesh State Archive Lucknow (UPSAL).
Department of Police, File No. RR 26, Uttar Pradesh State Archive Lucknow (UPSAL).
Department of Police, Serial No. 16/3, Uttar Pradesh State Archive Lucknow (UPSAL).
Englishmen, 17th July, 1924.
Executive Council Report, 9th April, 1928 (AMU Archive).
Explanation of Dr. Ziauddin Ahmad, Vilayat Manzil, Aligarh, 1928.
Fikr-o-Nazar, Vol. I.
Fikr-o-Nazar, Vol. II.
Fikr-o-Nazar, Vol. III.
File No, 51, 1937-38 (AMU Archive).
File No. XV/2, 1923-24 (AMU Archive).
File No. 1, 1920-21 (AMU Archives).
File No. 15, 1920-21 (AMU Archives).
File No. 4 (1), 1930-31 (AMU Archive).
File No. 4, 1942-43 (AMU Archive).
File No. 4/2 (I), 1924 (AMU Archive).
File No. 41/1, 1943-44 (AMU Archive).
File No. 41/3, 1939-40 (AMU Archive).
File No. 51 (I), 1930-31 (AMU Archive).
File No. 51, 1923-24 (AMU Archive).
File No. 51, 1924-25 (AMU Archive).
File No. 51, 1926-27 (AMU Archive).
File No. 51, 1939-40 (AMU Archive).
File No. 51, 1941-42 (AMU Archive).
File No. 51, 1942-43 (AMU Archive).
File No. 51, 1943-44 (AMU Archive).
File No. 51, 1945-46 (AMU Archive).
File No. 51, 1928-29 (AMU Archive).
File No. 51, 1929-30 (AMU Archive).
File No. 51, 1931-32 (AMU Archive).

File No. 51, 1933-34 (AMU Archive).
File No. 51, 1934-35 (AMU Archive).
File No. 51, 1935-36 (AMU Archive).
File No. 51, 1935-36 (AMU Archive).
File No. 51, 1935-40 (AMU Archive).
File No. 51, 1937-38 (AMU Archive).
File No. 51, 1938-39 (AMU Archive).
File No. 51, 1940-41 (AMU Archive).
File No. 51, 1942-43 (AMU Archive).
File No. 51, 1943-44 (AMU Archive).
File No. 51, 1945-46 (AMU Archive).
File No. 53/4, 1940-41 (AMU Archive).
File No. 6, Uttar Pradesh State Archive Lucknow (UPSAL).
File No. 604/36, Uttar Pradesh State Archive Lucknow (UPSAL).
File No. 62, 1938-44 (AMU Archive).
File No. 78/3, 1927-28 (AMU Archive).
File No. 78/4, 1929-30 (AMU Archive).
File No. 79, 1938-39 (AMU Archive).
File No. 82, 1936-37 (AMU Archive).
File No. II/7, 1922-23 (AMU Archive).
File No. IV/1, 1936-37 (AMU Archive).
File No. IV/1, 1924 (AMU Archive).
File No. IV/1, 1927-28 (AMU Archive).
File No. IV/I, 1926-27 (AMU Archive).
File No. V/2, 1931-32 (AMU Archive).
File No. XV/2, 1923-24 (AMU Archive).
File No. XV/3, 1925-26 (AMU Archive).
File No. XV/3, 1926-27 (AMU Archive).
File No. XVII/2, 1930-31 (AMU Archive).
File No. XX/42, 1920-21 (AMU Archives).
File No. XX/45, 1920-21 (AMU Archives).
Gazetteer of India, UP (Aligarh) Lucknow, 1987.
Hindustan Times, 25th January 1937.
Hindustan Times, 27th January 1939.
Indian Annual Register, 1921-22.
Indian Annual Register, Vol. II, 1931.
Indian Annual Register, Vol. II, 1935.
Indian Annual Register, Vol. I, 1937.
Indian Annual Register, Vol. II, 1941.
Indian Annual Register, Vol. I, 1943.
Indian Annual Register, Vol. II, 1934.
Indian Annual Register, Vol. II, 1935.

Indian Annual Register, Vol. II, 1938.
Indian Annual Register, Vol. II, 1939.
Indian Quarterly Register, Vol. II, 1927.
Minutes of the AMU Court, 1926 (AMU Archives).
Modern Asian Studies, Vol. 13, Part I, February 1979.
Modern Asian Studies, Vol. 8, Part II, 1974.
Modern Asian Studies, Vol. IX, 1975.
Muslim University Girls High School Magazine, 1964-65-66.
Muslim University Union Ministry Report, 1922-37 (AMU Union Hall).
Muslim University Union Ministry Report, 1945-46, 12th March, 1946 (AMU Union Hall).
Muslim University Union Ministry Report, 1945-46, 23rd March, 1946 (AMU Union Hall).
Muslim University Union Ministry Report, 1945-52 and 1946-47, 20th November, 1946 (AMU Union Hall).
Muslim University Union Ministry Report, 1945-52, 1945-46, 11th August, 1945 (AMU Union Hall).
Muslim University Union Ministry Report, 1945-52, 1945-46, 1st October, 1945 (AMU Union Hall).
Muslim University Union Ministry Report, 1945-52, 1945-46, 4th August, 1945 (AMU Union Hall).
Muslim University Union Ministry Report, 1945-52, 1945-46, 6th August, 1945 (AMU Union Hall).
Muslim University Union Ministry Report, 1946-47, 1st November, 1946 (AMU Union Hall).
Muslim University Union Ministry Report, 1946-47, 25th January, 1947 (AMU Union Hall).
Muslim University Union Ministry Report, 1946-47, 27th May, 1946 (AMU Union Hall).
Muslim University Union Ministry Report, 1946-47, 3rd March, 1946 (AMU Union Hall).
Muslim University Union Ministry Report, 1946-47, 9th November, 1946 (AMU Union Hall).
Muslim University Union Ministry Report, 1947-48, 2nd March, 1947 (AMU Union Hall).
Muslim University Union Ministry Report, 1947-48, 30th May, 1947 (AMU Union Hall).
Muslim University Union Ministry Report, 1945-52, 31st December, 1946 (AMU Union Hall).
Naqoosh, Lahore, January 1955.
Naqoosh, Lahore, October 1956.

Private Business Meeting Register 1937-44, 3rd March, 1944 (AMU Union Hall).

Private Business Meeting Register MU Union, 1937-1944, 17th February, 1941 (AMU Union Hall).

Private Business Meeting Register MU Union, 1937-1944, 1st April (AMU Union Hall).

Private Business Meeting Register MU Union, 1937-1944, 26th November, 1942 (AMU Union Hall).

Private Business Meeting Register, 1937-44, 27th January, 1939 (AMU Union Hall).

Private Business Meeting Register, 1937-44, 2nd February, 1939 (AMU Union Hall).

Private Business Meeting Register, 1937-44, 6th October, 1939 (AMU Union Hall).

Private Business Meeting Register, MU Union 1937-44, 8th September, 1939 (AMU Union Hall).

Proceedings of the Indian History Congress (55th Session Aligarh, 1994), Delhi, 1995.

Proceedings, Indian Legislative Council, Vol. LIX, (Uttar Pradesh State Library, Lucknow).

Report of the AMU Enquiry Committee (AMU Archive).

Select Committee Proceedings Book, 1935-44, 26th February 1939, (AMU Union Hall).

Tahzibul Akhlaq, 1st Rajab, 1289 H.

The Bombay Chronicle, 10th October, 1920.

The Bombay Chronicle, 16th October, 1920.

The Bombay Chronicle, 25 October, 1920.

The Bombay Chronicle, 26th October, 1920.

The Dawn, 15th June, 1946.

The Dawn, 17th June, 1946.

The Dawn, 23rd December, 1944.

The Dawn, 24th June, 1946.

The Dawn, 27th December, 1944.

The Dawn, 28th June, 1946.

The Dawn, 29th December, 1944.

The Englishman, 31st December, 1906.

The Hindustan Times, 20th January, 1937.

The Hindustan Times, 24th July, 1946.

The Hindustan Times, 2nd April, 1946.

The Hindustan Times, January, 11, 1946.

The Leader, 15th October, 1920.

The Leader, 18th October, 1920.

The Leader, 1st November, 1920.
The Leader, 20th October, 1920.
The Leader, 22nd October, 1920.
The Leader, 30th October, 1920.
The Leader, 31st October, 1920.
The Leader, 4th November, 1920.
The Pioneer, 11th January, 1888.
The Pioneer, 18th October, 1920.
The Pioneer, 24th October, 1920.
The Pioneer, 25th October, 1920.
The Pioneer, 30th October, 1920.
The Pioneer, 8th January, 1877.
The Times, London, 8th August, 1924.
The Tribune, 30th October, 1920.
The Tribune, 3rd November, 1920.
Urdu (Masood Number), 1937.
Young India, 10th December, 1919.
Young India, 1st January, 1928.
Young India, 3rd November, 1920.

Secondary Sources: Books

A.K. Fazul Haque, *Muslims Sufferings under Congress Rule*, Calcutta, December 1939.
Abdullah, Shaikh Mohammad, *Mushahidat-o-Taassurat,* Delhi, 1969.
Aggarwal, J.C., *Landmarks in the History of Modern Indian Education*, New Delhi, 1984.
Ahmad, Aijaz, *Indian Muslims Against British Rule,* New Delhi, 2014.
Ahmad, Aijaz, *Uprising of 1857: Some Facts About Failure of Indian War of Independence*, New Delhi, 2014.
Ahmad, Syed Tufail, *Musalmanon Ka Roshan Mustaqbil,* Delhi, 1945.
Anderson, Sir George, *Progress of Education in India 1927-32*, Delhi, (ND).
Ashraf, Mujib, *Hayat-ul-Bashir*, New Delhi, 1997.
Azad, Abul Kalam, *India Wins Freedom*, Madras, 1988.
Aziz, K.K., *Muslims under Congress Rule 1937-39*, Vol. I, Delhi, 1978.
Beg, Mirza Abdul Ghaffar, *Karachi Ka Tarikhi Muqadma*, Lucknow, 1985.
Bhatnagar, S.K., *History of the MAO College Aligarh*, New Delhi, 1869.
Chandra, Bipan, *India's Struggle for Independence*, Calcutta, 1992.
Coatman, J., *India in 1929-30*, Calcutta, 1931.
Coatman, J., *India in 1930-31*, Calcutta, 1932.
Coatman, J., *India in 1933-34*, Delhi, 1935.

Collins, Larry, & Lappiere, Dominique, *Freedom at Midnight*, New York, 1975.
Das, M.N., *A Contemporary History of the Indian National Congress*, Vol. 3, New Delhi, 1985.
Desai, Mahadeo, *Maulana Azad*, Delhi, 1946.
Dewar, Douglas, *Hand-book to the English Pre-mutiny Records in the Government Record rooms of the United Provinces of Agra and Oudh*, Allahabad (ND).
Dr. Ziauddin Ahmad, *Bayan*, Aligarh, (ND).
Dutta, Kali Kinkar, *Rajendra Prasad*, New Delhi, 1974.
Ghaffar, Qazi Abdul, *Hayat-i-Ajmal*, Aligarh, 1950.
Gilmartin, David, *Empire and Islam*, California, 1988.
Gopal, Ram, *Indian Muslims*, Bombay, 1959.
Gopal, S., *Jawahar Lal Nehru—A Biography*, Vol. I, Delhi, 1947.
Government of India, Ministry of Information & Broadcasting, *The Collected Works of Mahatma Gandhi*, Vol. 18, New Delhi, 1965.
Graham, G.F.I., *The Life and Work of Sayed Ahmed Khan*, Edinburgh, 1885.
Hadi, Syed Mohammad, *Ali Biradran Aur Unka Zamana*, New Delhi, 1978.
Hali, Altaf Husain, *Hayat-i-Javed*, Delhi, 1990.
Hasan, Abul, *AMU Aligarh, Addresses and Speeches*, Aligarh, 1987.
Hasan, Mushirul, *Mohammad Ali: Ideology and Politics*, New Delhi, 1981.
Hasan, Mushirul, *Nationalism and Communal Politics in India 1885-1923*, New Delhi, 1991.
Hasan, Mushirul, *Nationalism and Communal Politics in India 1916-1928*, New Delhi, 1979.
Husain, Mir Vilayat, *Aap Biti*, Aligarh, 1970.
Husain, Suraiya, *Sir Syed Ahmad Khan Aur Unka Ahad*, Aligarh, 1993.
Jain, M.S., *The Aligarh Movement*, Agra, 1965.
Jain, Naresh Kumar, *Muslims in India: A Biographical Dictionary*, Vol. II, New Delhi, 1983.
Jamiluddin, M.A. *Jinnah, Speeches and Writings*, (edited), Vol. I, Lahore, 1960.
Khan, Habibullah, *Hayat-i-Aftab*, Allahabad, 1947.
Khan, Syed Ahmad, *Asbab-e-Baghawat-e-Hind*, (Eng. Trans.), Patna, 1999.
Kumar, Kamlesh, *Role of Muslim in Indian Politics (1857-1947)*, New Delhi, 1985.
Lelyveld, David, *Aligarh First Generation*, New Delhi, 1878.
Low, Francis, *The Indian Year Book and Who's Who 1940*, Vol. XXVII, p. 885.
Luke, Sir Harry, *The Old Turkey and New*, London, 1955.
M.K. Gandhi, *An Autobiography or the Story of My Experiments with Truth*, Ahmedabad, 1945.
Manglori, Syed Tufail Ahmad, *Musalmanon Ka Roshan Mustaqbil*, Delhi, 1945.
Minault, Gail, *Khilafat Movement*, Delhi, 1982.
Mohsini, Shamsur Rehman, *Hayat-i-Abdullah*, Aligarh, (ND).

Mudholi, Abdul Ghaffar, *Jamia Ki Kahani*, New Delhi, 1984.
Mudholi, Abdul Ghaffar, *Jamia Ki Kahani*, Part-I, Delhi, 1964.
Muhammad, Shan, *Sir Syed Ahmad Khan*, Delhi, 1981.
Muhammad, Shan, *Sir Syed Ahmad Khan: A Political Biography*, Meerut, 1969.
Muhammad, Shan, *Successors of Sir Syed Ahmad Khan*, Delhi, 1981.
Muhammad, Shan, *The Aligarh Movement*, Vol. III, Meerut, 1978.
Muhammad, Shan, *The Growth of Muslim Politics in India,* New Delhi, 1991.
Muhammad, Shan, *The Indian Muslims (A Documentary Record)*, 1900-1947, Meerut, 1980.
Muhammad, Shan, *Unpublished Letters of Ali Brothers*, Delhi, 1979.
Muhammad, Shan, *Writings and Speeches of Sir Syed Ahmad Khan*, Bombay, 1972.
Mujahid, Al Sharif, *Qaid-i-Azam Jinnah*, Delhi, 1993.
Munawwar, Mohammad, *Dimensions of the Pakistan Movement*, Lahore, 1987.
Nehru, Jawahar Lal, *Selected Works* edited by S. Gopal, Vol. 15, New Delhi, 1984.
Nehru, Pandit Jawahar Lal, *An Autobiography*, New Delhi, 1962.
Nehru, Pandit Jawahar Lal, *The Discovery of India*, Calcutta, 1996.
Neimeijer, *Khilafat Movement in India, 1919-1924*, Nejheff, 1972.
Nizami, K.A., *Politics and Society during Early Medieval Period*, Vol. I, New Delhi, 1974.
Nizami, Khaliq Ahmad, *Sir Syed on Education, Society and Economy*, Delhi, 1995.
Panday, B.N., *The Indian National Movement 1885-1947*, Hong Kong, 1979.
Pirzada, Syed Sharifuddin, *Foundation of Pakistan*, Vol. II, New Delhi, 1982.
Pirzada, Syed Sharifuddin, *Qaid-i-Azam Jinnah's Correspondence*, New Delhi, 1981.
Quadiri, Khalid Hasan, *Hasrat Mohani*, Delhi, 1985.
Qureshi, Ishrat Ali, *Aligarh Past and Present*, Aligarh, 1992.
Ray, N.R., *Dictionary of National Biography*, Calcutta. 1986.
Rizvi, Khurshid Mustafa, *Hayat-i-Zakir Husain*, Delhi, 1949.
Robinson, Francis, *Separatism among Indian Muslims*, Cambridge, 1974.
Sarkar, Sumit, *Modern India 1885-1947*, Madras, 1983.
Sen, S.P., *Dictionary of National Biography*, (Vols. I, II, III, IV) Calcutta, 1974.
Shakir, Moin, *Khilafat to Partition, 1919-47*, New Delhi, 1970.
Sharma, Brij Kishore, *Introduction to the Constitution of India*, (7th Edition), Delhi, 1915.
Shaw Stanford, J., and Ezel Kural Shaw, *History of the Ottoman Empire and Modern Turkey*, Cambridge, 1977.
Sherwani, H.K., *The Aligarh Movement,* New Delhi, 1969.
Zakaria, Rafiq, *Rise of Muslims in Indian Politics,* Bombay, 1970.
Zuberi, Mohammad Amin, *Zia-i-Hayat*, Aligarh, 1970.

Index